AGING SLOWLY

The Prevention Total Health System®

AGING SLOWLY

by Myron Brenton and
the Editors of **Prevention**® Magazine

Rodale Press, Emmaus, Pennsylvania

Printed in the United States of America on recycled paper containing a high percentage of de-inked fiber.

Library of Congress Cataloging in Publication Data

Brenton, Myron.
  Aging slowly.

  (The Prevention total health system)
  Includes bibliographical references and
    index.
  1. Aged—United States—Life skills guides.
2. Aged—United States—Economic conditions.
3. Aging. 4. Health. I. Prevention (Emmaus,
Pa.) II. Title. III. Series.
HQ1064.U5B73   1983   305.2′4
83-13975
ISBN 0-87857-465-4 hardcover
    4   6   8   10   9   7   5   hardcover

The Prevention Total Health System®

Series Editors: William Gottlieb, Mark Bricklin
Aging Slowly Editor: Carol Keough
Writers: Myron Brenton with Carol Keough, Deborah
    Kaplan, Carl Lowe, Debora Tkac, Marian Wolbers
Research Chief: Carol Baldwin
Researchers: Christy Kohler, Holly Clemson, Christine
    Konopelski, Susan Nastasee, Joann Williams,
    Martha Capwell, Pam Mohr, Nancy Smerkanich,
    Pam Uhl
Art Director: Karen A. Schell
Associate Art Director: Jerry O'Brien
Designers: Lynn Foulk, Alison Lee
Illustrators: Susan M. Blubaugh, Joe Lertola
Art Production Manager: Jane C. Knutila
Project Assistants: Tom Chinnici, Linda Jacopetti,
    John Pepper
Director of Photography: T. L. Gettings
Photography Coordinator: Margaret Skrovanek
Photographic Stylists: Renee R. Grimes, Scott Schmidt,
    J. C. Vera
Photo Librarian: Shirley S. Smith
Staff Photographers: Christopher Barone, Carl Doney,
    T. L. Gettings, John P. Hamel, Mitchell T. Mandel,
    Margaret Skrovanek, Christie C. Tito, Sally
    Shenk Ullman
Copy Editor: Jane Sherman
Production Manager: Jacob V. Lichty
Production Coordinator: Barbara A. Herman
Composite Operator: Brenda J. Kline
Production Assistant: Eileen Bauder
Office Personnel: Diana M. Gottshall, Susan Lagler,
    Carol Petrakovich, Cindy Christman, Cindy Harig,
    Marge Kresley, Donna Strubeck

Rodale Books, Inc.
Editorial Director: Carol H. Stoner
Managing Editor: William H. Hylton
Copy Manager: Ann Snyder
Publisher: Richard M. Huttner
Director of Marketing: Eller Rama
Business Manager: Ellen J. Greene
Continuity Marketing Manager: John Taylor

Rodale Press, Inc.
Chairman of the Board: Robert Rodale
President: Robert Teufel
Executive Vice President: Marshall Ackerman
Group Vice Presidents: Sanford Beldon
                        Mark Bricklin
Senior Vice President: John Haberern
Vice Presidents: John Griffin
                 Richard M. Huttner
                 James C. McCullagh
                 Carol H. Stoner
                 David Widenmyer
Secretary: Anna Rodale

NOTICE

This book is intended as a reference volume only, not as a medical manual or guide to self-treatment. If you suspect that you have a medical problem, we urge you to seek competent medical help. Keep in mind that nutritional and health needs vary from person to person, depending on age, sex, health status and total diet. The information here is intended to help you make informed decisions about your health, not as a substitute for any treatment that may have been prescribed by your doctor.

Contents

Preface

Aging slowly does not mean doing battle with the passing years. It means enjoying them—to the hilt!

In many ways, we are far better equipped to relax and enjoy life as adults than as the kids we once were. Much of the confusion, insecurity and emotional turmoil of the early years are behind us. In its place are direction, confidence and yes, a certain toughness, too. We know what we want, and how we can best pursue it. We know how to pace ourselves. We know when to push, when to stand pat, when to shove and when to shove off. We know the overwhelming power of patience. We don't let ourselves be tricked into emulating someone else's pace, someone else's style. We are far less hysterical, self-righteous and boring than kids. We dress better, drive better and know all the best restaurants.

We know, in short, how to enjoy ourselves.

With all those qualifications for high-energy living, we needn't become discouraged about the negative aspects of aging. Science in recent years has taught us that nearly all the so-called inevitable problems of aging can be prevented, remedied or at least delayed by smarter living. These problems include everything from wrinkles to high blood pressure, and from a social circle that's gradually become too small to a house that's suddenly too big. The new generation of life-enhancement sciences has given us specific techniques, plans and just plain friendly tips that we can all use to wonderful advantage as we face these challenges.

The Fountain of Youth, when you get right down to it, then, flows with good information.

That's where *Aging Slowly* comes in. Here, we have marshalled the best information available about retaining and improving vigor throughout life. We have drawn from the fields of nutrition, exercise, psychology, gerontology (the study of aging), personal finance, even personal grooming, and more.

Our approach is holistic: No one part of life is necessarily more important than the others. And they all work better together than they do by themselves. No one food, no one exercise, not even one drug is worth very much by its lonesome. *Aging Slowly* shows you how to get your act together.

You'll find many questions you've wondered about answered in these pages. More important, you'll begin thinking about some new things. The essence of the youthful spirit, perhaps, is nothing more than learning.

We hope you'll find *Aging Slowly*—part of The Prevention Total Health System®—to be full of fresh ideas, practical tips and, best of all—inspiration.

Executive Editor, **Prevention**® Magazine

1

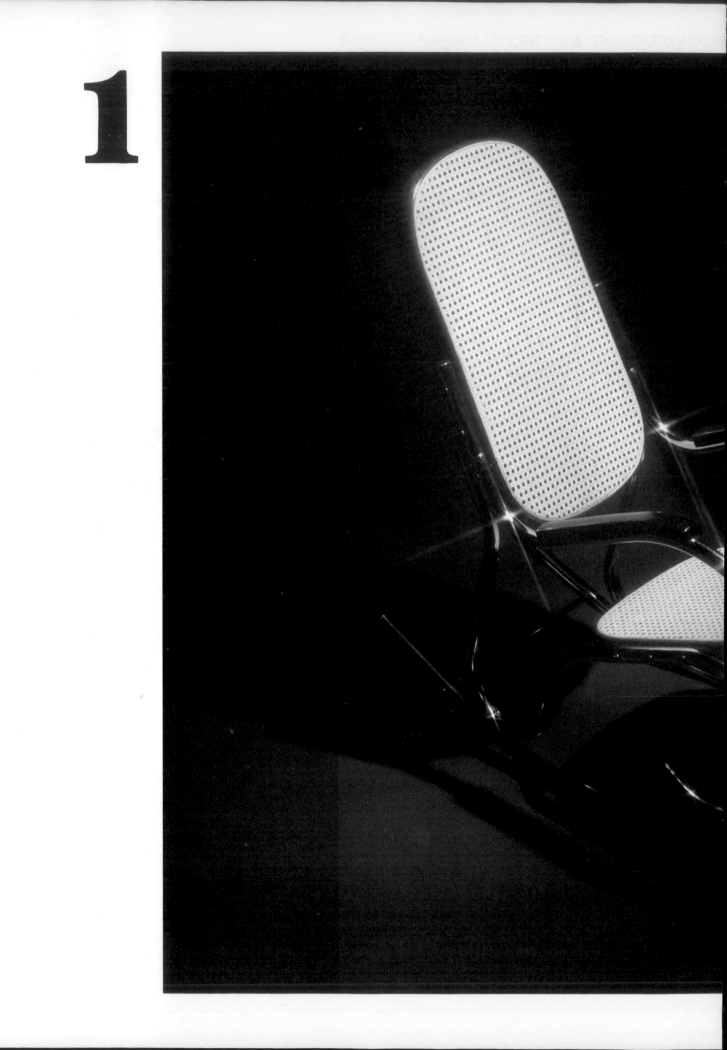

The Myth of Aging

We all have to *grow* old but we don't have to *be* old. Many "facts" about aging are just myths.

We are, as a nation, graying. The statistics are clear: 1 out of every 11 Americans is over 65. At the turn of the century, 20 of every 100 will be older than the traditional retirement age.

There's an irony to these statistics: We are, as a nation, entirely youth oriented. It's the young we admire, if not worship—their culture, their clothes, their songs, their spirit. Even those who should know better are hung up on youth—such as doctors who don't like to treat older people. Robert N. Butler, M.D., former director of the National Institute on Aging, points out that even older people are prejudiced against being old. Yet every day some 1,000 people reach the age of 65. Collectively and individually, our skins are beginning to wrinkle and sag. What can we do about it?

Happily, there's much we can do. For one thing, no matter how young or old we are, we can stop seeing aging as the enemy. It's a psychological principle that often when we stop fighting something and accept it—only then can we conquer it. Applying that principle, we can conquer our fear of aging. In a sense, we even can conquer aging. It's obviously impossible for us—as yet—to swallow a longevity pill or drink a potion from the Fountain of Youth. For now, the good news is that we already can learn enough from those scientists studying aging to slow down our personal clocks. These specialists point out that we're not even close to realizing humankind's current potential life span—a happy, healthy 110 or 120—but the possibility exists.

We can profit, too, from the example of the many older people whose physical fitness, mental alertness and enthusiasm about life exceed that of younger people. Living longer and staying younger—that's what this book is all about.

1

WHAT'S YOUR REAL AGE?

Meet a Chicago woman named Irene. She kayaks. She swims. She maneuvers through Chicago's dense traffic on a bicycle. She works as a hospital volunteer four mornings a week and lectures to groups on a subject she knows a lot about—namely, aging. Irene is 75 years old.

Meet a Des Moines man named Ted. He almost literally drags himself out of bed each morning. He usually drives to his office fighting off a headache. A sedentary type, he huffs and puffs if he has to climb a set of stairs. He drinks countless cups of coffee each day to keep himself awake and often collapses in front of his television set to eat a frozen dinner before he gladly turns in for the night. Ted is 47 years old.

The point is obvious but enormously important: Most of us erroneously lock ourselves into chronological age. Yet many specialists on aging no longer view age as a fixed number. They recognize that we possess an actual age, the number of years we've been on this earth. They also realize that the span from a birth date to today often doesn't reflect a person's true physical and biological age. Despite a couple of heart

attacks, Irene functions as vitally as people in their thirties and forties presumably do. Whereas Ted, sluggish and aching, seems older than his years.

In a purely biological sense, what we seem like on the outside and what we really are underneath may be entirely different. According to Nathan W. Shock, Ph.D., scientist emeritus of the National Institutes of Health and a pioneer gerontologist, "There are tremendous differences in the rates at which people age. And there can be great differences in the rate at which different parts of the body age."

Chronological age, biological age—there's yet another age to look at, the one that has to do with our attitudes. How open are we to new ideas, new ways of looking at things? How flexible? How enthusiastic are we about the work we do, our relationships, the life around us, the life we lead? There are people who retain an almost childlike enthusiasm all their lives; there are others whose flair for living seems to have been largely squeezed out of them by the time they're 40.

In the mid-1950s, several investigators working for the National Institute of Mental Health studied medically healthy older men and women who lived in their communities rather than in institutions. They were delighted to find that these people were psychologically flexible, resourceful and characterized by an upbeat view of life. In other words, we're not necessarily our "real" ages, either—but as young as we feel.

Maybe it's because of this youthful attitude that senior citizens show a comparatively high degree of well-being, despite the problems they face. This upbeat conclusion is drawn from a nationwide study of hundreds of men and women 60 and older. Sponsored by Americana Healthcare Corporation, the study stressed that three factors are crucial to the well-being of the older person: health, economic security and marital companionship with someone of equal physical capability.

Only 17 percent of those studied judged their health as poor. Most felt good about themselves, saying they always felt useful and had an

The large majority of the population is under age 55. However, as the baby boom grows older, the generation gap will narrow.

The Great Divide

OVER 55
21% OR 47,243,898

79% OR 179,260,927
UNDER 55

enduring sense of purposefulness. A whopping 84 percent talked enthusiastically about their special interests and hobbies. More than half said they were untroubled by sadness or depression.

One of the study's most significant findings was that age really doesn't have a bearing on a person's sense of optimism. You can be in your seventies or eighties and easily maintain a more optimistic view of life than someone much younger. In addition to finances and health, which are inextricably related to optimism, the health of your spouse matters greatly. The study was very clear about this: Regardless of age, the healthier you feel, and the healthier your spouse is, the more positive your outlook.

Birthdays are often greeted by derision. But consider the alternative to aging!

AGEISM IN AMERICA

The older person: decrepit, confused, ineffectual.

The older person: dependent, doddering, a drain on public funds.

This is ageism.

It was Dr. Butler who coined the term "ageism" in the late 1960s. For more than a quarter of a century, Dr. Butler has worked closely with older people in his roles as physician, researcher, psychiatrist and participant in community affairs involving the aged. He headed the National Institute on Aging from its start in 1977; now he's chairman of the department of geriatrics and adult development at the Mount Sinai Medical Center, New York City. His book, *Why Survive? Being Old in America* (Harper & Row, 1975) won a Pulitzer Prize. No one in America is more qualified to speak on behalf of the aged; no one is more offended by ageism.

"Ageism is the stereotyping, the prejudices, the discrimination that surrounds old age," he says. "All of which is really based on the underlying personal dread we have about growing old."

Very much steeped in the economic and political as well as the psychological and physiological aspects of aging, Dr. Butler came by his concerns early in life. He was still in medical school when he heard older people referred to as "crocks" and worse—and saw them being given short shrift. "I was amazed at how rapidly everyone wanted to get rid of an older person who had a stroke, for example, rather than have them be part of a teaching hospital and a medical school."

Later, when he lived in Washington, D.C., Dr. Butler saw more offensive ageism at work. He recalls a typical situation: Some very attractive apartments close to his own home were about to be made into public housing for older people. The reaction? A huge outcry from neighborhood residents and from the local civic association. "It was as though the very fact of being old was horrid to people," Dr. Butler says. There were other such incidents and experiences, and they helped shape his life into one that, essentially, serves the needs and concerns of the country's older population.

Has public attitude changed in the last 20 years? Dr. Butler says, "Yes, there has been some improvement," but then offers a list of examples of lingering, destructive effects. There's the age discrimination in the workplace, which often begins when a worker is only 40 or so. There are the compulsory retirement policies and the steady whittling down of benefits to older people.

"Ageism is the stereotyping, the prejudices, the discrimination that surrounds old age. All of which is really based on the underlying personal dread we have about growing old."
—**Robert N. Butler, M.D.**

Dr. Butler says, "I picked up a copy of a prominent business magazine a little while ago and the title on the cover was, 'Can We Afford Old Folks?' I don't believe people in other societies would say that."

Golden Age Achievers

The world rests in the hands of mature people. Most heads of state would have been long retired had they worked in a more usual occupation.

President
Rudolf Kirchschlaeger
(Austria)   Born 1915

Chancellor
Bruno Kreisky
(Austria)   Born 1911

President
Joao Baptista
Figueiredo
(Brazil)   Born 1918

Party Chairman
Hu Yaobang
(China)   Born 1915

President
Francois Mitterrand
(France)   Born 1916

Prime Minister
Andreas Papandreov
(Greece)   Born 1918

Prime Minister
Indira Gandhi
(India)   Born 1917

Prime Minister
Menachem Begin
(Israel)   Born 1913

President
Alessandro Pertini
(Italy)   Born 1896

Emperor Hirohito
(Japan)   Born 1901

Prime Minister
Pierre Werner
(Luxembourg)
Born 1913

King Olav V
(Norway)   Born 1903

President
Fernando Belaunde
Terry
(Peru)   Born 1912

President
Ferdinand E. Marcos
(Philippines)
Born 1917

President
Julius Kambarage
Nyerere
(Tanzania)   Born 1922

Party Chairman
Yuri V. Andropov
(USSR)   Born 1914

Queen Elizabeth II
(United Kingdom)
Born 1926

President
Ronald Reagan
(USA)   Born 1911

He talks about other examples of ageism—the tendency of some doctors to dislike treating elderly patients, the tendency of certain health institutes not to study older people. Aging research has been held back considerably, he says, because many decision makers are fearful that extending people's lives will mean increasing the number who will become dependent and unproductive.

"The most pernicious myth about the aged, in the broad sense, is that the old are useless, burdensome—that we'd be well rid of them," he says.

MYTH: Old and sick go hand in hand.

FACT: That's the popular belief—go past 65 or so and you're ready to fall apart. Not so. While it's true that the immune system doesn't work as well as we get older, aging is not synonymous with becoming sick, and there's much evidence to prove it.

As Dr. Butler points out, only 5 percent of older people at this point in time are in nursing homes, and most are over 80. The majority of older people are well able to take care of themselves.

In his book *A Good Age* (Crown Publishers, 1976), gerontologist Alex Comfort, M.D., explodes the commonly held belief that older people are constantly ill, citing statistics that show that people over 65 have roughly *half* as many acute illnesses per year as do men and women of all ages.

In fact, many serious medical conditions commonly ascribed to getting old really have nothing to do with the aging process—among them, arthritis, cataracts, heart disease, stroke and senility.

We can look at aging and illness still another way: Do older workers have more absences and on-the-job accidents than younger ones? A study sponsored by the Corporate Committee for Retirement Planning made it clear that they do not. An overwhelming number of personnel directors queried in this survey—97 percent, to be exact—said older workers have better attendance records than do younger workers. And more than half of the personnel directors said that older workers have fewer on-the-job accidents than younger ones.

It Could Be Better . . . It Could Be Worse

Age discrimination exists in America, we know. But would older folks fare better—or worse—in other countries in the world?

Japan

If you were a senior citizen today, during Japan's impressive industrial rise, you might wish you'd been born a century before. While life expectancy has increased, later years can be bitter and lonely. This nation's economic miracle has drawn young people to the cities and to heavy industry. The old have remained in the rural areas, only to find themselves alone, trying to cope. The traditional family support group has moved to the assembly line.

On the brighter side, people over 65 are offered free physicals, and health insurance covers most medical expenses.

Retirement can pose quite a financial dilemma because workers are asked to retire very early—sometimes as young as 45 and routinely at 55. A major problem for many is that pensions and Social Security-type allowances do not begin until after 60!

For many Japanese, however, these problems can be conquered somehow. What really is lacking is not so much money as the respect these lonely seniors paid their parents and expected to receive when their turn came.

Italy

Old age, Italian style, is very much a mixed blessing. A study of the lives of nearly 1,200 Italians done by American social scientists showed that the majority of seniors were healthy and strong enough to lead rich, productive lives. That's the good news. The bad news is that the older populace is jobless and isolated, despite financial dependence on their children.

Senior Italians are lucky to have the younger generation to support them because there's little they can expect from their government.

USSR

In Russia, retirement looks like a breeze. At least on paper. Senior citizens are provided state pensions that, while somewhat lower than their working salaries, equal at least half of the retiree's largest salary. Moreover, the pension dollar is stretched by excellent medical benefits.

So what's the catch? Russia's is not a consumer-oriented economy. Shortages abound, particularly in housing. As a result, most elderly live with their children—squeezing into already cramped quarters. They routinely take care of the grandchildren and maintain the home. They do all the shopping and cooking, and often have to share kitchen facilities with other families.

The Scandinavian Countries

Services and financial support for the elderly are among the best in the world in Sweden, Denmark and Norway. Take Denmark, for example. While the basic pension provided by the government is quite modest, it is often supplemented by a corporate pension, state-supported housing or rent allowances and medical care payments. What's more, all the Scandinavian countries also provide extensive home-help services that enable older people to live on their own.

In some ways, in fact, it may be easier to be old than young in the Land of the Midnight Sun. The Danish government, for example, heavily taxes its younger citizens in order to provide these generous old-age benefits.

China

And in China, things are rosy for golden agers. Mainland China has traditionally taken care of its elderly, but now the responsibility has shifted from family to state. In rural areas, a person's commune makes payroll deductions and distributes aid, while in cities it's the neighborhood or industrial groups that handle this function. Both programs guarantee basic allowances for food, clothing, fuel, housing and medical care. They require, in return, the payment of only nominal premiums during the working lifetime.

The elderly live either in their own houses—with repairs provided by the commune or factory—or in a "Home of Respect for the Aged."

The mandatory retirement age all over China is 60 for men and 55 for women. A typical yearly stipend amounts to about 70 percent of the worker's highest annual salary.

Another important point: Many of the ailments of midlife and old age that we regard as a "natural" consequence of growing old really aren't. They are, instead, the result of poor health habits developed in younger years.

MYTH: Older people are unproductive.

FACT: History belies this belief; every era has had its men and women in their seventies and eighties who made their marks upon society. George Bernard Shaw, the acid-tongued British playwright, was still writing witty plays when he was in his late eighties. Winston Churchill was 82 when he wrote his monumental book, *A History of the English-Speaking Peoples.* After retiring at age 55, the ruler of Parisian high fashion, Coco Chanel, made a successful comeback at age 71. And Giuseppe Verdi, one of the most famous composers of operatic music, was 74 when he wrote *Otello,* and 80 when he created the funny, intense *Falstaff.*

Want more proof? Konrad Adenauer, who guided Germany from war's devastation to the beginning of its current prosperity, was 73 when he was named its chancellor. Golda Meir became prime minister of Israel when she was 70. At 81, Benjamin Franklin worked out the compromise that led to the adoption of the U.S. Constitution.

Unproductive? Tell that to the thousands of older persons who are enrolled in formal classes at any given time. And those older students take their classes seriously. Observes gerontologist Barbara Ober, Ph.D., of Shippensburg State College in Pennsylvania, "Older people make excellent students, maybe even better students than the majority of 19- and 20-year-olds. One advantage is that they have settled a lot of the social and sexual issues that pre-occupy their younger classmates."

In addition, many older persons are gainfully, productively employed —nearly three million of them in 1980, according to the U.S. Bureau of Labor Statistics. Many more would be employed were it not for age dis-

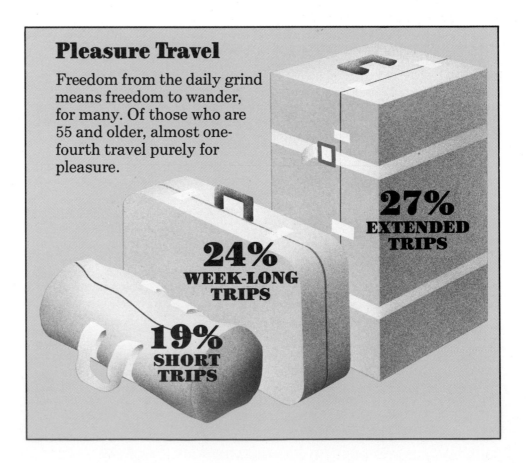

Pleasure Travel

Freedom from the daily grind means freedom to wander, for many. Of those who are 55 and older, almost one-fourth travel purely for pleasure.

27% EXTENDED TRIPS

24% WEEK-LONG TRIPS

19% SHORT TRIPS

crimination. The oldest volunteer for a federal government study of aging was a 92-year-old man, a vest maker whose main complaint about his age was, "I want a job and no one will hire me."

Far from being unproductive, older people are a tremendous national resource—when they're allowed to be.

MYTH: Old people are both poor and lonely.

FACT: The popular image of people over 65 has them languishing away in tiny rooms or nursing homes, with barely enough to eat and no one to talk to. And it is, unfortunately, an image that holds true for a portion of the older population. For example, more than 4.5 million older men and women living alone have incomes below poverty level. Living on fixed low incomes and dependent on their Social Security payments for their primary financial support, a segment of the older, retired population has become poor after retirement from work.

Nevertheless, a close look at the figures makes it clear that this is not the plight of most older Americans, who account for nearly 80 percent of all the money in savings and loan institutions. What's more, an estimated 28 percent of all discretionary money is held by older consumers. That's nearly double the amount held by persons under 34. What about people over 65? Most women and men in this age group own their own homes. The per capita income of households headed by someone over 65 is only $500 lower than that of the rest of the population.

Far from being universally poor, older people constitute America's new leisure class. A leisure class has money, has time and enjoys itself with both. That's what many older people are doing. The over-55 crowd is the major one on luxury cruises; it also accounts for a third of round-the-world excursions chartered in the United States.

As for companionship, the Americana Healthcare Corporation study revealed that more than half of the older citizens surveyed said they talk with or see their families almost every day. Nearly a quarter

more said they see them almost every week. And 62 percent see or talk to friends nearly every day. Most heartening, almost all senior citizens said they can count on family or friends to help them if they're sick and to give them advice on important matters.

MYTH: Sex after 60 is unenjoyable or just plain impossible.

FACT: Don't you believe it. None of the men and women in their sixties, seventies and eighties who lead active, satisfying sex lives do.

Cultural attitudes and the attitudes of physicians are responsible for the existence of this myth. Most physicians *assume* that both sexual interest and activity go into a gradual decline with age. As a result, a large part of the public expects their sexual drive to lessen sharply and inevitably with the passage of time. Men, especially, have been vulnerable to this myth. They no longer need to be. Recent surveys and clinical studies give a significantly different picture of sex and aging.

At Duke University two researchers, Linda K. George, Ph.D., and Stephen J. Weiler, M.D., questioned 278 married men and women (ages initially were 46 to 71) every couple of years for a six-year period. What the researchers found is that, in effect, the majority of us are in our later years what we were earlier. People whose sexual drive is strong and sexual activity vigorous throughout their middle years are likely to have a comparatively vigorous sex life well into their seventies. Conversely, people who have a fairly low level of sexual activity in midlife aren't apt to have much sexual interest later on.

In sum, sex after 60 is very enjoyable, very possible—if that's what it was right along.

Dr. George and Dr. Weiler sound another hopeful note. They found—as did earlier researchers—that most older people are less sexually active than are most young people. Nothing remarkable about that, one might think. However, the Duke University researchers believe this pattern may change. They say their findings suggest that as the number of couples

It's Never Too Late

Continuing research confirms the fact that both sexes can have a good and satisfying sex life well into the seventies, eighties and even beyond. In fact, one important study at Duke University's Center for the Study of Aging and Human Development shows that some men and women actually become more sexually interested and active as they get older. Other investigators have found that regular sex throughout adult life prevents problems later.

Not Older, Just Better

Fred Astaire, dancer *extraordinaire*, was born May 10, 1899. He began his career, which spans much of the 20th century, in 1916 as a dancer with his sister Adele, and continues in the 1980s as a television actor.

MYTH: As you grow older, you become unattractive.

FACT: Gaze upon the handsome faces of these older people, many of whom you will recognize.

Steve Allen, television funnyman and talented musician, was born in New York City on December 26, 1921. In addition to having a dynamic television career, Allen has written more than 3,000 songs, including "South Rampart Street Parade" and "This Could Be the Start of Something Big."

Ali MacGraw was born in 1939. Perennially young and fresh looking, she has starred in numerous movies, including *Love Story* and *Goodbye Columbus*.

Walter Cronkite, the legendary television news correspondent, was born November 4, 1916, in St. Joseph, Missouri. His dignified good looks appeared on CBS news broadcasts for almost 20 years.

Eddie Albert was born in Rock Island, Illinois, on April 22, 1908. He broke into the big time in 1935 with the radio show "The Honeymooners," acted on Broadway, and appeared on many television shows, including a starring role in the popular "Green Acres." Twice nominated for an Academy Award, Albert also has starred in a wide variety of films.

Angie Dickinson, television actress and movie star, was born September 30, 1931. Her lovely face and figure frequently appear in advertisements asking, "Would this body lie to you?"

Louise Bourgeois, French-born American sculptor, exhibited at prestigious museums while in her seventies. Her pieces are huge abstractions requiring both physical strength and creative energy.

(rather than widows or widowers) surviving to old age increases, there also will be increases in the number of older people reporting continued sexual behavior.

Additional research now confirms the fact that both sexes can have a good and satisfying sex life well into the seventies, eighties and even beyond. In fact, one important study at Duke's Center for the Study of Aging and Human Development showed that some men and women actually become *more* sexually interested and active as they get older. Other investigators have found that regular sex throughout adult life prevents problems later.

William H. Masters, M.D., and Virginia E. Johnson, the celebrated sexologists known for their pioneering clinical work, researched the changes that take place in the aging male and female. True, they say, the male produces less seminal fluid, takes longer to reach full arousal and, once he's reached his climax, quickly loses his sexual vigor, which takes longer to return than for the younger male. But this needn't be a problem—unless "he falls into the . . . trap of the cultural demand for constancy of male sexual performance and worries about possible loss of masculinity." The aging female also experiences changes. There's a slowing in the rate of production and a reduction in the amount of lubricating fluid, and the walls of the vagina lose some of their elasticity. The orgasmic episode may be shorter and less intense, but still pleasurable.

Masters and Johnson, too, state reassuringly that healthy men and women can enjoy an active sex life well into the eighties. In fact, they say, if sexual confidence isn't destroyed by unrealistic expectations, and if both partners are in reasonably good health and sexually interested in each other, a satisfying sex life can "and should" continue indefinitely.

MYTH: Older people are no longer creative.

FACT: You need only recall the painters, sculptors, writers, architects, scientists, mathematicians and others who produced major works in their sixties, seventies and eighties, and even beyond. There's Benjamin Franklin, who was 78 when he invented bifocal glasses. There's Louise Nevelson, the famous sculptor who put together a spectacular new exhibit of her work in 1979 when she was 78. Cecil B. deMille was 71 when

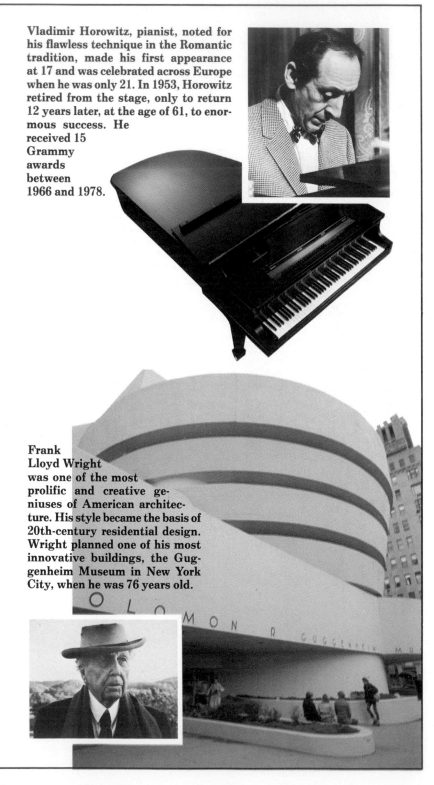

Vladimir Horowitz, pianist, noted for his flawless technique in the Romantic tradition, made his first appearance at 17 and was celebrated across Europe when he was only 21. In 1953, Horowitz retired from the stage, only to return 12 years later, at the age of 61, to enormous success. He received 15 Grammy awards between 1966 and 1978.

Frank Lloyd Wright was one of the most prolific and creative geniuses of American architecture. His style became the basis of 20th-century residential design. Wright planned one of his most innovative buildings, the Guggenheim Museum in New York City, when he was 76 years old.

he produced and directed the Academy Award-winning film, *The Greatest Show on Earth*. A quick glance at the list of notable American writers and playwrights in *The World Almanac & Book of Facts 1982* shows a total of 102 listed. Nearly two-thirds are over 60—among them Isaac Asimov, Taylor Caldwell, Harold Robbins and Irving Stone. Most are still productive; five were best-selling authors in 1980-81.

That creativity diminishes with advancing years first received official "documentation" in the studies of a social scientist, H. C. Lehman, in 1953. He tried to show that the crowning achievements of creative men came early in their lives—that, for instance, men of science did their most creative work before they reached 40, while those in the arts and literature did theirs before reaching 45. Other researchers since have come up with similar findings. Yet the studies remain controversial because of the obvious fact that some older persons produce their most creative work in what are sometimes called "the advanced years." For example, the mighty German writer Goethe completed his most stunning work—*Faust*—when he was 83. The studies are controversial, too, because of the assumption they make. The assumption is that someone who has a brilliant idea or two in his younger years—a great mathematician or scientist, say—should be expected to serve up brand new ideas endlessly. As Dr. Butler points out, that's unrealistic. "It may be that there aren't that many ideas in the heads of any of us," he says. "To use that as a way of measuring creativity is questionable."

Some years back, two social scientists studied the patent registrations of 89 chemists and chemical engineers who worked for the same organization. Did they find a decline in registrations as the men grew older? No. They actually noted a slight rise in registrations. The scientists were at least as creative as when they were younger, still churning out ideas new and brilliant enough in their fields to merit patenting.

In a certain sense, creativity blossoms best as we grow older,

Alexander Calder, sculptor, reached the peak of his career after age 55, when his hugely popular mobiles were installed in public places around the world. At age 66, Calder saw his delightful "Ghost" hung in the great well of the Guggenheim Museum. His last mobile, untitled, hangs in the East Wing of the National Gallery of Art.

Agatha Christie, the famed British writer, published until the age of 84. Altogether, her books sold more than 100 million copies. At age 62 she wrote the perennial hit *The Mousetrap*, which played for more than 24 years on the London stage. She died in 1976.

maintains Gay Gaer Luce, Ph.D., a psychologist who has worked closely with people in their later years. "As people grow older, they become more intuitive, sensitive and psychic," she explains. "This is one of the reasons why older people are often more religious. It's also why they can be more creative." Dr. Luce is one of the founders of SAGE— Senior Actualization and Growth

Steve Reeves, 57, exemplifies the benefits of lifelong exercise. The actor, perhaps best known for starring in a series of Hercules movies in the 1950s, developed an exercise called Power Walking. An adept Power Walker covers a mile in 12 minutes, often while wearing weights on the ankles, waist and wrists. Reeves advises: "Walk tall. Walk like you're going some-place and you *know* where you're going."

will finally paint what pleases them." When struggling to please themselves artistically, they are often most creative.

Few people think of truly brilliant ideas or produce masterpieces of any kind, of course. But leading a creative life is something else again. We can bring into our lives the things that please us without needing to feel selfish about it. As a subsequent chapter will make clear, many couples discover a richness to their lives after their last child has left home. No longer constricted by child-rearing responsibilities, they involve themselves in creative activities for which they had neither the time nor the energy before.

Summing up his research directed at older people, Dr. Butler says, "A great many older people are still leading extremely creative lives, changing their view of themselves, raising new questions about the world, addressing new issues or looking at them from a new angle."

MYTH: If you're old, the rocking chair has got you.

FACT: Two hundred older people competed in 13 field events sponsored by the Rhode Island Department of Elderly Affairs. More than 500 Virginians, aged 55 and up, vied for medals in 20 events, from hand-ball to high jump, in the Virginia Golden Olympics. Ruth Rothfarb, 81 years old, featured in *Running* magazine, runs 10 miles a day and ran the 1981 Avon International Women's Marathon in 5:37.

Old and sedentary? Bicyclist Fred Knoller, 86, was named by *50 Plus* magazine as one of the top older athletes of 1981. Older people are playing tennis, racquetball; going fishing, hunting, canoeing; playing golf; hiking, swimming, jogging, backpacking. They do everything that, according to the myth, they aren't expected to do at these ages.

At a scientific meeting held in conjunction with the 1972 Olympics, researchers presented evidence that can tell us a lot about the importance of exercise and the ability of older people to do it. They conducted a study of national athletes in the 40 to 75 age range. The results showed

Exploration—in San Francisco, which is the first program in the country that offers a holistic approach to aging.

An 80-year-old artist enrolled in SAGE is a prime example of the favorable influence of advanced years upon the creative spirit. Dr. Luce says, "Much has to do with an inner directedness that comes with age when we pay greater attention to seeking inner satisfaction." But doesn't such a focus on oneself amount to selfishness? Not at all, Dr. Luce says: "Because they refuse to seek endorsement and approval by a youth-oriented society, older artists that there was a significant difference between the training champions and the sedentary populations of the world. All the athletes had "excellent cardiovascular function and body composition characteristics."

Although all of us can't be Masters champions, all of us can certainly benefit from good exercise. For example, by following a special physical training program, 70-year-olds can achieve levels of vigor and fitness close to those of 40-year-olds. The program was developed by Herbert A. deVries, Ph.D., a leading specialist in gerontology and physiology.

More good news. Elizabeth Protas, Ph.D., of the Texas Women's University, and Christopher Bork, Ph.D., of Northeastern University in Boston, studied 80 runners and found that muscle and joint strength in their dominant knee didn't necessarily decline with age. What about muscle strength elsewhere in the body? Based on their research, Dr. Protas and Dr. Bork say it's quite possible that it doesn't decline with age, either, as long as proper, routine exercise is performed.

But along with the good news, there's bad news, too: Not enough older people exercise. The bad news came in a report by the President's Council on Physical Fitness and Sports. Forty-five percent of adult Americans don't exercise, the report said. It appears that older people are especially apt to remain sedentary because they feel the need for exercise disappears when they're older.

So while millions of older Americans keep themselves fit and hearty, millions still hold back. They relegate themselves unnecessarily to the rocking chair, which they could readily hide in the attic—with much greater benefit to themselves.

MYTH: Older people become senile.

FACT: As soon as we think of old age, many of us feel a stab of fear; we think, "That means senility." We think that with the advancing years we will become confused, disoriented and forgetful. Let's take an unemotional look at this scourge of old age.

Forget, for a moment, the sharpness of mind that has enabled so many persons in fields as diverse as architecture, music, business and many others, to make outstanding contributions while in their seventies and eighties. Let's concentrate on scientific facts. In strict scientific language, there isn't even such a disease entity as senility. It's a word commonly used, but it really describes a large number of conditions that have an equally large number of causes.

The basis for a lot of wrong notions about senility seems to be a related myth which holds that we possess a finite number of brain cells and that vast numbers—100,000 is a number often bandied about—die each day, never to be replaced. Information about the brain is still very limited. It is known that we're born with about 100 billion brain cells. It's also known that some parts of the brain don't seem to suffer cell loss no matter how old we get. And, insofar as those lost cells are concerned, our bodies have a built-in safety factor—a reserve that makes up for the loss. Research shows that living cells may be able to take up the functions of dead cells.

A GOOD, LONG LIFE

Advertising, Hollywood, television—they've done their share to perpetuate the myths of the older American as a somewhat pathetic—or invisible—figure. There's the youth culture; there's Madison Avenue's eagerness to cater to it. So the glamorous fashion and cosmetic ads are geared to young girls, the headache ads toward older folks. Protests beautiful over-50 model Kaylan Pickford, "We're more than people who use laxatives, hemorrhoid remedies, aspirins and dentures!"

Many women agree with her. When Compton Advertising, Inc., a major ad agency, interviewed people around the country about advertising's effect on them, many women in the 50 to 64 age group protested the profusion of such ads. "Everything," they asserted, "is for the young." Hollywood? Rarely does it make a film that features middle-aged (or

How Old Are You Really?

If you are uncertain of the answer, leave a blank. Place scores (given in parentheses) on lines provided in the + or − columns. Total the + and − columns and subtract the lower number from the higher to find the total (+ or −) for each section. Follow the instructions for calculating your medical age at the end of the Score Card.

PART I: Personal History
+ −

1. Weight. "Ideal" weight at age 20 was _____. If current weight is more than 20 pounds over that, score (+6) for each 20 pounds. If same as age 20, or less gain than 10 pounds (−3). ___ ___

2. Blood pressure. Under 40 yrs., if above 130/80 (+12); over 40 yrs., if above 140/90 (+12). ___ ___

3. Cholesterol. Under 40 yrs., if above 220 (+6); over 40 yrs., if above 250 (+6). ___ ___

4. Heart murmur. Not an "innocent" type (+24). ___ ___

5. Heart murmur with history of rheumatic fever (+48). ___ ___

6. Pneumonia. If bacterial pneumonia more than 3 times in life (+6). ___ ___

7. Asthma (+6). ___ ___

8. Rectal polyps (+6). ___ ___

9. Diabetes. Adult-onset type (+18). ___ ___

10. Depressions. Severe, frequent (+12). ___ ___

11. Regular* medical checkup. Complete (−12); partial (−6). ___ ___

12. Regular* dental checkup (−3) ___ ___

Subtotals ___ ___

PART I Total (+ or −) ___ ___

PART II: Lifestyle
+ −

1. Disposition. Exceptionally good-natured, easy-going (−3); average (0); extremely tense and nervous most of time (+6). ___ ___

2. Exercise. Physically active employment or sedentary job with well-planned exercise program (−12); sedentary with moderate regular exercise (0); sedentary work, no exercise program (+12). ___ ___

3. Home environment. Unusually pleasant, better than average family life (−6); average (0); unusual tension, family strife common (+9). ___ ___

4. Job satisfaction. Above average (−3); average (0); discontented (+6). ___ ___

5. Exposure to air pollution. Substantial (+9). ___ ___

6. Smoking habits. Nonsmoker (−6); occasional (0); moderate, regular smoking: 20 cigarettes, 5 cigars or 5 pipefuls (+12); heavy smoking: 40 or more cigarettes daily (+24); marijuana frequent (+24). ___ ___

7. Alcohol habits. None or seldom (−6); moderate with less than 2 beers or 8-oz. wine or 2-oz. whiskey or hard liquor daily (+6); heavy, with more than above (+24). ___ ___

8. Eating habits. Drink skim or low-fat milk only (−3); eat much bulky food (−3); heavy meat (3 times a day) eater (+6); over 2 pats butter daily (+6); over 4 cups coffee/tea/cola daily (+6); usually add salt at table (+6). ___ ___

9. Auto driving. Regularly less than 20,000 miles annually and always wear seat belt (−3); regularly less than 20,000 but belt not always worn (0); more than 20,000 (+12). ___ ___

10. Drug habits. Use of street drugs (+36). ___ ___

Subtotals ___ ___

PART II Total (+ or −) ___ ___

PART III: Family Social History
+ −

1. Father. If alive and over 68 yrs.; for each 5 yrs. above 68 (−3); if alive and under 68 or dead after age 68 (0); if dead of medical causes (not accident) before 68 (+3). ___ ___

2. Mother. If alive and over 73 yrs., for each 5 yrs. above 73 (−3); if alive under 68 or dead after age 68 (0); if dead of medical causes (not accident) before 73 (+3). ___ ___

3. Marital status. If married (0); unmarried and over 40 (+6). ___ ___

4. Home location. Large city (+6); suburb (0); farm or small town (−3). ___ ___

For Women Only
+ −

1. Family history of breast cancer in mother or sisters (+6). ___ ___

2. Examines breasts monthly (−6). ___ ___

3. Yearly breast exam by physician (−6). ___ ___

4. Pap smear yearly (−6). ___ ___

Subtotals ___ ___

PART III Total (+ or −) ___ ___

Calculations
+ −

Enter totals from PART I ___ ___

PART II ___ ___

PART III ___ ___

Totals ___ ___

Chart Totals (+ or −) ___

Enter current age here.

Divide chart total by 12, and enter + or − figure here. ___

Add or subtract above figure from your current age to find *your medical age.* ___

*"Regular" refers to well people who have thorough medical exams at a minimum according to this age/frequency: 60 and up, every year; 50-60, every 2 years; 40-50, every 3 years; 30-40, every 5 years; 25-30, as required for jobs, insurance, military, college, etc. More frequent medical checkups are recommended by other authorities. Dental exams: twice yearly.

From *How to Be Your Own Doctor (Sometimes)* by Keith W. Sehnert, M.D., and by Howard Eisenberg.
© 1975, 1981 by Keith W. Sehnert, M.D., and Howard Eisenberg. Reprinted by permission of Grosset & Dunlap, Inc.

older) lovers. As for television, Dr. Robert Butler says he conducted a study of public television shows a few years ago to determine how many older people were featured, "and you could have concluded that no one ever grows old in the United States."

There are signs that things may be changing. The fact that the over-55 age group represents more than $400 billion in annual personal income and that one-fourth of all consumer expenditures are made by people over 55 may be part of the reason why. The tourist industry, financial institutions, health clubs, even some cosmetics companies—and many others—have targeted the "maturity market" for a new look, for special attention and for the development of products specifically geared for it. The word on Madison Avenue is that this decade is seeing a significant shift of attention away from the young to the "mature" people. This new attention should help topple some myths!

It's vitally important that they *do* topple. Consider a survey of American attitudes toward aging, a survey that shows that one-fifth of the American population suffers from "gerontophobia"—the fear of old age. Fear of growing old is like all the other phobias. It won't slow down aging. Instead, it can have just the opposite effect. Dr. Butler tells the story of a patient of his who never had an illness—never a physical problem of any consequence. This man was extraordinarily ambitious and hard-working, in addition to being a runner all his life. He also ran from his aging, by refusing to celebrate his birthdays. So it went until he was 74. Suddenly he developed a terrible pain in his side and shortness of breath. Doctors thought it was a tumor, but it turned out to be something far less serious. He was given a reprieve, but he didn't act like it. He became profoundly depressed because, Dr. Butler says, "he thought he would never age, as if he were going to live forever. When he had to face aging and his fear of it, it was a profound shock."

Dr. Butler adds, "He didn't adjust to aging step by step throughout life. He had to adjust to it all at once, and it was very difficult." Part of the adjusting we can do is to prepare ourselves, condition ourselves for our later years. Getting the right nutrients, doing the right exercises, having the right outlook can be potent antiaging "drugs" of sorts, pushing our life expectancies beyond the probabilities.

Life span, life expectancy, the quality of life—these are the domain of gerontologists and other specialists in related fields. Life span refers to the inherent natural, maximum life length of an individual in a species—3 years for a rat, 110 years for a human. The life span hasn't changed for centuries—it's hard to know whether it ever will. Life expectancy now averages 73 years (69.5 for men, 77.2 for women), a dramatic increase from the turn of the century. Life expectancy has even taken a leap for people in the 60 to 80 age group. In 1900, 33 percent of those who reached 65 lived to 80; in the mid-1970s, 51 percent did.

We want to live longer—but we want to live well, too. As the English satirist Jonathan Swift wrote, "Every man desires to live long, but no man would be old." It's starting to happen. In her research of people at every age, Bernice L. Neugarten, Ph.D., of the University of Chicago, has found that our biological and social clocks have changed. People who are 40, 50 and 60 years old are starting new families, new jobs and new hobbies. Older people these days aren't conforming to the image they had of what a person of 60 is supposed to be like. Their expectations were of frailty, of a lack of curiosity, of dimmed enthusiasm. They're overjoyed to find how wrong they were. These are the "new" older men and women—vigorous, alert, eager to keep on seeing things, doing things, enjoying life.

2

Diets to Lighten the Years

The actual causes of aging are being revealed to science. Many can be slowed by dietary changes.

According to physician-scientist Denham Harman, M.D., Ph.D., the mysterious scientists of old, the ancient alchemists, worked zealously to produce two miracles—to transform base metals into gold and to concoct an elixir of youth—a potion that, once swallowed, would erase lines and years. Not a bad combination—getting rich and enjoying it forever.

As we all know, the alchemists failed in both respects. Modern scientists have given up on the transmutation of metals. However, using all the modern technological resources at their command, they are still hard at work, trying to uncover the mysteries of aging—and, in accomplishing this, to give us the means to longer, healthier and more productive lives. Gerontologists, the prime specialists in this quest, know that somewhere within ourselves—our bodies, our tissues, our cells, our genes—the key to the mystery is to be found. Working in laboratories all over the United States —all over the world—they search and they probe and they experiment. Some are trying to solve the puzzle of why we age by scrutinizing our hormones. Others are looking at our cells, at the chemical heart of life, DNA. Still others are looking for clues in our immune systems. Many are seeking answers, and finding them, in nutritional approaches to aging research. In particular, they're discovering how certain vitamins and minerals help protect our bodies from the more ravaging diseases we associate with aging—and how these nutrients may even more effectively prolong and protect our lives.

Gerontological theories are so diverse it would take a whole book to describe them all. Instead, we'll take a closer look at four current theories, two of which offer practical, nutrient-focused approaches to try right away.

THEORIES OF AGING

Consider that inside yourself you have a clock. A *real* clock, one that's genetically programmed to stop running at a certain time. One leading researcher in the field of gerontology, Leonard Hayflick, Ph.D., thinks there are trillions of such clocks inside each of us. Based on painstaking and ingenious experiments with cell cultures, he proposes that we have such a clock in the nucleus of each of the body's cells. At a certain point, the clock stops running—and that point, chemically set before birth, varies for different species, he theorizes.

The crux of Dr. Hayflick's experiments in this area is cell division. Simply put, prior to those experiments, it was generally believed that cells grown in a laboratory could be kept alive indefinitely—that they would undergo division after division. Dr. Hayflick proved that they have a limited life—one that appears to correspond to the normal life span of the species.

Gerontologist W. Donner Denckla, M.D., has another kind of aging clock on his mind. His exceedingly complex theory is based on the workings of two of the body's glands, the thyroid and the pituitary. The thyroid secretes two hormones that help to control the body's metabolic rate. Since older people manufacture about the same amount of these hormones as younger ones, the process of aging is not determined by the workings of the thyroid gland alone.

Enter the pituitary gland, which controls the body's growth and the hormone secretions of several other endocrine glands. Beginning at puberty, Dr. Denckla found, the pituitary starts to release significant amounts of a material which, over time, works destructively on the body's cells, keeping them from using the two vital hormones from the thyroid. In fact, Dr. Denckla has removed the pituitary from adult rats and found that their response to the two thyroid hormones was restored.

We can't turn back our genetic clocks (if they indeed exist), and we can't have our pituitary glands removed. But we *can* take advantage of work done by Dr. Harman with the "free radical" theory of aging. As you'll see, nutrition is the key.

Free radicals aren't extreme revolutionary leftists recently released from prison—though they do cause mayhem in our bodies. They are molecules—unstable molecules, dancing around inside us, swooping down at random on any unsuspecting molecule, creating reactions that are damaging to us. According to Dr. Harman, who is a professor of medicine and biochemistry at the University of Nebraska College of Medicine, the damage wreaked by free radicals is one of the main causes of aging.

Free radical reactions occur elsewhere in nature, too. Cut an apple in half, expose the two halves to air and watch them turn dark. Expose butter to the air, unrefrigerated, and it will turn rancid. Wet iron rusts. Untreated rubber turns hard. In each instance, free radical reactions are responsible. But now comes a basic question, and it's one that propelled Dr. Harman along on his antiaging search. What causes free radical reactions to occur in the first place? The one-word answer: oxidation.

Oxidation occurs whenever there's an interaction between matter and the oxygen in the air or elsewhere. Free radicals do their work anytime there is oxidation—which is why the apple turns dark, the butter rancid, the iron rusty. Oxidation is one of the consistent happenings in our bodies, as well.

HEROIC VITAMIN E

This was the mission: to decrease oxidation, to reduce those free radical invasions and to keep oxidation damage at a minimum. Impossible? Not at all. Industrially, it's been happening. Our cars are rustproofed, certain kinds of paper are specially treated to keep them from yellowing, special materials on leather and rubber products prevent them from deteriorating; in every instance, antioxidant compounds are what hold the free radicals at bay.

"In laboratory animals, vitamin E in the diet not only reduces aging damage caused by free radicals, it also cranks up their immune system."
—Denham Harman, M.D., Ph.D.

To slow down aging, we need something like rustproofing agents, or so the reasoning among Dr. Harman and a few other researchers goes. And it looks as if he has discovered some effective ones, including a vitamin that's an oxidation fighter of some renown.

As with most research stories, this one begins in the laboratory, with its science fiction equipment and its mice. Enter Dr. Harman and his colleagues, setting out to find out something about antioxidants and life span. Specifically, they wanted to know if mice would live longer when known antioxidants were added to their diets shortly after weaning. A number of such substances were studied. Two prominent ones were BHT (butylated hydroxytoluene) and vitamin E. Did the mice live longer? Definitely. Adding just one antioxidant to the mice's diet—only on a level of 1 percent or less by weight of total food intake—increased their life expectancy by 15 to 44 percent.

Dr. Harman experimented with fats, as well—and came up with another surprise. By now most Americans know the difference between saturated and unsaturated fat. Because saturated fat creates a buildup of cholesterol, which presumably leads to atherosclerosis, many millions of Americans have switched to unsaturated fat (most commonly, vegetable oils, which are polyunsaturated) for cooking. Dr. Harman fed groups of mice and rats diets containing various amounts and/or degrees of unsaturated fat, the highest being 20 percent by weight of the total diet. Presumably these diets should have made no difference in the animals' mortality rates. Yet they did. The group of mice that ate the most unsaturated fat had the highest death rate.

Despite all the publicity to the contrary, it seems any high level of fat, even unsaturated fat, can shorten life. And the reason is connected to those mayhem-causing free radicals. Here's how: Large amounts of unsaturated fat apparently increase oxidation reactions in the cells. A rise in the level of free radical reactions, in Dr. Harman's view, causes us to age faster.

Now let's bring vitamin E back into the oxidation picture. Does it help inhibit the oxidizing effects of unsaturated fat? Yes, studies suggest that it does—it seems to have a "rustproofing" effect. When Dr. Harman fed vitamin E to some of the mice whose diets were relatively high in unsaturated fat, its antioxidant properties went to work. The addition of 20 International Units (I.U.) of vitamin E per 3½ ounces of food significantly cut down the number of breast tumors the animals tended to develop as the amount of unsaturated fat in their diet was increased. Vitamin E also cranked up the immune responses of the mice, increasing their resistance to infection.

Vitamin E has figured as the nutritional hero in another approach to the riddle of aging. Jeffrey Bland, Ph.D., a chemist at the University of Puget Sound in Washington, studied red blood cells in older people. Among the old, a peculiar thing often happens to these cells—they take on a popcornlike shape, becoming "budded" cells. Dr. Bland theorizes that budding is the result of oxidative damage to the cell membrane. He could, in fact, make normal cells bud by exposing them to light and oxygen.

The Making of a Radical

The free radical reaction is the result of oxidation—when an organic compound meets with an oxygen molecule. The free radical reaction releases a free electron, which damages healthy cells. That damage can result in aging. The rate at which these free radicals form can be slowed—maybe even stopped—by preventing oxidation in the first place with the use of an antioxidant such as vitamin E.

Next, Dr. Bland studied the red blood cells of blood donors. Not ordinary donors, but those who'd received 600 I.U. of vitamin E every day for ten days prior to giving blood. When he exposed their blood to light and oxygen, only a small number of cells lost their original shape—while the ordinary red blood cells from people who hadn't taken the vitamin were totally transformed into budded cells. Vitamin E had kept most of those cells from aging.

Conclusive studies of vitamin E's antiaging effects with humans may be some time in coming. But even now we may be able to increase our functional life span. Our approach should be to limit *all* fats, including the polyunsaturated variety, and increase our intake of vitamin E by 300 to 500 I.U. a week.

How Long You Live, by Country

Life expectancy varies around the world. Twenty countries where people enjoy significant longevity are located in the Northern Hemisphere. These countries are shown below; each is labeled with the age you might expect to achieve if you lived there. (Statistics are for men only.)

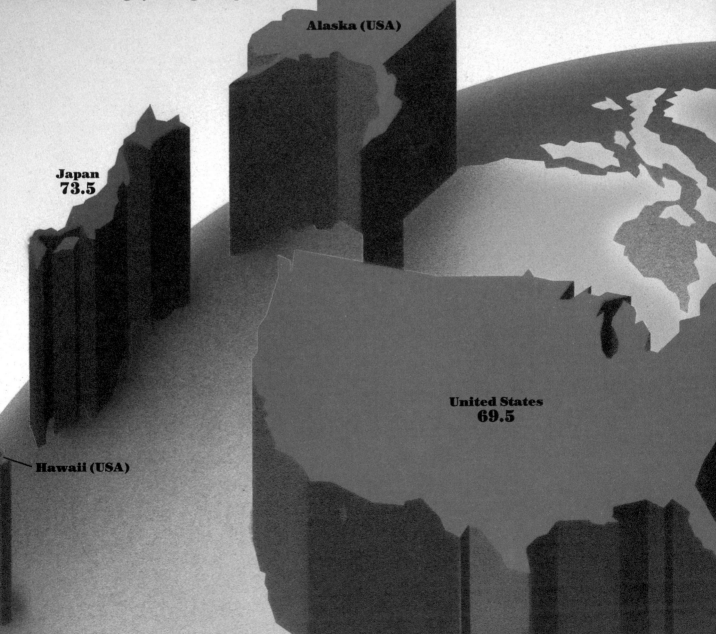

Alaska (USA)

Japan
73.5

Hawaii (USA)

United States
69.5

THE AGING DEFENDERS

The immune system is one of the most complex parts of our bodies. The effect of aging on the immune function is not completely understood, yet no system is more important to our health. It protects us from the infections and diseases to which even the youngest of us are vulnerable. It follows that if the immune system deteriorates, we're much more apt to become ill. The system is like a collection of stalwart fighters defending the castle against invaders. If the defenders weaken, the castle is overrun. Because our immune systems do deteriorate, our castles—our bodies—are more vulnerable to illnesses as we grow older.

To understand the immune

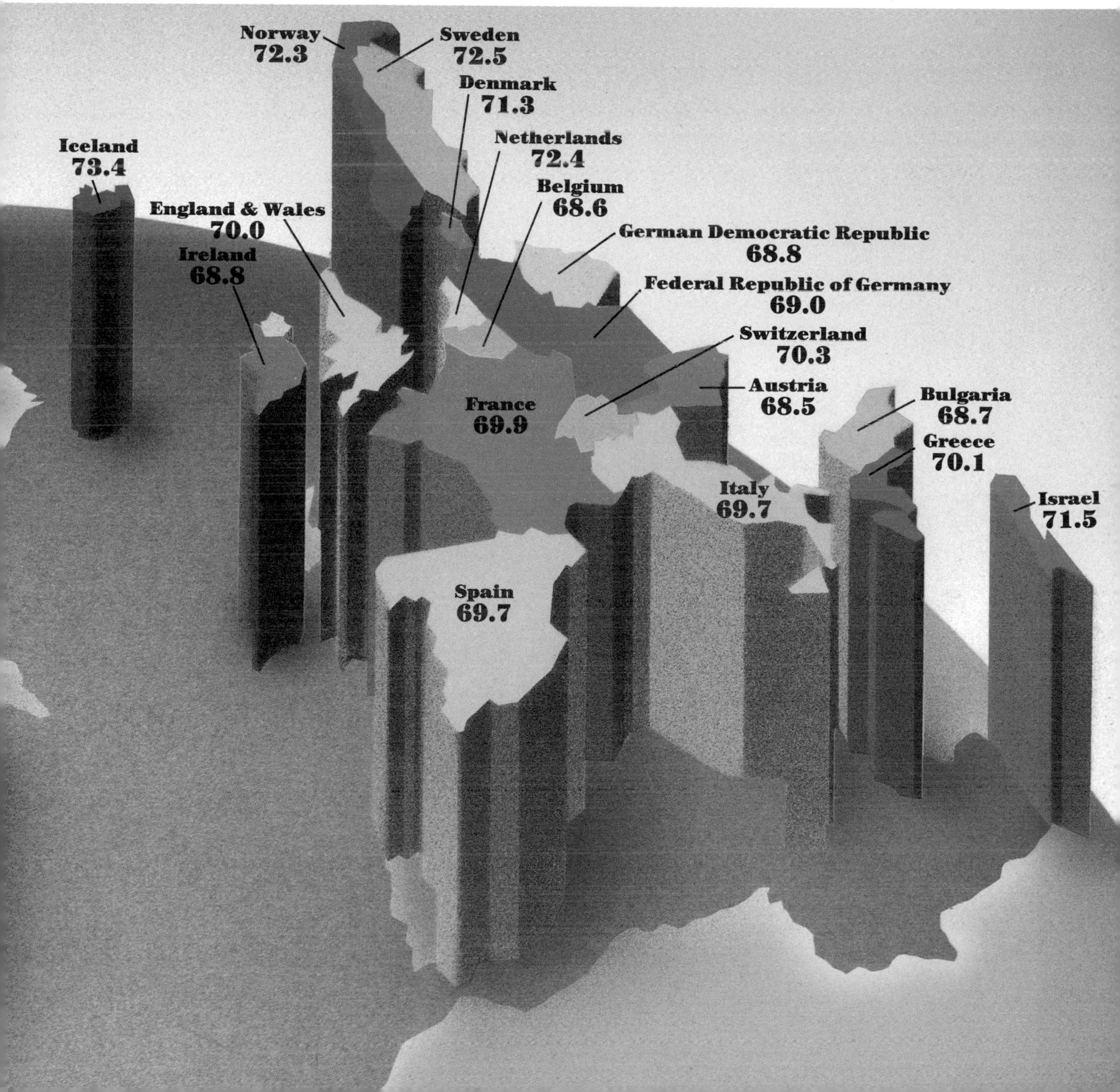

Iceland
73.4

Norway
72.3

Sweden
72.5

Denmark
71.3

Netherlands
72.4

Belgium
68.6

German Democratic Republic
68.8

Federal Republic of Germany
69.0

England & Wales
70.0

Ireland
68.8

Switzerland
70.3

Austria
68.5

Bulgaria
68.7

Greece
70.1

France
69.9

Italy
69.7

Israel
71.5

Spain
69.7

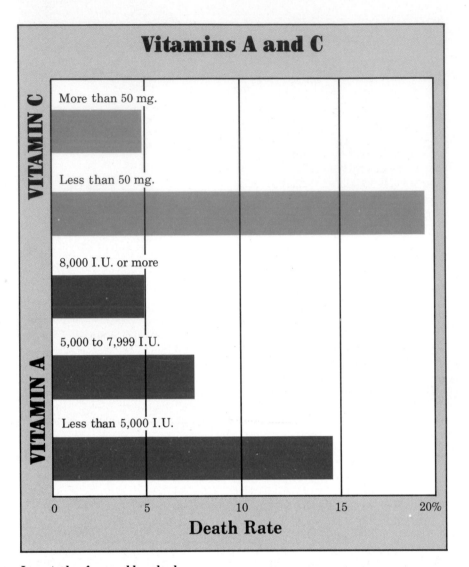

Vitamins A and C

VITAMIN C
More than 50 mg.

Less than 50 mg.

VITAMIN A
8,000 I.U. or more

5,000 to 7,999 I.U.

Less than 5,000 I.U.

0   5   10   15   20%

Death Rate

In a study of several hundred older people, a researcher found that as the intake of vitamins A and C increased, the death rate declined. Some scientists believe the reason for this relationship lies in these vitamins' ability to strengthen the immune system.

system, how it works and how we may be able to keep it defending us longer, let's see it briefly in action. Suppose you cut your finger and are a little careless about keeping the wound clean. That finger becomes slightly infected. An immune response is triggered. The action starts in your bone marrow, where an abundance of white cells called lymphocytes originate. There are two types of lymphocytes that circulate in the blood and lymph vessels, as well as in other parts of the body. One type of lymphocyte, referred to as the B-lymphocyte, is primarily responsible for the production of antibodies. These are your body's shock troops. They rush to the wound to destroy the bacteria in your infected finger as they rush elsewhere, when needed, to destroy other bacteria, viruses, fungi and parasites. The second type of

lymphocyte is the T-lymphocyte. These cells primarily work over the long haul, helping us to fight off viruses and maybe even cancer. As you might expect, something akin to a four-star general regulates this portion of the defensive system. It happens to be the little organ once thought to be useless—the thymus, which is found high up in the thoracic cavity, beneath the breast-bone at the base of the neck.

With age, the thymus shrinks; with age, the entire immune system's defense becomes less spirited. And another important phenomenon occurs, some gerontologists say—namely, our *auto*immune processes escalate. Autoimmunity is a complicated bodily event in which antibodies, our former defenders, suddenly betray us, turning on our own "good" cells and destroying them as if they were harmful outside substances.

How does the autoimmune response fit in with the aging process? Roy Walford, M.D., of UCLA School of Medicine, is the principal researcher of those whose works are grounded in this theory—that as we age two things happen to our immune systems: the systems become less effective, and our antibodies stray into autoimmune responses, destroying our healthy cells.

Whether or not our immune systems are really at the heart of aging is still a controversial subject—like all aging theories, this one has its believers and detractors—but promising research is going on.

BOOSTING THE SYSTEM

There's both direct and indirect evidence to show that the immune system can also be boosted when our diets are supplemented with certain nutrients.

A study from the Airedale General Hospital, Yorkshire, England, offered evidence of how proper nutrition can shore up the aging body's *entire* system of defenders, including the immune system. A. G. Morgan, M.D., and his colleagues tested 93 geriatric patients with acute medical problems for the vitamin levels in their bodies. Not one had a normal nutritional profile. Tests for vitamin A, thiamine (B_1), riboflavin (B_2), niacin, vitamins C, D, E and K and protein showed that for all patients the average number of abnormal test results was 29 percent. The most common deficiencies were in protein, niacin and vitamins C, E and A.

Dr. Morgan believes that nutritional deficiencies, such as the ones he found, are relatively common in older people. They do not necessarily have severe deficiencies that would result in diseases such as scurvy or beriberi. But what Dr. Morgan suggests is that "minor deteriorations of function or well-being" are caused by nutritional deficiencies. So in regard to the 93 patients in the study, it is possible that their poor nutrition came before their health problems—and brought them on.

Another researcher, Olaf Mickelsen, Ph.D., conducted a thorough review of vitamins and the aging process at Michigan State University's department of food science and human nutrition. One of his conclusions was that vitamin C in particular possesses impressive life-giving and life-extending properties.

Dr. Mickelsen cites a striking example: a 25-year study in which the average protein and vitamin C intakes of a group of 100 women were measured. This study found the women whose diets had higher amounts of vitamin C lived longer than those whose intake was lower. In a second study of 97 of the same women, Dr. Mickelsen found that those who consumed less thiamine, vitamin A and vitamin C looked older than others their age. Note, too, what medical examinations showed—that the younger-looking women consumed fewer calories and ate much less fat.

In 1948 and 1949 a classic study of the relationship between nutrition and aging was begun in San Mateo County, California: a survey of 577 people over the age of 50. Each participant's diet was carefully evaluated. Their general state of health and their specific medical problems were minutely recorded. Three years later Harold D. Chope, M.D., reexamined 306 of the participants and studied the records of the entire group to find out what role nutrition had played in the aging process.

What Dr. Chope found was dramatic evidence of nutrition's beneficial role. People whose diet had higher than average amounts of vitamins A and C and niacin tended to live longer than those with lower amounts. In some instances, the increase was startling. Among people whose daily vitamin A intake was less than 5,000 I.U., the death rate was 13.9 percent. But for those whose intake was between 5,000 and 7,999 I.U. the rate dropped to 6.9 percent. And, among people who consumed more than 8,000 I.U., the death rate was only 4.3 percent.

Even more striking data came from an examination of the group's vitamin C intake. Among those whose diet contained more than 50 milligrams per day, the death rate was 4.5 percent. For those who consumed less than 50 milligrams, the death rate quadrupled.

Linus Pauling, Ph.D., also points out that vitamin C may offer the benefit of longevity.

Dr. Pauling won the 1954 Nobel Prize in chemistry for his research on molecular bonds; his campaign against nuclear testing brought him, in 1962, the Nobel Peace Prize. But he's best

This microscopic view shows a normal red blood cell, which is disk shaped and healthy.

An aged or "budded" red blood cell resembles popcorn. This deformity results from exposure of the cells to light and oxygen.

Dr. Linus Pauling, twice winner of the Nobel Prize, says we could add 25 years to our lives if only we made proper use of the nutrients our bodies need. He especially endorses vitamin C.

known for his work on vitamin C—work that has earned him a maverick's reputation with the traditional medical establishment.

Dr. Pauling first gained fame for his enthusiasm about vitamin C's effect on the common cold. Large doses of vitamin C supplements taken on a daily basis, he maintained—and backed up with research studies—can and do prevent colds.

A cold is one problem; living longer and healthier is another. On the basis of the evidence he has seen and compiled, Dr. Pauling reaches an astonishing estimate—that at any given age the chance of getting any disease can be cut in half by regularly taking between 1 and 4 grams of vitamin C a day. And among those diseases he includes cancer and heart disease.

Dr. Pauling is convinced that vitamin C has considerable value in cancer therapy, a view thus far not shared by the medical establishment.

To B or Not to B
Signs of Possible B Vitamin Deficiencies

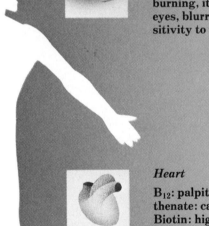

Nerves

Thiamine: irritability, poor reflexes, lack of initiative, insomnia. Riboflavin: nervousness. B$_6$: extreme nervousness, carpal tunnel syndrome, insomnia. B$_{12}$: disturbances of spinal cord and nervous system. Folate: tension headaches, "restless leg syndrome." Pantothenate: numbness, restlessness, irritability.

Lungs

A possible indication of a folate deficiency is shortness of breath. Breathing difficulties may also indicate insufficient B$_{12}$ in the diet.

Digestion

Thiamine: constipation, loss of appetite, nausea. Niacin: indigestion. B$_{12}$: sore tongue. Folate: intestinal disorders. Pantothenate: digestive disorders. Biotin: loss of appetite, nausea, vomiting and anorexia.

Eyes

A possible deficiency of riboflavin is indicated by burning, itching, teary eyes, blurry vision, sensitivity to bright light.

Heart

B$_{12}$: palpitations. Pantothenate: cardiac disorders. Biotin: high blood cholesterol.

Muscles

Thiamine: poor muscle function. B$_6$: tremors. Folate: fatigue. Pantothenate: poor muscle coordination, cramps. Biotin: muscle pains.

Skin

Riboflavin: cracks in the corners of the mouth or eyes, or on the genitals; scaliness, dandruff and oily hair. B$_{12}$: pale skin, which can signify anemia. Folate: inflamed gums. B$_6$: skin lesions. Biotin: rashes and pallor.

But there's plenty of research to back him up. At the University of Kansas Medical School, researchers found that vitamin C suppressed the growth of certain leukemia cells. Scientists from France and the United States studied vitamin C's effect on one particular type of cancerous cell—a melanoma cell. Working with mice, they extracted both cancerous and noncancerous cells from the animals. They placed the cells in two separate cultures and added vitamin C. The number of cancerous cells decreased by half.

Then there are Dr. Pauling's studies. In one, he and Dr. Ewan Cameron compared the survival time of 100 people with terminal cancer who were given massive intravenous doses of vitamin C over a five-year period with 1,000 other such people who didn't receive the vitamin. Those who did and didn't get the vitamin C were the same age and sex, and had the same type of tumor. The result? The patients who received vitamin C tended to live longer—some up to four times longer—than those who were not given the treatment.

How does Dr. Pauling explain vitamin C's good work? With cancer, he goes back to its effect on the immune system. He cites, for example, a study done by investigators at the National Cancer Institute that showed when humans ingest 5 to 10 grams of vitamin C per day it greatly increases the rate at which the body produces antibodies that fight off disease-carrying organisms.

As for vitamin E, its antioxidant properties make it a good preventive for clogged arteries. Dr. Pauling says that most people should take more of it as they grow older.

He personally takes 400 I.U. of vitamin E a day.

"If we make proper use of all the essential nutrients our bodies need," Dr. Pauling sums up, "we could live a quarter of a century longer than those of us who don't make proper use of them."

THOSE BENEFICIAL B's

Longevity studies that look to a nutritional basis for slower aging should stress the importance of B vitamins. They can help restore the health of people who have been ailing. Herman Baker, Ph.D., of the New Jersey Medical School in Newark, a specialist in metabolism and nutrition, has found striking proof in his studies. His subjects were 473 elderly people whose ages ranged from 60 to 102. Of them, 327 lived in nursing homes, the rest at home. When the study began, many of the participants couldn't be called spry or healthy. Roughly 8 percent showed signs of anemia, skin problems, cracked lips, nerve disorders, muscular aches and pains and poor visual coordination. What's more, about 39 percent suffered from what Dr. Baker termed "subclinical" vitamin deficiencies; that is, the problems were not yet noticeable. What did Dr. Baker's examination of these men and women show? First, their levels of vitamin B_6 (pyridoxine), niacin and B_{12} were markedly low. Also, they had inadequate amounts of other B vitamins, mainly folate and thiamine.

That's only half the story; the other half is more remarkable. To make up for these deficiencies, all of the participants received injections of the entire B complex every three months for a full year. After the first shot alone, people felt better. They began to shed their symptoms. At year's end, their physical complaints had vanished, and they were restored to good health.

A NUTRITIONAL STRATEGY

A nutritional strategy specifically designed for the years from 50 on may not break the life span barrier—but it can certainly slow down the aging processes.

This hopeful message comes from Myron Winick, M.D., director of the Institute for Human Nutrition, Columbia University. One of the world's leading experts on all aspects of nutrition, Dr. Winick begins by stressing two points: first, the earlier we develop that all-important strategy, the more we will be favoring our bodies as the years go on; second, no matter how old a person is, it's never too late to begin instituting sounder dietary habits.

"All older people, by definition, are overweight because the percentage of fat in our body increases. It means older people are more prone to develop obesity, especially if they lead a somewhat sedentary life."
—Myron Winick, M.D.

How? Start by reviewing your current diet. Are you overweight? If so, cut down on those calories. Most Americans, regardless of age, eat too much. But Dr. Winick says, surprisingly, that "all older people, by definition, are overweight." He hastens to admit to exaggeration, but, from a strict medical viewpoint, it's true. As we grow older, Dr. Winick explains, the percentage of fat in our bodies increases. This phenomenon happens to everyone—light eaters as well as heavy ones; the active as well as the sedentary. The reason is that, as we age, our bodies lose some of their muscle mass. What's left? Fat. Consequently, Dr. Winick says, "Older people have a higher percentage of body fat than younger ones do—even if they don't look fat. It means that older people are more prone to develop obesity, especially if they lead a somewhat sedentary life."

In a practical sense, it means that the older we become, the fewer calories we require. People in their sixties and above should limit their calories to around 2,000 a day, he advises.

Another question: How much fat are you eating? Evidence shows that eating a lot of saturated fats (those from meats and dairy products) can lead to heart disease, with older men especially susceptible. It's why the American Heart Association and other health-oriented groups have been advocating the use of polyunsaturated fats, those that come mostly from vegetable rather than animal sources. Unfortunately, the heavy publicity on this subject has given too many people the impression that it's safe to consume unlimited amounts of polyunsaturated fats. It isn't. As already noted, these fats are believed to stir up free radical reactions. Dr. Winick advocates cutting down on *all* fats for a variety of health-related reasons.

A third question: Do you have high blood pressure, or is there a history of high blood pressure in your family? If so, reduce your intake of salt drastically. In this context, Dr. Winick offers another surprise. Most of us believe that blood pressure naturally rises with age. But it's a misconception, he says, born of the fact that ours is a high salt-consuming society. In places where salt consumption is low—for instance, New Guinea—the blood pressure of older people isn't any higher than that of younger ones.

"Cutting back on calories, fat and salt will help ward off the killer diseases," Dr. Winick points out.

He suggests you calculate your overall diet as follows: 15 percent protein, 30 to 35 percent fat, 50 to 55 percent carbohydrates. Try to stay away from heavy red meats as a source of protein. If you're a vegetarian, be sure you eat enough high-protein foods to meet your requirements. Vegetarian or not, take your carbohydrates in complex form—fruits, vegetables and whole grain breads and cereals. Avoid the empty calories of sugar and other sweets.

EAT LESS, LIVE LONGER

Starve yourself and live longer. Though not quite so drastic, the principle of cutting down on food to increase our longevity is one that excites a number of scientists.

Serious work on this approach to slower aging and longer life began with a landmark study conducted in the 1930s. A Cornell University researcher, Clive M. McCay, Ph.D., fed one group of rats an all-you-can-eat balanced diet containing all essential nutrients, but shortchanged another group of rats of the same age. This group got the same diet but was never given the same calories. They were kept very thin. As it turned out, those animals weren't shortchanged at all—some survived almost twice as long as rats in the first group.

Scientific experiments can only be presumed to have validity if they can be repeated elsewhere, by other researchers. So often other scientists can't duplicate a particular experiment, thereby invalidating a so-called miracle. Not so with the underfeeding of rats. It has been repeated—with rats and with mice. And the results? They were always the same. Take the mice. In one experiment the control group had an average life span of about 34 months; experimenters extended it to as long as 41 months—simply by underfeed-

"As we age, two things happen to our immune systems—one, the systems become less effective; two, our antibodies stray into autoimmune responses, destroying our healthy cells."
—Roy L. Walford, M.D.

Eat Less, Live Longer

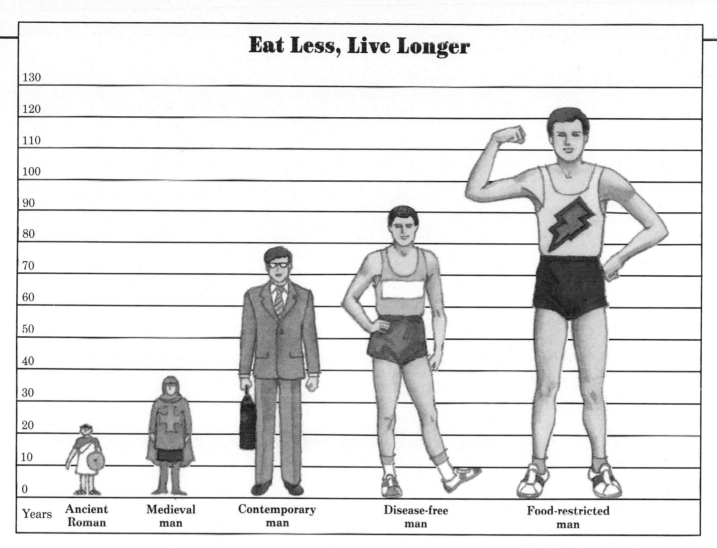

Years	Ancient Roman	Medieval man	Contemporary man	Disease-free man	Food-restricted man

The life span of humans has increased from the average 23 years of ancient Rome to a theoretical 125, under very special circumstances.

ing them, but also making sure that their diets were rich in essential nutrients.

Dr. Roy Walford, of the UCLA School of Medicine, a researcher who has studied the immune system in old age, also has used the underfeeding approach to slow aging. In most instances, the caloric content of the animals' diet is reduced by 25 to 50 percent—while making sure to supplement their diet with additional nutrients. "Undernutrition without malnutrition," he calls it. Dr. Walford found out that it is never too late to lengthen the life span. His studies show that even when the animals' diet is reduced starting at middle age, it results in a 10 to 20 percent average increase in their life span.

All these studies were done with animals. For ethical and health reasons, such studies obviously can't be done with humans. Nevertheless, there's some hint of what is possible. The scientists who work on limited-

diet projects have gone to their calculators and come up with some provocative figures. One group has estimated that if a middle-aged person's response to a limited—yet nutritionally adequate—diet were the same as it was for the animals thus far studied, the average life span would increase 20 years or more. Far fewer older people would suffer from the chronic, debilitating diseases we associate with old age. In the future, some scientists believe, there may well be restricted-diet studies with human beings.

No question about it, most of us should be eating less. There's a lot of proof—but there's a catch, too. Eating less can mean missing out on nutrition—not getting all the proteins, fats, carbohydrates, vitamins and minerals the body needs. Lots of nutrition experts have commented on the fact that even people who seemingly eat enough are often malnourished in the sense that they

27

are not meeting their nutritional requirements. This is especially true if they sup on a lot of "empty calories." The hurried, unbalanced meals that many of us eat hardly provide a diet for longevity.

Suppose we decide to get healthy. Suppose we take underfeeding to heart and decide to cut down on that rich American diet of ours—to eat meager but better-balanced meals. Will our new diet help us to ward off the diseases we associate with later life? Will that help us to slow down our aging? Maybe. And maybe not. Remember that in all those underfeeding studies the diet wasn't simply cut down, it was also supplemented with the nutrients essential to growth and health. We may have to do the same.

But don't rely on the mysterious RDAs to determine the nutritional value of the foods you eat. You know about RDAs—short for Recommended Dietary Allowance. You see the RDAs listed on many of the labels on the packaged foods you buy. The label on a loaf of bread, for instance, will tell you what two slices (one portion) contain in the way of protein, carbohydrates, fats, vitamins and minerals. Each will be listed as a percentage of the RDA.

In theory, the label listings make it easier for you to keep track of how nutritious your diet is. If, say, you eat five kinds of food containing vitamin B_6, and together they add up to at least 100 percent of the RDA for vitamin B_6, you know you've gotten enough B_6 for that particular day.

But have you really?

Alan R. Gaby, M.D., a biochemist and nutritionally oriented physician, points to the fact that a growing number of scientists and physicians seriously question it. They contend that for a variety of medical reasons, many people need more than the RDA of certain nutrients. And, they say, the easiest and surest way of getting those additional nutrients is to use nutritional supplements.

A panel of authorities in the field of nutrition researches the RDAs and revises them about every five years. Nutritionists who don't agree with their conclusions, Dr. Gaby says, aren't represented on the panel.

But he has far more serious reservations about the RDAs as currently set. They are supposed to "meet the known nutritional needs of practically all healthy persons." But Dr. Gaby asks, "What is meant by the phrase, 'practically all'? Researchers know that nutrient requirements vary widely from person to person—some need considerably more than others. Because of this variation, a small group of research subjects cannot be reliably used to predict the needs of an entire population."

There's another catch phrase in the official RDA definition—"healthy persons." People who suffer from metabolic disorders, infections or chronic diseases or who use medications are not considered "healthy persons." The definition says these people require "special dietary and therapeutic measures. These conditions are not covered by the RDA." Neither are heart disease, anemia, chronic diarrhea and the like. When it comes to that, how many of us are 100 percent healthy? The U.S. Surgeon General's 1979 report on the state of our health concluded that as a nation we're definitely healthier than we were some years back, but it also points out that "our 700 percent increase in health spending has not yielded the striking improvements over the last 20 years that we might have hoped for."

Dr. Gaby offers some examples, suggesting that at any given time, about a third of all Americans will develop heart disease, one out of five will die of cancer, millions of men will suffer from prostate trouble, millions of women will develop severe thinning of the bones, and so on. And, even if we remain quite healthy, as we grow older we begin to lose the ability to absorb vitamins and minerals efficiently. That means we need more of them. People who smoke and drink need more of certain nutrients at any age: Smoking depletes the body of vitamin C; heavy drinkers are often deficient in the B vitamins, especially thiamine.

A number of age-related physical conditions seem to respond well to amounts of certain nutrients greater than the RDA. Take a man who loves his steak, slathers plenty of butter on his baked potatoes, eats

"The Recommended Dietary Allowances may not meet the needs of many older people who suffer from chronic diseases. When planning your diet, keep the RDAs in mind, but remember that the ultimate in good health requires more than the bare minimum."
—Alan R. Gaby, M.D.

a couple of slices of bacon for breakfast every morning and enjoys too many of the other foods that shoot cholesterol levels up. He probably would do well to add vitamin C supplementation as well as niacin and calcium to his diet. These three supplements have been shown to lower the cholesterol count. Another example: Here's a woman who's often in excruciating pain because of kidney stones. The pain eases, she has a period of relative comfort— but then, to her utter dismay, the pain recurs. She's not alone. Each year, roughly 1 of every 1,000 hospital admissions in the United States is accounted for by cases involving kidney stones. People who get stones often have elevated calcium levels in their urine. Instead of passing out of the body in its dissolved state, it forms little pellets. How is the condition treated? By surgery, diet and substances that help keep the calcium dissolved. Magnesium, Dr. Gaby says, is one of those substances. According to a report in the *Journal of Urology,* a number of people who suffered from recurrent kidney stones were given magnesium as part of their therapy. The result? They had approximately 90 percent fewer stones.

And a third example: prostate trouble. This is one of the hazards men face as they grow older—the enlargement of the prostate gland. Among men 40 years of age and over, some kind of prostate problem is nearly inevitable. According to the Harvard Medical School, "by age 60 prostate enlargement is almost universal." The most common and obvious symptom is urinary obstruction. Here again, a nutrient taken in amounts greater than the RDA may come to the rescue, Dr. Gaby asserts. It's a mineral—zinc. Studies show that added zinc in the diet can relieve the urinary symptoms associated with an enlarged prostate. In one such test of zinc's healing properties, all the patients receiving zinc supplementation (34 milligrams per day for two months and then 11 to 23 milligrams daily thereafter) eventually reported an easing of their painful symptoms, and all but five actually showed a decrease in prostate size.

Daily Allowance for Aging Slowly

VITAMINS

	50+years
Vitamin A	10,000 I.U.
Thiamine (vitamin B₁)	10 mg.
Riboflavin (vitamin B₂)	10 mg.
Niacin	25 mg.
Vitamin B₆ (pyridoxine)	10 mg.
Vitamin B₁₂	10 mcg.
Folate	800 mcg.
Biotin	2 mcg.
Choline	10 mg.
Pantothenate	10 mg.
Vitamin C	1,000 mg.
Vitamin D	400 I.U.
Vitamin E	400 I.U.

Daily Allowance for Aging Slowly

MINERALS

	50+years
Calcium	1,200 mg.
Magnesium	400 mg.
Iron	10 mg.
Zinc	25 mg.
Selenium	75 mcg.
Chromium	75 mcg.

When planning your nutritional program, keep the RDAs in mind, Dr. Gaby advises, because "that way you will not forget to include at least the bare minimum for all the known essential nutrients. But remember that the ultimate in good health requires more than just the bare minimum."

MINERALS FOR LONGER LIFE

Studies delving into the relationship between diet and longevity often focus on vitamins and their marvelous potential for keeping us long-lived and healthy. Unfortunately, this emphasis may make it seem as though minerals don't play an equally important role. The fact is, they do. Many are vital to our general health, while deficiency of certain specific minerals can create serious medical problems.

If we take all the minerals in the world, we can divide them into three separate piles. The first we'll call the "major minerals"—those our bodies need in fairly large amounts. There are just a few of them, and they're quickly listed: calcium, phosphorus, potassium, sulfur, sodium, chlorine and magnesium. The second pile we'll label "trace minerals." They've been given this name because they're needed and present in the body in truly minute amounts; so minute they are specks, really. You wouldn't think a deficiency would matter. It does matter—very much.

In the third pile will go all the other minerals, the ones that don't seem to contribute to our bodies' well-being.

Let's just take a brief look at how some minerals help our bodies function well. Sodium and potassium regulate the body's water balance. Without those minerals that balance would go awry—to the point where we'd either swell up with fluid or, at the other extreme, dry out and perish. Iron, a trace mineral, helps make hemoglobin, the vital ingredient of our oxygen-carrying red blood cells. Calcium is the first-ranking mineral in the body, strengthening bones and teeth. Less well known is the fact that we need calcium for our nerves, too—to keep them functioning properly. As for the trace minerals copper, zinc and cobalt, among their other functions, they help keep the body's reactions buzzing along nicely.

Chromium, too, is important to our health. Even in trace amounts, it does the extremely important job of working with the body's insulin to keep our blood sugar levels balanced. Body chromium declines with age, so it's important to have a diet that includes foods rich in chromium, such as brewer's yeast and liver.

If you looked at vitamins and minerals under an electron microscope, you'd see how different their molecular structures are. But these differences don't keep them from getting along. Actually, some get along so well they bring out the best in each other. Phosphorus is one example; we absorb some of the B vitamins only when they're combined with phosphorus compounds. Zinc helps the liver release vitamin A. Vitamin C can triple the body's absorption of iron. Without vitamin D, our bodies couldn't make use of the calcium our bones so badly need.

Among the wonders our bodies perform is the actual manufacturing of certain vitamins. For example, we use sunlight as the source to produce vitamin D, and turn the beta-carotene found in vegetables into vitamin A. But that factory of ours shuts down when it comes to minerals. We can't make them from the inside. Our environment has to supply them all.

Ideally, every diet contains all the minerals we need to live longer and healthier. But this isn't an ideal world and it's quite possible to eat the foods that should give us the minerals we need, yet not be getting them in sufficient quantities. The reason? Refining grains drastically reduces trace elements like zinc and chromium. Canning vegetables robs them of much of their potassium. A high-protein diet washes calcium out of the body; alcohol and some diuretics wash out more. Even farming practices can come into play: Soil in at least 30 states is seriously depleted of zinc. So unless we eat organically grown foods or use mineral supplements, we're not getting enough of the minerals we need.

For all these reasons, many nutrition-minded health professionals say you should eat an excellent diet *and* take moderate amounts of nutritional supplements —just to be sure.

Of Mice and Men

Guess who smokes too much, drinks at least 3 martinis each and every day and is too lazy to exercise. Give up? It's a laboratory mouse.

The mouse in question belongs to Hans J. Kugler, Ph.D., gerontologist and author. He devised an experiment that wonderfully illustrates how nutrition, exercise and lifestyle factors can lengthen or drastically reduce our stay on this globe.

In his book, *Dr. Kugler's Seven Keys to a Longer Life* (Stein & Day, 1978), he admits his impatience to prove that these factors combine to have a powerful effect on our longevity. Rather than follow humans through the eons to see who lived longest and why, he chose to study laboratory animals.

The furry little creatures involved were rats, 3 strains of mice and some guinea pigs. In all, there were 700, which Dr. Kugler divided into 3 groups.

Group 1 received standard treatment for working rodents—animal chow and water, and life in a regulation-size cage.

The Group 2 animals were raised like the children of health-conscious parents. They were given vitamins and minerals and made to exercise even if they didn't feel like it. And like the pampered pets they really were, they also received toys and exercise wheels. In addition, their residences were designed to have cozy hiding places for privacy. In all, Group 2 had a pleasant and healthy environment.

Then there was the Group 3 bunch—a bad lot. If they were people, they'd be the kind you wouldn't let your daughter marry. Their diet was junky—about one-fifth sugar. And they breathed cigarette smoke. Even worse, they were boozers who drank every day, and didn't stop at just 1 cocktail but went on to lap up 2 or 3. Not surprisingly, they didn't exercise much. (Probably hung over!) In general, their health habits were abominable—and identical to those of many people!

You've probably already guessed that the lucky animals chosen for Group 2 lived the longest, and that the critters in Group 3 died young but ugly. What's surprising is the enormity of difference in the life span of the 3 groups.

Group 1 lived the normal number of years for its breed of laboratory animal. Poor Group 3 lived 30 percent less time. And good ole Group 2 had almost twice the life span of Group 3, and considerably more time than Group 1.

At the end of the experiment, Dr. Kugler concluded: "The results show that the genetic factor, which is often blamed for the aging process, is not the sole determinant when it comes to average and even 'maximum' life spans."

12 Plans to Keep You Young

These clear directives will help you maintain strong bones, a great body and good looks.

When you think of old age, certain pictures leap immediately to mind. The old guy with the shuffling step and the bent back. The woman whose lips are blue because of her heart condition. The man at the pool with the chalky white legs and the sagging chest. You think of false teeth, wrinkles, gray hair and baldness. The specter of chronic illness visits your daydreams. No wonder people fear growing old, with this depressing scenario stretching before them.

But many of the conditions and diseases considered to be an inevitable part of aging can, in fact, be either prevented or delayed.

How? Well, there's no magic pill or quick fix. But there *is* a lifestyle that includes good, nourishing food, exercise geared to your current fitness level (which will dramatically advance) and scrupulous attention to ferreting out bad habits such as smoking, or eating and drinking to excess.

Most of us don't realize it, but we can control many of the factors that affect our life expectancy and well-being. We have available to us a number of programs that can keep our internal organs functioning long and strong—and additional programs that keep us looking as young as we soon will feel.

This chapter includes 12 specific strategies that shape up and strengthen key parts of the body. All of the programs are completely natural and—as an added bonus—quite economical. (Several, in fact, will *save* you money!) Be aware, however, that some of these regimes require a sincere commitment on your part. You'll have to really work at them, so they can work for you. But consider the payoff! You'll have a healthy, supple, strong body. And when you look to the future you'll know that you will be "going like 80" until you're 80!

Strong Bones

It was a perfect spring Sunday. The sermon had been inspiring, and, coming out of church, Mrs. Sullivan had the wonderful feeling of everything being right with the world. Then it happened. She was holding on to Mr. Sullivan's hand, starting to go down the short flight of steps—when she slipped. Mr. Sullivan tried to steady her, but couldn't. So she fell, clutching at him and making him lose his balance, too. Both tumbled headlong, Mrs. Sullivan first, her husband right behind, bouncing on the concrete steps until they landed on the pavement.

Miraculously, Mr. Sullivan suffered no injury except for a few bruises on his hands and arms. Mrs. Sullivan wasn't so lucky. She experienced a lot of pain, and when she was brought to the hospital a short while later, X rays showed that she had fractured both her hip and her right wrist. In one respect this 68-year-old woman was lucky, though. She developed no complications during her hospital stay and the fractures healed well.

When she talks about the accident, Mrs. Sullivan says, "I'm glad John wasn't hurt, but it still amazes me—he took as nasty a fall as I did and came away with just a few black and blue marks. How lucky can you get?"

Maybe a bit of luck was clinging to John Sullivan as he took his tumble, but there's a reasonable *physical* explanation as well to account for the difference in the severity of their injuries. Mr. Sullivan doesn't have osteoporosis; Mrs. Sullivan does.

Osteoporosis is a condition in which bones become weak and riddled with holes. So weak that they can snap like dry twigs at the slightest bump or bounce. But how do bones get so fragile? Aren't they made to last for life? They are—*if* you know how to take care of them. And the first step is understanding the factors that can weaken bones.

Osteoporosis usually develops after menopause. At this time of life, the body stops producing estrogen, the female sex hormone. And in women, estrogen acts as a sort of chemical dam, holding calcium in the bones. Without it, the mineral slowly drains away. This low-calcium condition was probably responsible for what happened to Mrs. Sullivan. Weakened by osteoporosis, her porous, brittle bones couldn't bear the force of her fall.

But if misery loves company, Mrs. Sullivan has plenty of it. Over 150,000 women with osteoporosis break their hips each year. The hip isn't the only target, though. About 25 percent of women past 60 have spinal vertebrae that have been so weakened by osteoporosis that the result is a spinal fracture. And even these statistics are only the tip of the iceberg. It's estimated that some *6.3 million Americans* suffer from osteoporosis. Not all of them are women, of course. Men get osteoporosis, too, but usually in their late seventies and eighties.

In addition to a lack of calcium, a number of other factors, alone or in combination, may account for this condition. Some women have a genetic predisposition. A flood of hormones from an overactive parathyroid may be responsible. So may a vitamin D deficiency (more about this important vitamin later). Women who don't get enough exercise are very much at risk. So are women who have eaten the typical American diet for many years; it's almost sure to be low in calcium. But even those who

Osteoporosis Explained

Osteoporosis does not necessarily make bones smaller or thinner. Rather it makes them porous and brittle, so that they break easily; it is often responsible for the hip fractures that so often occur when older people fall.

It's natural for the body to both create and break down bone. But until the age of 40, the body generally creates more than it destroys. After 40, however, bone loss is common. It accompanies the aging process and begins to affect women at menopause and men at age 50.

eat excellent diets can also develop problems because the intestines, as we age, simply don't absorb as much nutrition from food as they did when we were younger. Calcium can come and go—unused.

Is this threat to health an inevitable part of aging? Of course not. Proper diet, vitamin and mineral supplements and exercise can prevent osteoporosis from ever developing. And, if you already have the disease, this program can keep your bones from getting any worse than they are today. In fact, if you really work at the combination of diet and exercise, you actually can *reverse* the disease.

BEGIN WITH CALCIUM

Our skeletons, the girders that support and protect the interior parts of our bodies, are mainly composed of calcium, phosphorus and a protein called collagen. Of all these components, calcium is the most important. You see, it's the crystals of calcium that bond with collagen to give our bones their fantastic strength.

Each day that passes without sufficient amounts of calcium in the body is another day of bone loss. If, for example, a postmenopausal woman consumed only 500 milligrams of calcium per day, she would experience a bone loss of about 1.5 percent per year. Like checks being drawn on a bank account into which insufficient funds are deposited, the deficit grows larger and larger.

Unfortunately, we are losing a mineral we don't get enough of in the first place. Dietary surveys show that the average woman who's 45 or older takes in the bare minimum of 450 to 500 milligrams of calcium a day. This fact may come as a big surprise to the many who think that, with a glass of skim milk and a dab of cottage cheese a day, they're getting all the calcium they need. And 500 milligrams is far below the Recommended Dietary Allowance of 800 milligrams of calcium for women and men over 19—which, many investigators in this field believe, is itself much too low.

For instance, Robert P. Heaney,

M.D., professor of medicine at Creighton University School of Medicine in Omaha, Nebraska, says that women past the age of menopause should probably *double* the amount of calcium they consume. "The RDA for adults is 800 milligrams, but our studies indicate they should be getting a gram [1,000 milligrams] or a gram and a half a day," Dr. Heaney suggests.

Another reason extra calcium intake is so important is that our bones were designed to be a storehouse for this mineral, keeping calcium available for various crucial body functions like muscular contraction. Therefore, the mineral doesn't simply stay in this respository; there's a constant inflow and outflow. When calcium is needed in another part of the body, a hormone ferries some calcium from our bones to our blood, nerves, muscles or other areas. Blood, in turn, delivers new calcium back into the bones for their vital needs. So the calcium composition of our bones is constantly in flux, with

Body Maintenance CHECKLIST

☐ Eat foods high in calcium, such as milk, cheese, sardines and kale.

☐ Get outdoors into the sun for a few minutes each sunny day.

☐ Exercise regularly. It strengthens your bones.

☐ Avoid a high-protein diet based on meat or fish. It washes away calcium.

☐ Cut down on coffee, tea and cola because the caffeine found in these drinks acts as a diuretic and may flush calcium out of the body.

☐ Eliminate excessive fat and salt from the diet.

☐ Give up the use of antacids.

☐ Get out of the chair and get moving.

the mineral flowing to other parts of our bodies or staying in the bones to replenish the storehouse.

During early adulthood, when calcium is "borrowed" from the bones, new bone forms in proportion to the amount that was lost. But as we age—or if our diets don't supply enough new calcium—more calcium leaves than returns. It's like an inventory shrinkage, and the shrinkage literally comes to pass. By the time a woman has her seventieth birthday, she may have lost 30 percent of her bone mineral mass.

Fortunately, calcium can help prevent this terrible degeneration. It works safely and has the great virtue of avoiding side effects. One long-term study showed not only that supplementation with this mineral can prevent osteoporosis, but also that it actually can *reverse* the bone loss so painfully experienced by people with osteoporosis. This study was done by a team of American researchers headed by Anthony A. Albanese, Ph.D., at the Miriam Osborn Memorial Home in Rye, New York, and the Burke Rehabilitation Center in nearby White Plains. Twelve elderly women, all living in a nursing home, were given 1,200 milligrams of calcium a day. The calcium came both from their diets and from calcium tablets. Vitamin D was also given so that their bodies could more easily accept the calcium. These women were compared to another group of elderly women who weren't given supplemental calcium.

After three years on this high-calcium regimen, the women in the experimental group had denser bones. Though they were three years older, their bones now were as strong as those of younger persons. What about the elderly women who hadn't been taking extra calcium? They didn't fare so well. As they grew older, their bones became even thinner.

This experiment is not the only success Dr. Albanese has seen. Over about a ten-year period he administered various calcium supplements (in doses of 750 to 1,000 milligrams per day) for different periods of time to 526 women in White Plains and Rye. He charted their bone density by quantitative radiodensitometry. That means he had X rays of people's bones read by a machine, rather than relying on subjective human eyes to rate the X rays for bone density.

His findings should convince even the most skeptical. Those people given calcium supplements developed stronger bones. Those given placebos kept deteriorating.

Osteoporosis is of sufficient complexity that no two women responded in the same way to these supplements. In some, only a mild increase in density resulted after more than three years. In others, density increased remarkably. One 62-year-old woman, who started out with bones more porous than those of six other women aged 36 to 54, ended up, three years later, with bones denser than those of the youngest of the six.

In general, the women's bones did not respond with calcification until six to nine months of day-in, day-out supplementation had elapsed. "In some of those women, bone loss had been going on for 20 years. You can't expect to put it back so fast," Dr. Albanese says.

Now for the bottom line. How much calcium do *you* consume a day? Make a special chart that shows all the foods you eat, plus the quantities, and compare them with the chart on page 39 showing foods high in calcium.

If your comparison reveals that your diet is somewhat low in calcium, it may be wise to take a calcium supplement.

THE SUNSHINE VITAMIN

In addition to seeing that your bones get enough calcium, make sure they get enough vitamin D, too. This remarkable substance is synthesized by your skin when you're out in the sunshine. If you don't get outdoors often or if you are faced with long, gray winters, lack of sunlight on your skin can result in a steady drain on your vitamin D supply. In fact, recent studies show many people experience a sharp decline during the winter. One such study was conducted by doctors at the University of Dundee, in Dundee, Scotland, where levels of ultraviolet light in

Women past the age of menopause should probably double the amount of calcium they consume. "The RDA for adults is 800 milligrams, but our studies indicate they should be getting a gram [1,000 milligrams] or a gram and a half a day."
—Robert P. Heaney, M.D.

Vitamin D:
Where the Rays Are

The sun shines East, the sun shines West, but let's see where the sun shines best. According to information published by the U.S. Department of Commerce, the states in the red area receive the most sunshine per year. The orange areas get about 95 percent of that amount, yellow receives about 85 percent, green gets only around 75 percent, blue a low 65 percent and purple a dim 60 percent.

Normally, ultraviolet rays in sunshine strike your bare skin, helping the body turn a fatty substance into a precursor of vitamin D. It actually takes 3 or 4 days to produce the vitamin. But Jolly Ole Sol isn't the only factor determining how much sun shines on your shoulders, because fog, smog, dust and volcanic ash can veil the earth from those vitamin D-producing rays.

Remember, of course, that *too much* sun can be harmful. But do enjoy a few minutes of fun in the sun every day.

sunshine are "very low or negligible" from November through February. Over a year's time, the researchers studied the vitamin D status of three groups of people by measuring their serum levels of the major circulating form of vitamin D, 25-hydroxyvitamin D, or 25-OHD for short.

The groups were divided according to occupation and amount of exposure to sunlight: A group of gardeners in the local parks department who worked outdoors all day; hospital staffers who got their sunshine mostly on weekends or after work; and a group of elderly patients, confined indoors, who received virtually no sunlight at all.

The results showed that "in each group the seasonal changes were highly significant," with the highest 25-OHD levels recorded during the late summer and autumn and the lowest during the late winter or early spring.

What all this means to your health was demonstrated in another study conducted by a trio of doctors in Leeds, England. Over a period of five years, the doctors examined biopsies from hip bones of 134 patients who had suffered suspicious fractures of the thigh bone. They concluded that 37 percent of the patients were suffering from a bone disease caused by a vitamin D deficiency. But what was most disturbing was the fact that by far the largest number of fractures occurred in a period stretching from February through June.

Keeping your vitamin D stores in order really shouldn't be too difficult, even if you rarely venture into the sun. A study in Norway—at latitude 70 degrees north, where the sun hangs below the horizon a full two months of the year—is a case in point. Over a period of a year, serum 25-OHD levels were examined in 17 healthy adults living in Tromso. Though the lowest concentration was found in March, blood levels overall remained "at a constant and fairly high level" throughout the year. The researchers attributed this sunny finding to good nutrition and the widespread consumption of dairy products fortified with vitamin D.

Actually, vitamin D isn't very common in the natural food supply. The foods that contain it in high amounts are all of animal origin, especially saltwater fish high in oil, such as salmon, sardines and herring. Fish-liver oils are highly concentrated sources of vitamin D. Egg yolks and liver also contain substantial amounts.

While you're adjusting your diet, keep an eye on the amount of coffee you drink, because caffeine may affect our bones in a bad way. Dr. Heaney and Robert R. Recker, M.D., of the Creighton University School of Medicine, examined some 168 women whose ages ranged from 36 to 45—women who had not yet reached menopause—and found that even a moderate amount of caffeine, the equivalent of a couple of cups of coffee a day, was associated with a loss of calcium from the body. Also be wary of eating too much protein. During the course of the same study, investigators found that a diet loaded with protein can lead to a calcium imbalance, where more of the mineral is excreted than is replaced. Try to eat more of your protein from vegetal sources like grains, beans and potatoes.

ESSENTIAL EXERCISE

While changing your diet can help to prevent or even reverse osteoporosis, there is another equally important step you can take to prevent the problem. And that is, simply, to take steps. Lots of them.

Exercise keeps bones healthy and strong. For example, researchers have found that people who are bedridden suffer from bone loss. People who are active, who engage in regular exercise, enjoy thicker, healthier bones. A study of 50- to 59-year-old cross-country runners, for instance, found that they had a 20 percent greater bone mass in their thighs and upper arms when compared to nonrunners of similar age, weight and height.

Those Antagonistic Antacids

What does a stomach remedy have to do with your bones? Plenty. Here's the story of one 60-year-old woman who was admitted to the hospital in great pain. Hospital X rays showed she had osteomalacia—adult rickets. A bone in her lower leg had fractured. Others were pitted with holes. Blood tests showed the woman had extremely low levels of phosphorus, a mineral that keeps bones strong.

It turned out she had been taking large daily doses of a non-prescription antacid for half a year and smaller amounts for the previous 12 years. The antacid contained aluminum hydroxide, which blocks the absorption of phosphorus. She was taken off the antacid. Within a month, she could walk a bit, and within 3 months she could walk normally.

Exactly what happened to this poor woman? According to Herta Spencer, M.D., of the Veterans Administration Hospital in Hines, Illinois, antacids cause the body to excrete large amounts of phosphorus.

In a similar study reported in the *Annals of Internal Medicine,* 18 women past menopause were divided into two groups. Nine did warmups, conditioning and circulatory exercises for an hour a day, three times a week. The other 9 remained sedentary. At the end of a year all of the women were tested. There was an increase in body calcium in every one who had exercised, but a decrease in all the sedentary women.

"The skeleton will adapt to the mechanical loading that you put on it," explains R. Bruce Martin, Ph.D., director of orthopedics research at West Virginia University in Morgantown, West Virginia. "If you increase the force, the bones become stronger. If you decrease the force, the bone weakens."

DANGEROUS TREATMENTS

Why don't more people know about these natural cures for osteoporosis? Because, until recently, most doctors treated women suffering from osteoporosis with supplemental doses of the hormone estrogen. Estrogen works. It slows the rate of bone loss and helps in the formation of new bone, restoring the balance between calcium outflow and return. But it doesn't strengthen bones that are already weak and thin. More important, estrogen has been related to a significant problem—namely cancer.

"For 30 years," said one survey published in the British medical journal *Lancet,* "from 1940, the incidence of endometrial cancer in the United States was more or less stable, but a marked rise was noted for the period 1969 to 1973 in data from a number of cancer registries. This rise exceeded 10 percent per year in some areas and was greatest in women aged 45 to 74 years. It was suggested the increase might relate to use of estrogens, sales of which had risen fourfold in the years 1963-73." Also, "a fall in estrogen prescriptions in early 1976 was followed by a fall, within a year, in endometrial cancer incidence. . . ." Other studies have shown that long-term estrogen therapy places women at greater risk for cancer of

the ovaries, uterus or breasts. Three studies, for example, showed that the risk of getting cancer of the uterus was four to eight times greater among women taking estrogen than among those who weren't. A study of 908 women on estrogen therapy showed the risk of developing ovarian cancer was two to three times higher than for women who weren't using it.

Patrick Ober, M.D., an endocrinologist at the Bowman Gray School of Medicine in Winston-Salem, North Carolina, uses calcium and vitamin D instead of estrogen. "When there are two kinds of treatments and one, like calcium, is benign and just as effective, then I'm inclined to go with it," he told us.

Is estrogen worth the risk of cancer? "Maybe, if it really works," you might say. Ah, but there's the catch. If estrogen therapy is used and then stopped, bone loss will be faster than ever, eventually catching up with the losses experienced by those people who never took estrogen at all. Why gamble on a risky long shot like estrogen when you can be a safe, sure winner with calcium, vitamin D and exercise?

Foods Naturally High in Calcium

Food	Portion	Calcium (mg.)	Food	Portion	Calcium (mg.)
Sardines, drained	4 oz.	494	Pizza, cheese	⅛ of 14-in. pie	144
Yogurt, skim	1 cup	489	Collards, cooked	½ cup	110
Salmon, drained	4 oz.	365	Kale, cooked	½ cup	103
Milk, skim	1 cup	302	Almonds	¼ cup	83
Swiss cheese	1 oz.	272	Chick-peas, dried	¼ cup	75
Monterey Jack cheese	1 oz.	212	Cottage cheese, low-fat	½ cup	69
Muenster cheese	1 oz.	203	Broccoli, cooked	½ cup	68
Mozzarella cheese, part skim	1 oz.	183	Artichoke	1 med.	61
Dandelion greens, cooked	½ cup	147	Filberts	¼ cup	60
Tofu	4 oz.	145	Eggs	2 large	56

A Healthy Heart

"**A** good heart is better than all the heads in the world," wrote Edward Bulwer-Lytton, a 19th-century novelist. Witty and true, for all that our hearts and circulatory systems do for us. The human heart, an engineering marvel, pumps 7,200 quarts of blood each day. Actually, the heart is not one pump but two—two pumps and two circulatory systems working in beautiful harmony with each other. The first carries blood to the lungs, the other pushes oxygen and nutrient-laden blood to the rest of the body's cells. The return of the blood to the heart is accomplished with the same marvelous efficiency. Small blood vessels collect it from the tissues, then they empty into larger veins that return the blood to the heart to be recirculated. The heart, too, nourishes itself with blood.

Yet it's true that the heart, like any mechanical device, shows some wear with age. The question is: How much wear? Well, that depends on what you *do* with (and to) your heart.

You see, not all hearts, even if they're the same age, are in the same condition. That's because the heart is not only machine—it's muscle. And like all muscles, it needs exercise and the right foods to stay in good shape.

Unfortunately, many people take the heart for granted and neglect its needs. As a result, a heart can become sluggish or lose its timing and become subject to skipped beats or flutters—what doctors call arrythmias. And atherosclerosis can do its slow and deadly work, blocking and hardening the arteries until the heart turns into a time bomb, ticking out the moments before it explodes in a heart attack.

But if heart disease is still "the nation's number one killer," the day may come when newspaper writers have to pin that cliché on some other disease. In recent years the mortality rates have been dropping steadily. In fact, since 1968, deaths from cardiovascular disease among American men have fallen by some 25 percent.

The figures make one thing startlingly clear, says one team of doctors, who point out that advances in the treatment of heart disease account for only a small part of the decline. The trend results mainly from preventive measures, they say, which include "changes in diet, cigarette smoking and exercise habits."

In fact, it may very well be that changes in our health habits have added to that statistical slide. If that's the case, what have we learned about heart attack prevention over the past few decades? What are we doing right?

For one thing, we're cutting down on the saturated fat we eat. The worst thing about fat is not what we see on the outside—the spare tire and extra chin—but what medical researchers believe happens on the *inside:* the manufacture of cholesterol. This substance travels in the blood, and can build up on the walls of the blood vessels, leading to hardening of the arteries and ending with a heart attack or a stroke.

But a low-fat diet is only part of the story. There are other, *special* foods that can keep cholesterol in check.

FOODS THAT HELP KEEP CHOLESTEROL HONEST

Let's look first at the eggplant. When Austrian scientist G. H. A. Mitschek of the University of Graz fed supplemental amounts of eggplant along with a cholesterol-rich diet to laboratory animals, there was a remarkable degree of protection against the development of fatty plaques in their blood vessels. The eggplant owes this effect, observes Dr. Mitschek, to certain constituents that slow the absorption of cholesterol in the intestine. And the good news is that its effects are most impressive when it is eaten not by itself but along with a fatty diet. In other words, it's the perfect accompaniment to cholesterol-rich foods.

The onion, too, can take the cholesterol sting out of other foods. To test the effect of onion as a cholesterol-lowering agent, K. K. Sharma and three colleagues associated with S. N. Medical College in

Agra, India, gave a group of men 3½ ounces of butter spread on four slices of bread first thing in the morning, after a 13-hour fast. On subsequent days, the men got their bread and butter with various accompaniments: once with 50 grams (about 1¾ ounces) of raw onions and another time with boiled onions. On another occasion raw onions were not given until 2 hours after the bread and butter.

The results? When butter alone was given, cholesterol levels two hours later increased from an average of about 211 to 232. Four hours after eating the butter fat, cholesterol was all the way up to 241, for a total rise of 30 points. But when raw onion was eaten at the same time, the total rise was only 9.4 points. Numerous studies have also shown that garlic has a similar protective effect.

Yogurt, too, actually reduces the amount of cholesterol in the blood. This was discovered by George V. Mann, M.D., Ph.D., at the department of biochemistry, Vanderbilt University School of Medicine, during a study of the diets of Masai tribesmen.

These primitive African people have very low blood cholesterol levels to begin with, but when they consumed large quantities of yogurt, even though some of them gained weight, blood cholesterol levels dropped significantly. Dr. Mann suspects that the yogurt bacteria produce or enhance a substance in milk that blocks cholesterol production in the liver.

While low cholesterol levels are considered an indication that you're doing something right, high levels don't necessarily indicate trouble ahead. In fact, if your cholesterol is high in the HDL fraction (high-density lipoproteins) as opposed to the LDL (low-density lipoproteins), your prognosis may be excellent. It is the LDL fraction that seems to get stuck in your arteries and is linked to heart disease. The high-density guys, however, appear to be very protective of your heart and arteries. The trick is to increase your HDL and decrease your LDL. How? One of the best dietary aids for encouraging this

Body Maintenance CHECKLIST

☐ Eat less fat, especially animal fat.

☐ Eat eggplant, yogurt and onions frequently to combat cholesterol.

☐ Eat apples and citrus fruit often and supplement the diet with soybean lecithin to fight cholesterol.

☐ Take extra vitamin C to protect arteries, and magnesium to prevent coronary spasms.

☐ Drink hard water.

☐ Exercise, exercise, exercise—at least 3 times a week for a half hour each time.

favorable ratio may be soybean lecithin, say Marian Childs, Ph.D., and four colleagues from the Northwest Lipid Research Clinic at the University of Washington in Seattle, who tested the substance on 12 volunteers with normal cholesterol. After three weeks, the researchers discovered that the volunteers' overall cholesterol levels had not been lowered. But what they did find was that a dose of 36 grams (more than 3 tablespoons) of lecithin daily lowered the LDL cholesterol and, at least in women, raised the relative amount of HDL cholesterol.

That an apple a day can keep the doctor away has never been proven by scientific testing. But, because of its pectin content, an apple a day might help to keep high cholesterol levels away.

Several researchers have reported findings showing the effectiveness of pectin. One of the most recent studies conducted by Mei Ling W. Chang, Ph.D., at the U.S. Department of Agriculture's Human Nutrition Research Center in Beltsville, Maryland, revealed that pectin helps lower cholesterol levels by slowing down the digestion of cholesterol-rich fatty foods. But that's not all.

Pectin is often used in making jams and jellies because it has gel-forming properties. Dr. Chang believes these same characteristics may help convert cholesterol into a

form not readily absorbed by the body.

The white membrane beneath an orange peel is also a good source of pectin. But oranges may also protect the heart because they're a good source of vitamin C.

Getting the Fats Straight

Fat goes by a lot of names these days: saturated, polyunsaturated and hydrogenated, to cite a few. How can you tell which are the good guys and which are the bad?

Each type consists of carbon, hydrogen and oxygen in various combinations. Saturated fat is constructed so that it contains all the hydrogen it can possibly hold. Hence, it's called saturated fat. You can spot a saturated fat, because it is *solid* at room temperature.

Polyunsaturated fats are not filled to the brim with hydrogen. In fact, the carbon molecules of polyunsaturated fat have room for more than one (hence the "poly-") hydrogen atom. This type of fat can easily be identified because it is *liquid* at room temperature.

A large body of research indicates that too much saturated fat in the diet is not good for your heart. Some studies have shown that by substituting poly-

unsaturated fat for saturated in the diet, cholesterol levels may drop enormously, decreasing the chance of a heart attack.

And so, it seems, one need only avoid all fat that is solid, instead substituting fat that is liquid. But what about products like margarine or Crisco? They claim to be vegetable oil and yet they are solid. A manufacturer who wants to turn, say, corn oil (a liquid) into margarine (a solid) chemically adds hydrogen to the oil. The process hydrogenates (or partially hydrogenates) the oil, converting it into a semisolid fat. Hydrogenation changes the fatty acids, increasing saturation and altering some of their components into "unnatural" arrangements.

Hydrogenation can create an abnormal type of fatty acid, which, research with laboratory animals has shown, tends to collect in the heart.

VITAMIN C AND A HEALTHIER HEART

Vitamin C, researchers have found, is a good defense against cholesterol, hardened arteries and heart disease.

One study of vitamin C and heart disease was conducted in England, where 11 elderly hospital patients with coronary artery problems took 1 gram (1,000 milligrams) of vitamin C daily, decreasing total blood cholesterol levels in only six weeks. That prompted reseachers to assert that "atherosclerosis and ischemic heart disease are not inevitable features of aging." And that's not all they found.

When the patients started their gram-a-day supplementation, most of them had vitamin C deficiencies; the men also had correspondingly low levels of HDL cholesterol. "After six weeks' treatment with ascorbic acid [vitamin C], the mean [average] HDL cholesterol concentration had increased," the study noted. What's more, the benefit was not restricted to the heart patients; all 7 men in the 14-member control group enjoyed it as well.

The evidence that vitamin C can protect as well as defend, that it is as beneficial to high-risk subjects as to those already afflicted with heart disease, may be the most compelling aspect of the British investigation. The research team has entered a plea for higher recommended daily intake of vitamin C because "latent ascorbic acid deficiency may be one of several preventable 'risk' factors contributing to the present epidemic of ischemic heart disease in the western world."

And a vitamin C deficiency is more common than you might think. The heart patients in the British experiment weren't the only ones suffering vitamin C deficiencies at the outset: Some of the 14 "healthy" control subjects were deficient, too.

The study noted that "low blood ascorbic acid levels are often found in elderly patients."

THE SPASM THEORY OF HEART ATTACK

It had long been assumed that atherosclerosis was the prime (and perhaps only) suspect in anginal pain and heart attacks. Today, however, a growing body of research indicates that coronary artery *spasms,* which can starve the heart of oxygenated blood as surely as fatty plaque or a wandering clot, may indeed be an important factor in heart attacks and angina. Just how important, or how common, is unknown, though one leading researcher estimates that a staggering 40 percent of all fatal heart attacks may be caused by spasms. And what causes spasms? Another debated point. But there is convincing evidence that the culprit may be a deficiency of the vital dietary mineral magnesium.

One of the earliest clues was the observation that the incidence of sudden death from ischemic heart disease (SDIHD), which is caused by a blockage of blood flow, is highest in areas where the drinking water or the soil contains only small amounts of magnesium.

Finland, for example, has one of the highest SDIHD rates of any country in the world; there are also distinct differences in mortality rates from region to region. Studies of the mineral content of soils from various districts in Finland showed that magnesium, calcium and potassium were much scarcer in the east, where mortality rates are highest, than in the southwest, where they are the lowest. The most pronounced difference, researchers reported, was in magnesium levels.

Both magnesium and calcium are the main components of hard water, and calcium is sometimes considered the protective "water factor" that shields people in hard-water areas from heart disease. But a more recent Finnish study showed that the Finns' consumption of calcium is actually *higher* than that of most other peoples; the geographical distribution of heart disease and

Fish Oil: Good Heart Food

Scientists have discovered a special substance in fish oil that lowers blood fats and may stop heart-threatening clots.

Interest in the relationship of fish oil to cardiovascular disease began with a study of Greenland Eskimos, who eat a high-fat, high-cholesterol diet—a diet that ought to promote atherosclerosis. Yet, among Eskimos, atherosclerosis, stroke and heart disease are rare. Noting that the main source of fat in the Eskimo diet is fish, scientists studied the fat and found it unique.

Fish fats contain relatively high amounts of omega-3 fatty acids and researchers found that fish-loving people have high levels of this acid in their blood. It reduces a substance that causes blood platelets to stick together, leading to blocked arteries and eventual stroke or heart attack. If Eskimo arteries are clearer than those of the average North American, it might be because of the fish they eat.

"Unfortunately, the average North American diet seldom contains foods rich in these omega-3 fatty acids,"

says William Harris, Ph.D., at the Oregon Health Sciences University.

In an experiment with 5 men and 5 women, Dr. Harris found that a diet based on salmon and salmon oil as the only sources of fat seemed beneficial for the heart. "After a month on the salmon diet, average blood cholesterol levels went down 17 percent. But triglyceride levels also dropped 40 percent, which is exciting. There's something unique about the effect of fish oil on triglyceride metabolism."

Another study by a team of researchers at University of Michigan Medical School, Ann Arbor, shows that eating fish may also prevent or lessen the severity of strokes. They found that a diet high in fish oil enabled laboratory animals to survive a stroke. It seems the diet prevented small blood vessels from constricting, allowing them to take over the function of the larger, blocked arteries.

How can you include these beneficial fats in your diet? A teaspoon or two of cod-liver oil daily would do the trick.

Can't Jump Rope? Then Take a Walk

Exercise, quite simply, does not have to be hard in order to be good for you. Some very interesting studies have been done with heart attack patients to bear this out.

When 32 victims of coronary artery disease, for example, were put on a 13-week moderate exercise program, researchers observed a marked increase in their HDL (the blood component that helps protect against heart disease by clearing excess cholesterol out of the bloodstream). The amount of exercise responsible for this result was a modest 1¾ miles of walking/jogging 3 times a week.

magnesium scarcity make a much tighter statistical fit. The researchers suggested that "inadequately low intake of magnesium in the industrialized countries in general, and in certain geographical areas in particular, may be one of the reasons for the present high incidence of cardiovascular diseases."

Another observation reported in a number of different studies: Samples of heart muscle taken from victims of heart attacks contain anywhere from 10 to 35 percent less magnesium than the hearts of those who died from other causes. Depleted magnesium levels in both humans and animals have also been associated with elevated blood pressure, that prelude to heart disease.

In the United States, one of the leading researchers on magnesium and the heart is Burton M. Altura, Ph.D., of the Downstate Medical Center in Brooklyn, New York, who with his wife, Bella T. Altura, Ph.D., and others, has been exploring this intricate mystery.

In one experiment, Dr. Altura and associate Prasad D.M.V. Turlapaty, Ph.D., used four different coronary vessels taken from dogs to test the idea that magnesium deficiency is indeed linked to SDIHD. Each of the vessels was exposed to a solution containing low, medium and high concentrations of magnesium; they were also studied when all magnesium was suddenly drawn out of the solution. Result? High concentrations of magnesium decreased the tension of the arteries, and sudden withdrawal of magnesium resulted in "rapid, increased tension development in all coronary vessels tested," Dr. Altura wrote in *Science*, a leading research journal.

"These data support the hypothesis," they concluded, "that magnesium deficiency, associated with sudden death ischemic heart disease, produces coronary arterial spasm."

If magnesium deficiency really is one of the devils behind heart attacks, what factors affect the levels in our bodies, besides what we eat and what we drink? Well, it now appears that stress, that bugaboo of modern life, can have a marked effect on cellular magnesium levels. Dr. Bella Altura suggests, for example,

that the hard-charging, competitive behavior we call "Type A," known to be associated with an increased risk of heart attack, is really "a state of more or less constant self-induced stress"—and that what makes it so deadly is the self-induced depletion of magnesium.

Beginning to wonder how *you* stack up in all of this? Well, the Recommended Dietary Allowances for magnesium range from 300 to 450 milligrams a day for adults—but three studies in the United States showed an average daily intake among both men and women of 250 to 280 milligrams, or marginally low. With improved methods for measuring magnesium in body fluids, writes Maurice Shils, M.D., director of clinical nutrition at the Memorial Sloan-Kettering Cancer Center, "it has become obvious that human depletion [of magnesium] occurs much more commonly than had been assumed previously."

Why? A study published by the National Research Council of Canada suggested the main reasons for dietary magnesium shortages, especially in industrialized countries: soft water, home cooking and commercial processing practices that leach the mineral out of foods and the widespread use of synthetic fertilizers that do not replace the magnesium that crops have drawn from the soil.

Magnesium occurs widely in foods, especially plant foods, in their natural state. The very richest sources are nuts, beans and legumes, such as peas. One-half cup of raw kidney beans, for example, packs 151 milligrams of magnesium, while ½ cup of soybeans contains nearly 200. Whole grains, such as wheat, barley and corn, are also richly endowed with magnesium. Green, leafy vegetables —spinach, kale and beet greens, for example—contain good amounts, but these should be steamed or briefly boiled because it's easy to leach the mineral right out of them.

EXERCISE FOR A STRONGER HEART

Elderly men who have bicycled vigorously for most of their lives are ten times less likely to develop heart disease than are others their age, says a report in the *British Medical Journal*. Dr. H. K. Robertson studied the health records of approximately 300 members of the Fellowship of Cycling Old Timers, a club for cyclists over 50 years of age. Most had cycled thousands of miles in their younger years on extended tours of the countryside. Seventy-five percent were still cycling regularly.

When compared with figures for noncyclers in the same age groups, the older cyclists had less heart disease and fewer heart attacks. Those over age 75 appeared to enjoy the greatest protection as a result of their lifelong exercise: a tenfold decrease in heart disease.

And in a similar study on this side of the Atlantic, researchers who studied 36,500 male alumni of Harvard University who enrolled between 1916 and 1959 found that those who continued to engage in vigorous physical activity after college were at less risk of heart attack.

In fact, those who were not active in sports during college but *later* became physically active were better protected than the beefy

Cholesterol-Fighting Foods

If you're working to clean your arteries of cholesterol, you already know what foods to eliminate. But do you know the foods you should add?

Here is a list of cholesterol fighters guaranteed to work *for* you: 100 percent bran cereal, oat bran, apples, oranges, bananas, eggplant, alfalfa, salmon, sunflower seeds, yogurt, skim milk, dry curd cottage cheese, beans, onions, garlic and raw green peppers. And don't forget your brewer's yeast.

fellows who charged across the goal lines at the university and later settled into sedentary lifestyles. While warning that diet and psychological factors can't be completely ruled out as elements involved in heart attack risks, the researchers stressed that the protective influence of exercise is very important.

Smoking and Heart Disease

One disease either caused or complicated by cigarette smoking is atherosclerosis. Two components in cigarette smoke seem to do the dirty work: nicotine and carbon monoxide. Nicotine speeds up a bodily mechanism—platelet aggregation—that may trigger the formation of blood clots. Carbon monoxide (CO) also hassles your heart, by luring hemoglobin into shirking its duty.

To help minimize the danger of carbon monoxide, take vitamin C, which offers some protection.

To help your body counter some of the damage caused by nicotine, consider taking vitamin E. Two researchers found that it can *decrease* platelet aggregation caused by nicotine.

In this study, one doctor collected blood samples from several normal, healthy volunteers. He then isolated the platelets from the blood samples and mixed them with various chemical agents known to trigger rapid platelet aggregation—and vitamin E. The results?

The more vitamin E that was added to the platelet samples, the greater was the reduction in platelet aggregation.

So if you must smoke, a bit of vitamin E may help to protect your arteries.

But, most important, quit altogether.

Breathing Easy

Take a deep breath. Hold it. Now slowly exhale. Become aware of your respiratory system and of the crucial organs at its center—your two lungs. Basically working on the principle of an air pump, our lungs draw oxygen-rich air into our bodies, exchanging it for the waste material carbon dioxide, which we remove from our lungs by exhaling. How much of this breath of life we need to fuel us depends on the activity in which we're engaged, our body size and how efficiently we breathe. An adult goes through an inhalation/exhalation cycle around 16 to 20 times a minute.

As we grow older, our lungs, like our hearts, go through changes. Part of the change has to do with the aging process itself. It's clear that our lungs have a lot of elasticity, expanding and contracting when we breathe in and out. The bony cage that houses them also has lots of give. But with the passing of the years, our lungs lose some of that elasticity and the compartments that house them become more rigid. Less play, less give, obviously mean less efficiency.

We experience this lessened efficiency when we put extra demands on the lungs—when we exercise, for example. Between the ages of 30 and 75, the volume of air taken in and out by the lungs drops by about 45 percent, while the amount of oxygen passing into the blood decreases by about half.

If You Must Smoke, at Least Do This

One of the greatest dangers of smoking is that it leads to the possible development of lung cancer, a disease which would seem too formidable for natural treatments like vitamins.

Not according to a massive study in Norway, which indicated that there is a strong link between the amount of vitamin A in your diet and the incidence of lung cancer.

A paper summarizing the study, "Dietary Vitamin A and Human Lung Cancer," written by E. Bjelke of the Cancer Registry of Norway, reported that 8,278 men were followed for several years and the amount of vitamin A in their diets estimated.

"Thirty-six cases of cancer of the bronchus or lung were found . . . A lower lung cancer rate in those with the high values of the vitamin A index is seen in all groups . . ."

That means if you do smoke, and you *also* eat foods rich in vitamin A, your chances of getting lung cancer may possibly be lessened.

Herbert Sprince, Ph.D., chief of research biochemistry of the Veterans Administration Hospital, Coatesville, Pennsylvania, suggests that other nutrients, too, may help. Dr. Sprince and his associate described how they gave rats *lethal* doses of the killer acetaldehyde and then tested the protective value of various nutrients and combinations of nutrients. The winning combination—vitamin C, thiamine and an amino acid called cysteine.

What do the lungs need in order to keep them healthy and effective over the longest possible period in our lives? Two things—proper exercise and proper nutrition.

Exercise helps ward off deterioration, and even people who are in their seventies or so respond well to a program of moderate exercise. In his physical fitness program for older people, Herbert deVries, Ph.D., found that even those who have been fairly sedentary for many years improve their breathing capacity by a surprising 35 percent with proper exercise.

Unfortunately, more efficient lungs can mean breathing in more pollution as well as more air. However, the problem is minor, and can be countered with proper nutrition.

At Tulane University, James C. S. Kim, D.V.M., Sc.D., compared the effects of nitrogen dioxide, a major pollutant, on three groups of hamsters. The first was deficient in vitamin A; the second was adequate in vitamin A. The third group was highly supplemented with vitamin A. Here's the intriguing outcome of Dr. Kim's experiment: Many of the deficient hamsters showed signs of pneumonia and some developed precancerous cells. Too, there was serious damage to the lungs, resulting in rapid and labored breathing when they were exposed to the pollutant. All the well-nourished hamsters, by contrast, survived easily. The nitrogen dioxide did some damage to their lungs, too, but normal tissue grew back—the lungs repaired themselves. All from vitamin A.

This kind of research is important for all of us. Nitrogen dioxide is emitted from our car exhausts; it's also a component of industrial wastes. Many of us are constantly exposed to it, and it's associated with the onset of emphysema. However, vitamin A can help our lungs mend, Dr. Kim says.

The question then arises: Do we get enough vitamin A in the course of our day-to-day lives? The evidence mounts: A surprising number of us don't. One reason has to do with lifestyle. As Michael B. Sporn, M.D., of the National Cancer Institute, points out, "There are groups in the United States that don't eat well, that don't get enough vegetables and milk products, which are good sources of vitamin A, and thus have marginal vitamin A intakes. For example, women trying to lose weight are probably missing vitamin A as well as other vitamins and minerals." Supplementing our diets with vitamin A can obviously do a great deal to keep our lungs in good repair.

Exercise and vitamins are a plus to the lungs. But a minus also is needed: lungs minus smoke. Of all the pollutants we are likely to breathe, tobacco smoke is the one most in our control. Studies at the Gerontology Research Center have made it very clear that cigarette smoking—particularly heavy smoking—is related to reduced lung function. On the average, the respiratory system of a heavy smoker performs the way a nonsmoker's does—but a nonsmoker who's ten years older than the smoker. However, there's good news, too: When that heavy smoker gives up the habit, his lung function recovers to nearly normal within 18 to 24 months.

Thus, the complete program for drawing a deep, cleansing breath involves exercise, diet and the discipline to refrain from smoking.

Body Maintenance CHECKLIST

☐ Exercise every day to make your lungs work efficiently.

☐ Take 5,000 I.U. of vitamin A daily to protect your lungs against pollution.

☐ Take 30 I.U. of vitamin E daily to protect against free radical formation.

☐ Give up smoking to prevent emphysema and lung cancer.

Strong, Firm Muscles

You sit down on the couch as you've always done, when suddenly one of your legs takes on an unwanted life of its own—it goes into a tremor. Or a sudden spurt of energy after a long lazy period propels you to do a super housecleaning job—and the next day your muscles are so cramped and sore you can hardly move.

Muscles. We don't think about them (unless they hurt) or about the body movements they trigger, but they work through a remarkably complicated system that uses elec-trical, chemical, thermal and mechanical elements.

To understand why muscles sometimes fail us, let's watch them closely as they go about their jobs. Say you want your hand to grasp an object. You may think the "command" you give your hand is instantaneous, but that's not so. The tiniest split of a split second elapses from the time you think the command until your hand executes it. In this speck of time, a signal speeds along your brain's nerve cells and those of your spine to the appropriate nerves that will carry the message to the proper muscle. When the muscle fibers receive this chemical code, they convert this chemical energy into mechanical energy. Stored muscle fuel is used to produce the end result, a muscle contraction.

The chemical sequence of events differs depending on how much we exert ourselves. Normally, if our oxygen supply is adequate to the energy demands of the body, carbon dioxide and water are the waste products. But when the oxygen supply isn't sufficient, as when we engage in heavy exercise, lactic acid instead becomes the end product of the muscle's energy-making process. The more lactic acid that's concentrated in our bodies, the more tired we become. Fatigued, we have to rest until there's enough oxygen back in the system to restore the balance. Why oxygen? Because oxygen helps in the further breakdown of lactic acid. The demand for oxygen is why we breathe heavily after we've exerted ourselves.

When we are out of condition, our lungs, heart or blood vessels don't deliver enough oxygen to the working muscles, causing lactic acid to build up earlier than it should. Thus, the conditioned person's brisk walk becomes the unconditioned person's strenuous exercise.

Lack of exercise, chronic illness, not eating properly and therefore not supplying the muscles with the proper nutrients—all these factors contribute to being out of condition. Then there's the aging process, which hits some people harder and sooner than it does others.

Some loss of muscle mass and

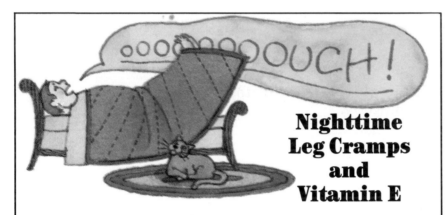

Nighttime Leg Cramps and Vitamin E

Two doctors, Samuel Ayres, Jr., M.D., and Richard Mihan, M.D., report they treated 125 of their patients who were suffering from nighttime leg and foot cramps with vitamin E.

"More than half of these patients had suffered from leg cramps longer than 5 years," the doctors write.

But vitamin E made short work of even these long-standing cramps. Of the 125 patients, 123 found relief after taking E. About 100 of these patients had "excellent" results.

If you find vitamin E does work, stick with it. "In a number of instances . . . cramps recurred when treatment was stopped, but promptly responded again when treatment was resumed," the doctors explain.

All in all, the doctors feel confident that vitamin E will do the job. "The response of [nighttime] leg and foot cramps to adequate doses of vitamin E is prompt, usually . . . within a week," they assert.

strength may be inevitable, but we can all stave off some of the more unpleasant things that can happen to our muscles with proper exercise and a nutritional program that takes muscle needs into account.

Muscle cramps are a case in point. "For muscle contraction to be normal, adequate levels of calcium must be present in the body," notes Ralph Smiley, M.D., of the Environmental Control Unit at Brookhaven Hospital in Dallas, Texas. Yet whether they're young or old, in or out of condition, what almost everybody doubled up with pain from muscle cramps or spasms seems to have in common is a low blood level of calcium.

Dr. Smiley and his colleagues found that some patients suffering from tetany—severe muscle spasms —needed calcium to relieve the pain. A daily maintenance dose worked to reduce seizures and helped keep tetany from recurring.

But man does not live by calcium alone. Consider studies at the biology department, Old Dominion University, Norfolk, Virginia, which indicated the importance of vitamin B_6 to keep our muscles functioning smoothly. The experiments were done with rats on exercise wheels. Forty of the animals were fed identical diets, except that 20 of them were dosed orally with vitamin B_6 on a daily basis. The result: The animals given B_6 seemed to have increased stamina because their muscles worked longer and harder than those of the rats who weren't on B_6.

A number of researchers believe that iron is integral to the proper functioning of the muscles. We all know it prevents anemia, but its good work goes far beyond that. Experiments have shown that even when they weren't anemic, iron-deficient animals were markedly impaired in their running ability. Once they received supplemental iron, their disability vanished within days.

Many people may have an iron deficiency without realizing it because of a problem in absorbing the mineral. A study conducted by doctors at the University of

Body Maintenance CHECKLIST

☐ Exercise daily to provide muscles with oxygen that breaks down lactic acid, and to maintain muscle mass and tone.

☐ Eat foods rich in calcium to keep muscles working smoothly.

☐ Eat foods rich in vitamin B_6 to increase stamina.

☐ Supplement the diet with iron for strength and endurance.

☐ Avoid caffeine and eat foods high in magnesium to help muscles relax.

☐ Eat foods rich in iron to keep muscles functioning properly.

☐ Eat foods rich in the B vitamins to help eliminate tremors.

Washington and the Kansas University Medical Center, however, showed that absorption of iron is greatly enhanced when it is accompanied by vitamin C.

As for the tremors and twitches that some older people experience, a number of vitamin and mineral deficiencies seem to be partially responsible. A potassium deficiency, for example, can upset the muscles' mineral balance. Then there's magnesium, which, when deficient, may be responsible for many a tongue, arm or leg tremor. Finally, there are the B vitamins, which are so important to the health of the central nervous system. A multivitamin/mineral tablet should ensure that you're getting enough of the nutrients to satisfy your muscles' requirements. For potassium, though, look to potatoes, raisins and avocados.

Good Digestion

Most people don't give a thought to whether nutrients from the food they eat are actually absorbed by their bodies. They mistakenly take this process for granted. Yet, a number of conditions can result in malabsorption.

Digestion begins with the act of putting food into our mouths. Saliva helps the digestive process by moistening and softening the food that's on its way to the stomach. Once there, gastric juices go to work on the food, breaking down every morsel into simpler substances that can be absorbed by the bloodstream. Eventually, the food is converted into a thick liquid called chyme, which slides along our digestive conveyor belt, first into the small and then into the large intestine. All told, the intestines are about 26 feet long, and

every millimeter is designed to carry food through that digestive process.

A series of complex chemical reactions that involve bile from the liver and enzymes from the pancreas and the small intestine accomplish this. It's from the small intestine, too, that our now-digested food in its final liquid form is absorbed to provide our trillions of cells with the nutrients they need.

Food absorption takes place through the villi, which are millions of microscopic fingerlike projections that line the walls of the small intestine. Proteins and carbohydrates wend their way to our cells via the bloodstream; fats, too, travel in the bloodstream, but are stored. What remains is bulk and liquid. The large intestine absorbs the liquid from the waste and delivers it to the blood-

Mealtimes that are unhurried, pleasant and free of quarrels and complaints contribute to good digestion as well as to good family relationships.

stream. Elimination takes care of the rest.

Proper absorption means we're properly fueled for all our bodily processes. Malabsorption, on the other hand, means we lose those precious nutrients because they just keep streaming along until they are excreted.

We can suspect malabsorption if we often feel abdominal discomfort or have loose bowels. Some people bruise easily after long periods of malabsorption. For others, the symptoms also include fatigue and night vision problems.

Malabsorption has many causes. It's a fact of life for people who have had intestinal bypass surgery, as well as for people who have celiac disease (gluten intolerance) and for those with diseases of the pancreas. However, malabsorption can result from far more common factors. A viral infection in the gastrointestinal tract, spoiled food or "irritable bowel syndrome" (or any other condition that causes frequent or considerable diarrhea) can cause nutrients to pass through the intestines without being absorbed. In addition, emotions have a direct effect on digestion. As John W. Erdman, Jr., Ph.D., of the department of food science at the University of Illinois elaborates, "People who have emotional difficulties, who are 'hyper,' often suffer from frequent diarrhea. This condition can have a significant effect on absorption."

In general, too, the older we are, the more likely problems will occur with the way we absorb nutrients, because with aging secretions of stomach acids and digestive enzymes decline. However, some older people absorb their food far more efficiently than others. Their secret lies in exercising, consuming plenty of raw foods, whole grains and vegetables and making mealtime a relaxed experience.

To further ensure sufficient nutrition, it also helps to take vitamin and mineral supplements. However, you may be wasting your vitamins and minerals by not taking them in partnership with other foods or nutrients that aid in absorption.

Body Maintenance CHECKLIST

☐ Take vitamins A, D, E and K with foods containing a little fat to help them become absorbed.

☐ Take vitamin C and the B complex group with meals to prolong absorption time.

☐ Take calcium with vitamin D to maximize benefits.

☐ Take iron with vitamin C to increase absorption.

☐ Eat lots of raw foods, whole grains and vegetables for bulk and to prevent bowel disease.

☐ Make mealtime pleasant. Never eat when you are upset.

☐ Exercise every day to stimulate efficient digestion.

Vitamins A, D, E and K are fat soluble, and most thoroughly absorbed when accompanied by a little fat. At breakfast, for example, don't simply gulp down a vitamin E capsule or multivitamin tablet along with a cup of coffee. Instead, take the capsule with a *real* breakfast that includes buttered toast or whole milk. Because the B complex and C vitamins are *water* soluble, it's best to take these vitamins with meals, too, because a full stomach slows the rate of absorption—also with beneficial effects.

Minerals, too, need other nutrients to help them escape from the digestive tract. We absorb only half the calcium we take in, unless we consume foods containing vitamin D or D supplements along with it. Iron deficiency—which is very common in this country, especially among older people—is at least partly linked to a poor absorption of this vital mineral. Studies show that when you take vitamin C along with iron, the combination dramatically enhances iron absorption.

From all this, it's clear that we need to amend an old saying. We're not so much what we eat as what we absorb.

Good Elimination

Some people define constipation as a disease. It isn't. It's a symptom of an underlying disorder that is sometimes serious, but more often is not. It consists of having infrequent bowel movements or of having them only with great difficulty. The first thing you should know about constipation is that a lot of people—older people in particular—worry about it needlessly.

The fact is that what's normal for one person isn't necessarily the regular ("normal") pattern for another. As the National Institute on Aging points out, "There is no accepted rule for the correct number of daily or weekly bowel movements. 'Regularity' may be a twice-daily bowel movement for some or two bowel movements a week for others."

How do you know if you're truly constipated? The appearance of certain regular symptoms will let you know. The National Institute on Aging suggests you ask yourself the following questions: Do you often have fewer than two bowel movements a week? Do you have difficulty passing stools? Is there pain? Are there problems—for instance, bleeding?

If your answers to most or all of these questions is yes, you probably are constipated.

What are the underlying causes of constipation? Sometimes it's a reaction to a medicine—for instance, certain antidepressants, antacids that contain aluminum hydroxide, antihistamines, diuretics and drugs used to treat Parkinson's Disease. Sometimes it's lack of exercise. On the other hand, active, busy people

---

Say Goodbye to Laxatives

More than 41 million Americans use laxatives. In fact, they spend hundreds of millions of dollars on the over-the-counter brands. Some people become so heavily dependent on laxatives they actually become "hooked," and cannot function normally without them.

What, exactly, are laxatives?

Laxatives work in a variety of ways. One group works to increase the bulk of the stool and *prevent* constipation. Products in this category include Metamucil and Serutan.

Another category is made up of laxatives that stimulate the intestine to work by irritating the mucous lining and acting on the nerves in the intestinal muscle. Depending on the dose, the results can range from mild action to all-out warfare. Products in this category include the old-time unfavorite, castor oil, along with Dulcolax, Senokot and Carter's Little Pills.

Mineral oil (not to be confused with castor oil) is a lubricant laxative, as are Agoral and Haley's M-O. This group prevents the intestine from reabsorbing water from the stool as well as absorbing the fat-soluble vitamins A and D.

Products like Colace and Surfak are softening agents, which work by causing liquid and fatty substances to combine with the stool. These drugs are useful in certain specific instances, such as after rectal surgery. They are not everyday laxatives—and should never be taken along with mineral oil.

The last large group of laxatives is based on either magnesium hydroxide (Phillips' Milk of Magnesia), or another magnesium salt (magnesium citrate, magnesium sulfate). They cause the intestine to retain fluid until it is stimulated into activity.

Regardless of which type of laxative you're taking, you probably could do without it altogether.

who are so rushed they develop the habit of "putting off" a bowel movement also can become constipated. At times, this relatively minor problem can signal the onset of an intestinal disorder. But, most of all, poor diet is the crux of the problem.

A lot of the food we eat is simply too processed to provide the roughage we need. Our digestive systems suffer the consequences. Our flour and bread is made snowy white by processes that remove not only nutrients but also the bulk we need for good digestion and elimination. By contrast, dietary fiber—those parts of food that we neither digest nor absorb—naturally leads to evacuation of the bowels.

What about laxatives and enemas? Beware. All too often they perpetuate constipation rather than cure it. Americans spend an estimated $250 million on nonprescription laxatives each year. Older persons are especially prone to using them. But the National Institute on Aging cautions, "heavy use of laxatives is usually not necessary and often can be habit forming."

What's the best—the healthiest—approach when bouts of constipation mar our days? First, have your doctor look you over, just to make sure no serious disorder is the cause. In most instances serious disorders can be ruled out, so take a close look at your diet next. You'll probably be surprised at how little fiber you actually are consuming.

To illustrate the point, consider the typical meals this Los Angeles man, a 64-year-old film editor, healthy in every respect except for bouts of constipation, outlined for his doctor.

"For breakfast I have a couple of eggs, sunny-side up, half an English muffin and a cup of coffee. For lunch, a meat or cheese sandwich and a cup of coffee. For dinner I'll have soup, a main dish of meat or fish, vegetables and some dessert. Won't that give me enough fiber?"

The physician smiled, shaking his head. "I doubt if you get *any* fiber to speak of, unless the portion of vegetables you eat at dinner is very large."

There's widespread agreement

Body Maintenance CHECKLIST

☐ Eat fruit, vegetables, grains and other foods high in fiber.

☐ Check to see if a medication that causes constipation (certain antacids, for example) can be switched for one that does not.

☐ Exercise daily to stimulate bowel function.

☐ Do not "put off" visits to the bathroom.

☐ Reduce and eventually give up the use of laxatives and enemas.

☐ Take 1 to 2 tablespoons of bran every day, and drink lots of water.

in the medical community that dietary fiber—especially bran—is a most effective and safe way of warding off constipation.

The medical literature is replete with literally hundreds of bran-related studies. One of the most important was conducted by I. Taylor, M.D., and H. L. Duthie, M.D., surgeons at the University Surgical Unit, Royal Infirmary, in Sheffield, England. What did they find? That bran actually normalizes bowel function in diverticular disease. In fact, bran can correct a number of different bowel disorders, including constipation and diarrhea. It acts as a stool softener in cases of constipation, shortening the time it takes for food to pass through the bowels and be eliminated. With diarrhea it works incredible reverse magic, hardening the stool and lengthening the transit time.

Denis Burkitt, M.D., a renowned researcher and fiber enthusiast, recommends adding the following to your diet: whole grain breads and cereals, nuts, dried fruit, beans, carrots, peas, and a tablespoon or two of bran. Drink at least one extra glass of water a day—you want to provide the bran with enough moisture to absorb.

Diverticulosis

Martha C., a 60-year-old schoolteacher, called her doctor for an appointment because she wasn't feeling well. When the internist questioned her about her medical problems, she described intermittent abdominal cramps that were getting worse. Constipation also was a problem, Martha said—but, when the physician questioned her closely, it seemed that what she called constipation often turned out to be small and difficult bowel movements. Occasional diarrhea was yet another problem, as were gas and a frequent bloated feeling. Worst of all, she told the doctor, she noticed some blood when she moved her bowels.

Martha was understandably frightened. Yet, her doctor was properly reassuring; the medical workup she received was even more so. Yes, she had a problem, the physician told her, but it wasn't serious and could be corrected by an addition to her diet.

The problem was diverticulosis.

"The X rays showed me that tiny pouches have developed in the wall of your large intestine," the doctor explained. "It's very common among people over 60, though most go along for years—or forever—with no symptoms or very few of them. There's no inflammation and I'm not going to prescribe any drugs for you. The only thing I'm going to ask you to do—and I want you to be sure to do it—is to alter your diet somewhat. I want you to make it a high-fiber one."

What is the cause of this disease? Once again, a consistent, lifelong low-fiber diet is the most likely candidate. The first comprehensive—and by now widely accepted—explanation was given by the English surgeon Neil S. Painter. Dr. Painter stated that the colon might well be likened to a series of little segments. Contractions normally move food from one segment to the next. As this happens, any given segment containing food residue tightens at both ends and contracts with sufficient strength to push that residue on. If the segment contains a sufficient amount of material to propel onward, all's well and good. But if it doesn't, problems begin because the less material there is, the more pressure that segment has to apply in order to move the material along. When this excessive pressure occurs repeatedly over a long period of time, it causes those little pouches (called diverticula) to pop out of the

The Cure That Didn't

For more than 50 years diverticulosis—which strikes 1 out of every 3 people over 60—was treated with a low-residue diet. And it took 50 years to realize that this diet was actually the *cause* of the disease.

Before 1900 diverticulosis was almost unknown. However, with the advent of processed foods, people ate fewer whole grains, fruits and vegetables (all good sources of fiber) and more meat, dairy products and sugar (all low in fiber). Along the way, they developed diverticulosis.

But researchers investigating the disease found that it was uncommon among rural people who ate lots of high-fiber foods. Going against medical tradition, they added bran to the diets of patients with diverticulosis.

Surprise! Ninety percent of the patients' symptoms were relieved.

Diverticulosis and Fiber

intestinal walls.

But those who do develop diverticulosis needn't reconcile themselves to living endlessly with the problem. As Dr. Painter's experience —and that of many other physicians —bears out, it's curable, and without surgery. How? With fiber. With bulk. The more fiber in the colon, the fewer and less forceful the contractions that are needed. The fewer the contractions, the less pain and other symptoms there are.

This success of dietary fiber has been wonderfully borne out by the many patients who recovered because of it. At Manor House Hospital in London, for example, Dr. Painter's theories were put to a crucial test when 62 diverticular disease patients were put on a diet high in fiber. Their regimen consisted of bran, whole wheat bread, an increase in the amount of raw fruits and vegetables the patients consumed daily and an extra pint of fluid per day. At the same time, their intake of sugar and sugary foods was kept at a minimum. Before the fiber therapy, about half of this group of patients were irregular in their bowel movements. Movements were infrequent and accompanied by a lot of straining. Several had small stools and attacks of diarrhea. Most were used to taking laxatives. What's more, at least 10 of the group had pain severe enough to indicate a problem requiring surgery.

After having been on the high-fiber diet for a while, however, all of the patients began to have regular bowel movements. The vast majority reported that they no longer had to strain. Most gave up laxatives and the few who didn't resorted to medication only infrequently.

Most striking of all, the patients for whom surgery had been indicated no longer experienced their severe pain. According to Dr. Painter's report, "all recovered without surgery and remain well since on bran."

These amazing recoveries were not isolated phenomena. Consequently, other British doctors and hospitals started to prescribe simple, ordinary bran to their patients and saw amazing improvement in their conditions. For instance, at the

Body Maintenance
CHECKLIST

☐ Add high-fiber foods, such as spinach, corn, peas, broccoli, whole grains and berries, to the diet.

☐ Take 1 level tablespoon of bran 3 times a day; gradually increase the amount until it works in treating the condition. Maintain that amount daily.

☐ Drink an extra 8-ounce glass of water each day.

☐ Cut down on sweet and processed foods.

Royal Berkshire Hospital in Reading, a specific operation for diverticular disease—which previously had been performed about once every three weeks—was being done just once a year or so after the patients were put on a bran/fiber diet.

Dr. Painter suggests people "start by taking 2 teaspoonfuls of bran three times a day. After two weeks, increase the bran intake slowly until the stools are soft and [you can] defecate without straining." Because of differences between English and American spoon sizes, Americans with a diverticular problem might want to begin by taking a level tablespoon of bran three times a day, slowly increasing the amount they take in until it becomes effective in treating the condition, then maintaining that level for good. If you have diverticulosis or diverticulitis, your physician will probably indicate how much bran and other high-fiber food he wants you to add to your diet.

A diversified high-fiber diet also includes vegetables and fruits high in fiber. Spinach ranks very high—1 cup of spinach contains 11.4 grams of fiber. A cup of peas has 8.4 grams; a cup of blackberries has 10.6, or about half the amount in a cup of 100 percent bran cereal. Broccoli, zucchini and summer squash are also realtively high in fiber.

Sex

Their mid-sixties are for Kathy and Joe M., a just-retired couple living in Madison, Wisconsin, a complete and joyous surprise. They are enjoying their leisure activities. They are enjoying each other far more than they'd ever thought they would. Sex, too, is fun—more vibrant and enjoyable than they'd ever expected it to be at their ages.

Sylvia and Larry F. are also recent retirees. They gave up their New York City apartment and live in a Miami condominium, which they love. In many ways their lives are as satisfying to them as Kathy's and Joe's. Where they differ—and differ strikingly—is in their sex life. There's very little of it.

Two older couples, two strikingly different experiences insofar as their sexual lives are concerned. Unfortunately, the second couple reflects what all too often happens as the years advance. Sexual activity becomes less and less frequent; sometimes it stops altogether. Often, too, there's the feeling among such couples that sexual desire "after a certain age" is embarrassing.

As the section on sexual myths in chapter 1 pointed out, ageism is largely to blame for these attitudes. You already know that sexual desire and activity in the later years are perfectly normal and possible. In fact, experts in medicine and gerontology agree that sex has a beneficial effect on older people. This doesn't mean people who have no interest in or enjoyment of sex ought to force themselves into it. It does mean that people who have sexual urges shouldn't deny their existence or be ashamed of them. On the contrary, good sexual functioning—and enjoyment of sex—requires a positive attitude. Equally important is keeping oneself in reasonably good physical condition.

Though many women do undergo changes in relation to lubrication in the vaginal area following menopause,

Do Oysters Really Make You Sexy?

Folk legend says that oysters make you feel sexy. Could it possibly be true?

Yes, it could. Possibly. Oysters, you see, are high in zinc—a mineral of primary importance to a healthy sex life. The pituitary gland, which stimulates our bodies to produce both egg and sperm, needs sufficient zinc to function well.

In addition, zinc helps keep the male prostate gland and female vaginal tissue in good shape. Moreover, doctors have found that a deficiency of this mineral can result in impotence. Scientists have found, however, that zinc supplements help this problem to disappear.

The Recommended Dietary Allowance for zinc is 15 milligrams a day. A 3-ounce serving of Atlantic oysters contains more than 64 milligrams!

What else is in oysters? Iodine, which is essential for good thyroid function. And, when functioning well, the thyroid puts your libido in drive. They also contain vitamin A, which is needed to produce sexual secretions.

It seems a bed of oysters may actually contain enough of the right nutrition to deserve its reputation!

the heartening news from Robert N. Butler M.D., and Myrna I. Lewis, in *Sex after Sixty* (Harper & Row, 1976) is that "women in good health who were able to have orgasms in their younger years can continue to have orgasms until very late in life, well into the eighties."

If you're a man reading this, your own outlook may well become more positive in light of one set of heartening findings that came out of the National Institute on Aging. Contrary to popular belief, they show that levels of the male sex hormone testosterone do not decrease with age. On the contrary, they found that "healthy old men maintain their production of sex hormones at levels found in younger men." Among the oldest subjects in this study—men aged 70 to 89—those with the highest testosterone levels were also those who maintained the highest levels of sexual activity.

To enjoy sex, many follow these specific rules of good health and good nutrition:

1. Climb on the wagon. Tolerance to alcohol varies and a glass or two of wine may be a fine way to relax and get "in the mood"—but the more alcohol that's drunk, the more problematic sex becomes. Also, alcohol lowers the testosterone level in men, creating potency problems; in women it delays orgasm.

2. Go light on sweets. In a research study with men having potency problems and women having problems reaching orgasm, it was found that an unusual number of these subjects tended to be hypoglycemic—to have a low blood sugar problem.

3. If you're a coffee drinker, try to cut down or even switch to herb tea. Caffeine affects the entire nervous system, including sexual functioning.

4. Zinc is helpful in the maintenance of male sexual health and vigor. In one widely reported experiment originating at Georgetown University, four impotent kidney patients treated with zinc showed striking improvement of

their potency, while four others treated with a placebo (a dummy pill) did not. Is a zinc deficiency likely in the average American male? It is if he smokes or drinks; heavy smokers and heavy drinkers may be especially prone to zinc deficiency. Liver, sunflower seeds, oats, nuts and cheese are good sources of zinc.

5. If you're taking drugs, ask your doctor whether they can cause impotence (in a man) or a lessening of sexual desire (in both sexes). Tranquilizers and antidepressants sometimes fall into this category, as do some drugs used to control high blood pressure.

6. Engage in regular, appropriate exercise. The less we do physically, the less we want to do physically, and that includes engaging in sexual activity. Conversely, the more active we are generally, the more invigorated we feel in *every* respect.

Body Maintenance
CHECKLIST

☐ Realize that sexual activity at any age is normal and appropriate.

☐ Retain a positive self-image.

☐ Get in shape with a daily aerobic exercise. Walking is good.

☐ Refrain from drinking alcoholic beverages.

☐ Cut down on eating sweets.

☐ Cut down on coffee and other drinks containing caffeine.

☐ Get adequate amounts of protein.

☐ Eat zinc-rich foods.

☐ Check with your doctor to see if any of your medications has an effect on your love life.

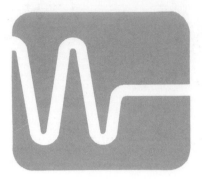

An Easy Menopause

For Brenda P. the onset of menopause came when she was 41. That's when she began to experience some of the early symptoms—irregular menstruation, hot flashes, fatigue, a hot temper that she found harder than usual to control. These symptoms lasted for about six years.

For Ellen K., menopause began when she was 49. Her menstrual periods, too, became irregular and—for a woman with lots of energy—she sometimes found herself unusually tired. But that was the extent of her problem. When she was 54, her periods quietly stopped altogether. As she puts it, "It was so calm, I was surprised."

As Brenda's and Ellen's experiences illustrate, menopause—the "change of life"—is an event whose configurations differ from woman to woman. For some, the onset is earlier; for some, later; the average age, at least in the United States, is about 51. For a relative few, it begins much sooner. It's not unusual for a woman to experience the symptoms of menopause for a decade or longer before her periods cease altogether. Roughly 25 percent of menopausal women suffer few symptoms, while another 25 percent are more cruelly afflicted. The remaining 50 percent have mild difficulties.

When seen as a biochemical event, the pattern for all women is the same. Ovulation stops. The menstrual flow becomes irregular. There's a reduction in the amount of estrogen, the female sex hormone, that the body produces.

This lessening of the sex hormone has its effects—if not on sex, then on the sexual organs. The walls of the vagina become thinner and less elastic; they also become more easily irritated, more prone to infections and less readily lubricated. Intercourse may become more difficult, scratchy or painful.

Menopause, whether easy or difficult, is a major change in the life of a woman. How can she most constructively handle this change? For many physicians whose female patients do suffer severely from the symptoms of menopause, estrogen replacement therapy (ERT) is the "cure." This therapy does alleviate some menopausal symptoms— especially the hot flashes, the vaginal dryness and the night sweats. But as the section on osteoporosis made clear, ERT is a very controversial treatment because of reports linking it to an increased risk of uterine cancer, gallbladder disease and high blood pressure.

Fortunately, there are other approaches for the relief of the more distressing menopausal symptoms— approaches that are safe, natural and in harmony with the body's needs.

In this context, let's consider hot flashes.

These episodes are essentially harmless, but they do cause a lot of discomfort and embarrassment. For

Hot! Flash!

One moment you're perfectly comfortable. The very next, inexplicably, you feel as though an invisible heat ray were beamed at your face and neck. You begin to sweat—not just politely perspire, but really sweat. But even before you can pick up the phone to call your doctor, the sensation passes.

Congratulations. You've just experienced a hot flash.

What causes this bizarre phenomenon? Nobody really knows, but one theory suggests that hot flashes are caused by a drop in the production of estrogen along with a simultaneous increase in the hormone production of the pituitary gland.

A British study of several women who experienced hot flashes revealed that the skin temperature does, indeed, shoot up abruptly—but usually just a couple of degrees.

Here's how to take some of the heat out of these symptoms. Wear clothes in layers, so you can peel off something when a flash starts. Drink ice water during an episode. In addition, some physicians report that vitamin E may help.

women who don't want to risk ERT or for whom ERT isn't indicated—for instance, those who have a history of breast cancer in their families or who themselves have breast nodules—an alternative is found in taking vitamin E. After interviewing hundreds of women who had gone or were going through menopause, Rosetta Reitz, author of *Menopause: A Positive Approach* (Chilton, 1977), discovered that many of these women found quick relief by taking 800 I.U. of this vitamin. Ms. Reitz writes, "I have seen flashes disappear completely when the vitamin E is also accompanied by 2,000 to 3,000 milligrams of vitamin C (taken at intervals throughout the day) and with 1,000 milligrams (also at intervals) of calcium. When the flashes have subsided, usually after a week, the woman reduces the vitamin E intake to 400 I.U." (See "Hot! Flash!" for additional recommendations.)

The dryness in the vaginal area that often occurs after menopause also can be safely overcome without estrogen. Many women find the use of a lubricating jelly effective in dealing with the problem.

Some women have a rough time of it emotionally after the onset of menopause. Quite a few women labor under the misapprehension that after menopause sex won't be good. From a medical point of view, nothing could be further from the truth. Many women find menopause a great relief, in the sense that they no longer have to worry about birth control. Consequently, they enjoy sex far more than they did before; there's more of a sense of "letting go." Yet, some women do become less responsive sexually after menopause. Psychotherapist Claire Leighton, who has worked with many older patients on issues of loss and change, theorizes, "Some women become depressed partly because they feel that, in the eyes of men, they have lost their desirability as women. But there are other reasons for menopausal and postmenopausal depression, too—because of the physical symptoms, and because it really means having to face that one is growing older. Today we hear less

Body Maintenance CHECKLIST

☐ Take 800 I.U. of vitamin E daily to treat hot flashes. Reduce the amount to 400 I.U. after 1 week.

☐ Take vitamin C and a brewer's yeast tablet daily.

☐ To help cope with depression, eat foods high in vitamin B_6, such as halibut, chicken, tuna and bananas.

☐ Eat foods high in vitamin E, including sunflower seeds, salmon and peanut butter.

☐ Exercise daily for fitness and emotional release.

about women being subject to depression during menopause or afterwards because women today have invested themselves in new roles, interests and activities."

Fortunately, there is a nutritional approach to the emotional symptoms that's safe and healthy. That approach is B vitamins. Studies show that many older women are deficient in B vitamins, especially B_6. Yet the B vitamins—and B_6 in particular—are necessary for the healthy functioning of the central nervous system, which governs our emotions. Try to eat foods high in vitamin B_6—freshly cooked fish, chicken (white meat), liver, sunflower seeds, canned tuna, bananas.

What else can help? Ms. Leighton suggests: "Look at your symptoms as normal rather than as an 'illness,' and they may become easier to live through. Keep yourself fit by engaging in sports or exercises you enjoy and channel your energies into interesting pursuits. The more you do to make yourself feel good, the easier menopause will be."

Eyes

Did you know that each of your eyes weighs ¼ ounce and is about 1 inch in diameter? Or that when you were born, your eyes were closer in size to what they were to be when you became an adult than any other part of your body? Or that there's an intimate connection between good sight and good nutrition? A poor diet, in fact, can have a destructive effect on the eyes in a variety of ways. More and more studies related to vision bear this out. The leading cause of blindness in children, for example, is brought on by malnutrition in general and lack of vitamin A in particular. In adults, a poor diet may not lead to total blindness, but it does affect our vision after dark. When a Florida optometrist tested 100 patients at random to determine how well people see at night, 26 of them failed some portion of the test. Night vision depends on a light-sensitive pigment called rhodopsin—and the main source of rhodopsin is vitamin A. Other research has shown that zinc

deficiencies, too, can cause night blindness in some people.

Glaucoma also may be helped with certain nutrients. This disease, which is all too common in those over 40, is the result of an increase in fluid pressure in the eye. Chronic glaucoma —the most common type—is usually painless, but as the pressure inside the eye mounts, it damages the retina and leads to loss of side vision. Eventually the optic nerve is damaged. The result is a severe loss of vision and, finally, blindness.

If chronic glaucoma is detected early, vision often can be saved through the regular use of medication. (Closed-angle or acute glaucoma, which *does* cause eye pain, requires surgery.) Everyone over 40 should have a routine eye examination that measures pressure in the eye.

Some doctors emphasize that medicines and surgery aren't an absolute cure for glaucoma; in too many people, the condition just continues to get worse. After review-

---

Eye Problems

Below are 4 variations of the same scene. The first represents normal vision; the others show the scene as it would appear to people with certain eye problems.

Normal
With normal vision, you have a clear, complete view of whatever's in sight.

Glaucoma
With chronic glaucoma, it seems as though you are looking down a gun barrel. Side vision is lost, and what remains is foggy. Often you see colored halos around bright lights.

Cataracts
With cataracts, vision is blurred. Some people experience double vision, "ghost images" or spots, as well. You may require a brighter light for reading and close work. Night driving may become difficult.

Myopia
Myopia is the medical term for nearsightedness. A person with this problem has trouble clearly seeing objects in the distance or even certain closer items such as small print. Images of these things appear blurry.

ing the literature on glaucoma and nutrition, W. Marshall Ringsdorf, Jr., D.M.D., and E. Cheraskin, M.D., D.M.D., of the University of Alabama in Birmingham, offer another kind of hope. They note the therapeutic value of vitamin C. In just about every study undertaken with glaucoma patients, vitamin C supplementation (usually in large doses) resulted in sometimes dramatic drops in pressure. In one of the studies cited, the high eye pressure of glaucoma patients dropped four or five hours after they received a single, massive dose of vitamin C. This lowered pressure remained for more than eight hours.

Reporting on this study in the *Journal of Holistic Medicine,* Dr. Ringsdorf and Dr. Cheraskin concluded vitamin C "is effective in reducing intraocular tension in glaucomatous eyes."

Even eyes that are in excellent shape and not affected by specific diseases can show some changes with age.

Many of us still see fairly well no matter how old we are—though often with eyeglasses; and there are people who have lived close to a century with 20/20 vision. But aging of the eye does occur, and for most of us, poorer vision results. The cornea tends to flatten, which either creates or worsens astigmatism, a condition that causes our vision to become distorted.

As we age we see more "floaters" —dots, lines or cobwebs that come unbidden to hover in front of our eyes. Some people are frightened by them when they first make their appearance, but these little blips in vision are just normal signs of aging. (Floaters accompanied by flashes of light are something else again, calling for a checkup by an eye specialist; this condition sometimes indicates a detached retina, which can lead to blindness.)

Additional changes that come with aging may have a serious impact on our vision. The lenses of the eyes become clouded, and the pupil grows smaller. These older eyes react more slowly to changes in light. As a result, less light reaches the

Body Maintenance CHECKLIST

☐ Get adequate amounts of vitamin A to counter night blindness.

☐ After age 40, have a glaucoma examination with every physical examination.

☐ Make sure your diet is high in vitamin C for healthy eyes.

☐ If you experience "floaters" accompanied by flashes of light, have an eye examinaton.

☐ Be sure to provide adequate lighting in your home.

retina—meaning you need brighter light to see well. At the same time, the eye can lose its ability to focus well on objects that are close—a problem easily corrected with prescription lenses.

Researchers at London's St. Bartholomew's Hospital measured how well 56 older Britons (average age, 76) could see in their homes, then compared these findings with how well the same people could see in well-lit environments. They concluded that "general levels of lighting are often so poor in the homes of elderly people that the number of people functioning as 'blind' is twice what it need be." Just increasing the wattage of existing lighting, they discovered, improved vision in 82 percent of the subjects.

For better Hearing

Near the Sudanese-Ethiopian border in Africa lives the primitive Mabaan tribe. Theirs is virtually a Stone Age existence, but that isn't the only unusual thing about them. Even more unusual is their hearing. When a team of doctors tested the Mabaans, they found that young or old, Mabaans retain their ability to hear remarkably well. Why are they blessed with such excellent hearing? Because they respect quiet—and consequently, respect their ears. They speak quite softly. They don't fire guns. They don't beat on drums. Except for the sounds of nature, theirs is a wondrously hushed setting. They also have a diet that seems to protect their hearing, but more about that later.

The contrast between the Mabaans and ourselves in our advanced, industrialized society is clearly startling. Without even counting workers in industry, 40 million

people are exposed to potentially harmful noise levels. Moreover, about one-third of all those over 65, while not deaf, have problems with their hearing. Not surprising. Few of us reside in hushed surroundings. What we experience is usually a never-ending assault on our ears. The toll all this noise takes, both in loss of hearing and in other serious problems, is increasing.

Much of this hearing loss may be preventable and controllable with proper diet and good care of the ears. New theories, as you'll see, link hearing to stress and to dietary deficiencies. Consider, first, what your ears are really like and how it is we hear. Think of your outer ear as a kind of trumpet that gathers sound. A canal that's slightly over an inch long runs from it to the eardrum. Thousands of hairs and wax glands line the walls of this canal, guarding the more delicate parts of our ears from irritants. The eardrum seals off

Are You Hearing Less?

- Do you have trouble understanding what is said from the stage or pulpit?
- Do you tend to lip-read or watch gestures of speakers?
- Do you have to ask people to repeat what they say?
- Do you have to lean forward or sit on the edge of a chair to hear?

- Do you lose the thread of conversation at the dinner table?
- Do you socialize less because of anticipated difficulty in listening situations?

- Is one ear better than the other?
- Do you miss the telephone bell or the doorbell?

- Does your family repeatedly ask you to turn down the TV or radio?
- Do people seem to be mumbling?

one end of the middle ear; a flexible membrane closes off the other. This tiny middle ear is an air-filled space inside of which are three tiny bones called the anvil, hammer and stirrup because those are the shapes they vaguely resemble. Sound waves funneled into the outer ear reverberate against the eardrum, which begins the process of transforming them into mechanical vibrations. These go through the middle ear for amplification, then are passed on to the inner ear.

It's here that the sounds we hear are converted into electrical impulses which, in turn, register in the brain as sound. The inner ear is also our internal gyroscope, helping us to maintain our balance and our equilibrium.

As with all organs of the body, people do vary a great deal in the extent to which they lose hearing as they grow older. Some doctors who specialize in the anatomy, physiology and pathology of the ear have questioned whether the hearing loss we may sustain is actually due to aging, or is the result of a lifetime of exposure to noise far greater than the human ear can stand. They point to the Mabaans, where 75-year-old tribesmen hear as well as—or better than—35-year-old Americans. And they've found that this isolated tribe has more than a quiet environment to help their hearing.

The scientists who examined them noticed that high blood pressure and heart disease were extremely rare among them, their cholesterol levels were low and their diet was low in saturated fats. To find out whether common nutritional elements accounted for their excellent hearing, low cholesterol levels and healthy hearts, these scientists observed the results of a unique experiment conducted in Finland. For a five-year period, the inmates of a mental hospital there were fed the usual Finnish diet, high in animal fats. At the same time patients in another mental hospital were fed quite a different kind of diet—one in which the fats were unsaturated, thus making it similar in nature to the Mabaans' traditional diet. As might be ex-

Body Maintenance CHECKLIST

☐ Don't put anything in your ears, not even swabs.

☐ To help with tinnitus (noise in the ears) avoid aspirin, caffeine, nicotine and refined foods.

☐ Use protection against noise, such as earmuffs or plugs that fit the shape of the ear canal.

☐ To prevent swimmer's ear, wear a bathing cap.

☐ After showering, shake water from the ears and towel gently.

☐ To get relief when your ears "pop," swallow often or chew gum.

☐ To prevent frostbite of the ears, wear a hat.

☐ Limit salt and fat. Take vitamins A, C and E.

☐ Wear head protection when playing sports.

pected, this second group of patients had healthier hearts than the first group, but what else? Their hearing was significantly better, too. But the story doesn't end here. At this point the diets of the two groups were reversed; four years later the patients in both groups received another hearing test. This time the patients who'd had the best hearing now had the worst. And those who'd had the worst hearing before had the best!

Indeed, proper diet is a most effective way to keep your hearing in as good shape as possible—both in terms of preventing problems and of reversing some when they do occur. Paul Yanick, Jr., Ph.D., a holistically oriented audiologist, explains that the dietary minerals sodium and potassium are integral to the optimum transmission of sound. The reason is the inner ear fluid in which those thousands of sensory cells so vital to our hearing reside. Those two minerals constitute the chief ingredients of that fluid. (They're also called electrolytes.) They have to be in balance; when they're not, Dr. Yanick says, it can interrupt the passage of sound and cause hearing loss. But in our salt-eating society, it's pretty certain that an imbalance *does* occur. To help regain the necessary balance, be sure to cut down on salt and eat foods with plenty of potassium, such as sardines, flounder, salmon, potatoes, avocados, raisins, chicken, cod, beef liver, orange juice and bananas.

Dr. Yanick points to the B vitamins, so important to nerve function, as essential to our ears; B_6, especially helps prevent sodium retention. "In an electrolyte imbalance problem, I might want to give a person B_6 three times a day," he says. He also recommends vitamin A, explaining that "the cilia cells in the ear, which are the cells that give rise to hearing, are dependent on vitamin A."

Dr. Yanick generally urges patients with hearing problems that result from high levels of cholesterol and triglyceride to eat a lot of raw fruits and vegetables, cut down their fat intake and take lecithin three times a day. Lecithin helps to lower levels of these fats in the blood. Going easy on fatty foods is excellent advice for everyone, not just from the standpoint of the heart and circulatory system, but for the maintenance of good hearing, as well.

In addition to diet, factors like loud noises or even the way we clean our ears can have an effect on our hearing. Loud noise causes, for example, degeneration of the hair cells that are so vital to hearing. Animal studies offer striking examples. In one experiment a team of investigators took six chinchillas to a disco. There the little animals were exposed to live disco music for more than two hours, positioned at a distance of 3½ feet from a loudspeaker. A few hours after this exposure, the ears of four of the chinchillas were examined, and the other two were studied a month later. In all of the animals many of the crucial hair cells were destroyed by the music—something that held as true for the animals studied after a month's interval as for the ones examined immediately. Here's a very important point: The damage was permanent. It was irreversible. Now, you probably don't spend much time in a disco like those poor chinchillas, but the basic point still applies: Loud noises cause hearing loss. Evaluate your environment for certain sounds—like the whine of power tools, overhead airplanes, traffic and the like. Of course, you can't muffle an airplane, but you can close the window or put cotton in your ears. Awareness of the problem is half the solution.

In fact, by taking certain preven-

Choosing the Right Hearing Aid

A wide variety of hearing aids is available, but just 2 types account for 80 percent of all those in use: the crescent that fits behind the ear or the kind hidden in an eyeglass frame.

When you go to a store for a fitting, give the hearing aid a trial. Some stores allow you to rent one for as long as a month. If you find such a store, take advantage of the rental offer. A trial allows you to get used to wearing the hearing aid, and also to adjust to the new, strange sounds you'll be hearing. Once familiar with wearing an aid, you can better determine how well a particular model suits you.

Keep the following tips in mind:

• Be sure the aid you choose distorts sound as little as possible and that the loudest sounds don't hurt your ear.

• Be sure the hearing aid works when you're using the telephone or when you're in a large group.

• Be sure it's sturdy enough to take everyday wear and tear.

Sound Levels and Human Response

	Sounds	Noise Level (dB)	Effect
	Carrier deck jet operation Air-raid siren	140	Painfully loud
	Jet takeoff (from 200 feet) Thunderclap Discotheque Auto horn (from 3 feet)	120	Very annoying; hearing damage possible after 8 hours
	Garbage truck	100	
	City traffic Heavy truck (from 50 feet)	90	
	Alarm clock (from 2 feet) Hair dryer	80	Annoying
	Noisy restaurant Freeway traffic Man's voice (from 3 feet) Inside a classroom	70	Evidence of a stress response may begin
	Air-conditioning unit (from 20 feet)	60	Intrusive
	Light auto traffic (from 100 feet)	50	Quiet
	Living room Bedroom Quiet office	40	
	Library Soft whisper (from 15 feet)	30	Just audible
	Broadcasting studio	20	
		10	
		0	Hearing begins

tive steps, we not only save our hearing but also spare ourselves from certain other destructive reactions. One such is what the psychologists call a "generalized stress reaction." When we're highly stressed, you remember, our bodies mobilize. Adrenaline flows. Blood pressure rises. In Amsterdam, Holland, a researcher studied the effects of airport noise on nearby residents. The investigator found that where aircraft noise was high, residents were more likely to be treated for heart trouble and high blood pressure than residents of areas not exposed.

All this information points to one significant—really, inescapable—conclusion. As a very important part of our aging slowly program we should give our ears the best health care possible. One aspect of that care is to avoid or protect ourselves from loud noises. Be especially careful not to expose yourself to loud noise while drinking alcohol (or having alcohol in your system) because it can create an immediate hearing loss that's greater than it would have been without alcohol. Don't ever put a hard object like a hairpin, nail file or paper clip into your ears to clean them; you can cause a lot of damage—pushing the wax further in or perforating the eardrum. Besides, a certain amount of earwax has a protective function—it acts as a lubricant and as a barrier against foreign objects like dust that enter the ears. Do you have an earache or a consistent ringing in your ears or other ear-related problems? Or do you notice that you can't hear as well as you used to (a sign: You ask "what?" more often)? Then don't hesitate to see your physician or a hearing specialist.

Aging and Your Skin

Most of the signs of aging we can keep to ourselves, but our wrinkles are something else again. They're a very visible sign of the passing of the years.

Yet there's much we can do to keep our skin looking young. While some dermatologists (physicians who specialize in the skin and its disorders) believe wrinkles are an inevitable part of aging, others don't. Albert Kligman, M.D., Ph.D., professor of dermatology at the University of Pennsylvania Medical School and a foremost researcher in this field, is one who doesn't. Dr. Kligman is convinced that what produces wrinkles is mostly the environment.

He explains: "Apart from looseness, every skin change that you can see with your eyes and feel with your hand is due to an environmental insult." As for the environmental factors that produce these changes, he holds responsible excessive sunlight and wind, cold, harsh soap and all sorts of traumas that the skin has to endure. "Sunlight and heat wreck the skin's collagen and elastic fibers," he says. Wrinkles develop when our facial movements repeatedly fold skin that's no longer as elastic as it was.

To prove his point about the destructive combination of sunlight and heat, Dr. Kligman sometimes asks his female patients to look at the underside of their breast or upper arm. "That's the way the skin on their faces should look," he points out. "And the only reason it doesn't is that it's not protected from the environment the way the underside of the breast is."

We can't turn back the years and undo all the effects that sunlight and heat have had on our skin. But, dermatologists say, we can do a good deal to prevent further aging of the skin. Their tips follow.

Avoid harsh cleansers and astringents. Dr. Kligman advises that a mild soap is best for your skin. After washing, apply a moisturizer to help fight dryness and wrinkles.

Another noted dermatologist, Irwin I. Lubowe, M.D., stresses how important it is for older people to *maintain a proper diet* as one approach to good skin care. He emphasizes

Washing for a Youthful Glow

Step 1: Start with a cleansing lotion. Pour about a teaspoon of it onto a washcloth. Massage into the skin using a gentle, upward motion from the center of the face to the sides. Include the neck, also using upward strokes. Rinse thoroughly with warm water.

Step 2 (optional): If you enjoy using soap, follow Step 1 with your usual washing. Be sure to use a mild, nonalkaline brand that will not destroy the skin's delicate acid balance. (Any oatmeal or transparent soap will do.)

Step 3: Saturate a cotton ball with a mild skin freshener made of equal parts of witch hazel and cucumber juice. Dab gently on the skin.

proteins, unsaturated fat, fruits, vegetables and an increased intake of certain vitamins and minerals. Sardines and/or shellfish help in the development of amino acids, he says, which help firm aging skin. Dr. Lubowe believes, too, that the B complex vitamins have a beneficial effect on collagen and the fibrous tissues beneath the skin. Additionally, he also routinely suggests that his patients take vitamin A, vitamin C and an all-purpose vitamin/mineral tablet "for the production and maintenance of skin integrity in aging." Be sure your mineral intake is sufficient, too; a number of minerals are essential for the maintenance of healthy skin—zinc, to avoid rough and scaly skin; manganese, as an essential ingredient in the building of body proteins that make up the connective tissues of the skin; magnesium, because it's basic to the breaking down and building up of cells.

Protect yourself from the harmful effects of the sun's ultraviolet radiation. The sun's effect is insidious in that often the damage it causes—especially to the elastic fibers beneath the skin's surface—may not show up for many years.

To prevent dryness, *wear rubber gloves* when you're washing dishes or using strong cleansing agents.

Body Maintenance CHECKLIST

☐ When in the sun use a sunscreen or wear a wide-brimmed hat.

☐ Avoid using strong soap or astringents.

☐ Use a moisturizer every day.

☐ Maintain a proper diet, with lots of fruits and vegetables.

☐ Eat foods rich in vitamin A (carrots, sweet potatoes) and vitamin C (citrus juices, green peppers, broccoli).

Step 4: Splash with cold water to rinse off any remaining freshener and to close the pores and stimulate the circulation.

Step 5: Gently pat dry with a towel. Then, when the skin is dry, apply a light moisturizer. This step is important because it helps the skin retain moisture while protecting it from dirt and pollution.

Step 6: Stand back to admire that youthful glow.

4

Exercises for Vim and Vigor

What's the difference between youth and age? Quickness of step and strength of hand. Exercise.

If, on one side of a room, you lined up a dozen people who exercise regularly and on the other side you lined up a dozen sedentary people, you'd find an enormous difference between the two groups. The exercisers would *look* better. They'd exude an aura of health, vigor and well-being noticeably greater than those who didn't use their bodies in the same way.

Exercise—here a shorthand word for any physical activity that tunes our hearts, muscles and other body parts—is in a sense like a potion that keeps us young. And scientists are finding out how that potion works. Researchers at the University of California at Berkeley suggest one main reason why active people usually look and feel so much better than others is that their hearts are better able to pump blood throughout their bodies, nourishing each cell with oxygen. (Hence the glow.) Their muscles defy gravity, remaining taut and strong. And there are lots of benefits you *can't* see. For instance, people who exercise regularly use the protein from their diets more effectively and have higher levels of vitamin C and iron in their blood.

These are just a few of many examples of how exercise benefits us. And besides making us feel good, participating in sports helps keep us "socially fit," too, because we do them with others.

If you haven't been exercising thus far, don't think it's too late to begin now. Zebulon Kendrick, Ph.D., assistant professor of physical education at Temple University in Philadelphia, stresses that unless there's a compelling medical reason against it, it's never too late to start.

Where should you exercise? Structured fitness programs for older people abound, but there's much we can do on our own, as well—from walking to lawn mowing to light calisthenics.

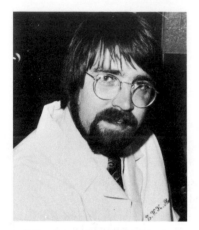

"It's never too late to start exercising . . . Even a 'low-level' exercise like walking can be beneficial if done regularly."
—Zebulon Kendrick, Ph.D.

THE BODY OF KNOWLEDGE

Everett Smith, Ph.D., assistant professor of preventive medicine at the University of Wisconsin Medical School, offers some provocative statistics. After we reach the age of 30, those of us who are sedentary lose about 1 percent of our capacity to work or exercise—in effect, our strength—each year. Over a 40-year period, most of us become at least 30 percent less fit than we were at 30. This loss of fitness presents itself in subtle ways: Maybe there's still a spring in our step, but our hearts don't function as efficiently, our ability to take in and use oxygen to promote bodily processes declines, our bodies lose some of their flexibility, and some of our muscle strength slips away.

If this decline were inevitable, aging would be a melancholy process, indeed. But just as a proper nutritional approach can help slow the aging process, so can exercise. Dr. Smith's sad figures are based on those of us who lead sedentary lives; it appears that deterioriation of function is due as much to lack of exercise as to the passage of the years.

How does exercise shackle Father Time? Exercise requires oxygen; we can't work long and well without getting it to our bodies' tissues. Fitness, therefore, really has a lot to do with our capacity to draw in the amount of oxygen we need to work easily. This capacity declines with age. But an older person who exercises regularly can achieve the maximum oxygen intake of a person 15 years younger. In a sense, the more active we are, the younger we become.

Aging Slowly. Dr. Smith's own research bears out this essentially optimistic conclusion. He and his research assistant, Charles Morse, studied 28 men and women whose ages ranged from 62 to 85, all of whom were quite sedentary. For 12 weeks this group participated in a walking exercise program in which they started out walking for ¼ mile, then stopped to do brief upper body exercises—arm rotations and the like. Over time the pace of the program was stepped up. Dr. Smith observes that at the beginning of the program many of the participants were so out of shape they had to catch their breath at short intervals. By the time the program came to an end, the participants could walk from 1 to 3 miles. By testing various body functions before and after the program, researchers found that their fitness level had improved by 24 percent. In fact, they were functioning at a level comparable to that of the average sedentary 30-year-old.

You might be thinking that although exercisers are younger in some ways, their joints are probably *older*—all that bending and bouncing! Well, moving those joints—keeping active and exercising—keeps them far fitter, far longer. This was borne out in a study conducted by Elizabeth Protas, Ph.D., of the Texas Women's University, and Christopher Bork, Ph.D., Northeastern University of Boston. What they did was to measure the muscle strength in the dominant knees of 80 marathon runners, aged 18 to 58, who had run some 52 miles a week for an average of four years. They were divided into two groups—one under and one over age 40. As it turned out, the strength in the knees of both groups was nearly the same, especially at lower speeds. Dr. Protas and Dr. Bork speculate that exercise may slow down the decline of muscle and joint strength in other parts of the body, too.

A Stronger Heart. What about that great muscle we call the heart? And what about our lungs, our respiratory systems? Study after study has shown the importance of exercise in maintaining the health and efficiency of our hearts, our circulatory systems and our lungs. Experiments at Baltimore's Gerontology Research Center offer direct evidence, for instance, that "the tendency of the aging heart to stiffen, to take longer to contract, and to spend less time relaxed can be overcome by a relatively light exercise regimen."

There's evidence, too, that prolonged exercise lowers total cholesterol levels and elevates high-density lipoproteins, the form of cholesterol that protects against the buildup of fatty deposits. In other words, exercise can protect us from coronary artery disease.

A Firm Body. The issue of exercise in weight reduction is rife with myth and misconception. Many people believe exercise won't decrease weight. However, more and more evidence has surfaced in medical literature to make a strong case for exercise as a weight reducer. Contrary to popular opinion, it does not whip up an appetite. Animal experiments have shown just the opposite. Moreover, the harder you exercise, the *less* hungry you later feel.

There's no question that exercise burns calories; the more vigorous and prolonged the exercise, the more are burned. But you don't have to work up a tremendous sweat in order to lose weight. Moderate exercise is also effective; you just have to keep at it longer. For example, walking burns fewer calories over the same distance than running; when you extend the walk, though, you burn the same number of calories.

Whether you're working out to lose weight, to build up your cardiovascular system or just to have a good all-around feeling about yourself, Dr. Kendrick stresses how important it is to do it regularly. The exercise can be "low level," he says—walking is an example—but it has to be done in a regular and continuous way. "The lower the level of intensity, the more work you have to do, but there's no reason why people can't build up to walking, say, 3, 4 or 5 miles a day, four days a week. Their heart rate and blood pressure will come down and there will be marked changes in their skeletal muscles."

With walking still as his example (though his comments would apply to other exercises as well), Dr. Kendrick suggests starting at three times a week. Less than that and the exercise won't make any improvement. Once you do start to feel the beneficial results of exercising, don't slacken off or stop. After three days, those good effects start to wear off. If you stop, all the gains you've made will be gone within 8 to 12 weeks and

Prevent Joint Aging through Exercise

The best reason to exercise is to increase the strength of your heart, lungs and bones. But what if your joints have become a bit creaky and moving around hurts? Is exercise still safe? Most doctors answer with a resounding yes!

James Nicholas, M.D., director of orthopedic surgery at Lennox Hill Hospital in New York, says that the way to *prevent* joint aging is to maintain motion. Why? Because the cartilage inside a joint has only one way of getting nourishment —from the fluid that surrounds the joint. And the only way that fluid can get inside is through exercise.

Let's begin at the beginning, by testing each joint to see what it can do. Next, focus your attention on getting them all back into shape with the stretching routine on pages 76 and 77.

A word of caution: Do *not* use painkillers when you are exercising. They too easily mask pain, so that you can unwittingly damage a joint by pushing it too fast or too hard.

you'll be back where you started. For good health, he says, exercise should be a "lifelong, sustained activity."

ACTION FOR EVERYONE

For Leslie Pawson, the 1982 Senior Olympics held at Brown University in Providence, Rhode Island, was a doubly memorable occasion. First, this 78-year-old master athlete (a three-time winner of the Boston Marathon in the 1930s) was the person selected to light the torch signaling the beginning of those games. Second, competing with other men in the 65-and-over category, he was first-place winner in the 6.2-mile run. Clocking 51.54 minutes, he beat out two competitors who were more than a decade younger.

Pawson has been running since 1924 and still runs an average of 5 miles a day. "For me it's almost like a therapy," he says. "You get running, and if you have any problems, you seem to run them away." Leslie Pawson is an outstanding example of the older person as athlete. But he and many more hundreds of thousands of older people also exemplify by their lives a most important point—namely, that an active life is the right kind of life for all of us, not just for the young. As the old saying goes, *use* it or *lose* it.

There hardly seems to be a physical or emotional aspect of ourselves that doesn't benefit from exercise. Improved reflexes, for instance. Studies have shown that we become less coordinated as we grow older, and that our reaction time—the time it takes us to respond to a stimulus—slows down after age 60. Both good coordination and rapid reaction time are obviously extremely important to athletes, but they're pretty important to the rest of us, too. A reaction time study at San Diego State University asked volunteers to respond to a light by lifting their fingers from the appropriate light switch as swiftly as they could. As expected, the older volunteers' reaction time was slower, with one important exception—*those older people who exercised regularly did not show the same slow reactions.* And they probably were nimble, too. Experts in exercise physiology say that reaction time and maneuverability are closely tied: If you're quick to react, you'll likely be more agile, as well.

It's self-evident that a good exercise routine keeps our bodies flexible in a way they couldn't possibly be if we were inactive. When we lose flexibility as we grow older,

Exercise not only firms the body, it also quickens the mind. Whatever your choice of activity, the exhilaration it provides can send spirits soaring. Whether your sport requires the split-second agility of skiing or the more leisurely coordination of horseback riding, you share an additional benefit: communion with the great outdoors.

it really means we lose the full range of motion we had (and took for granted) when we were younger. But many exercise physiologists are convinced that a lot of the muscle and joint problems generally ascribed to aging are actually the result of disease. Proper exercise relaxes tense muscles, stretches tight ones, strengthens those that are weak.

Another important plus for exercise is that it has an invigorating effect overall, toning up our minds as well as our bodies. In fact, there's usually a big difference in the way we look at things, depending on whether we lead a sedentary or an active life. This is what half of 32 people, volunteers for a research project at the Duke University Preventive Approach to Cardiology Program, discovered. Their ages varied from midtwenties to early sixties, but they shared a common trait. They all led sedentary lives. Sixteen of these people were given an exercise program to follow, one that involved walking or jogging three times a week for a total of ten weeks. The other 16 persons were the control group, simply going along in their usual sedentary way. Tested for vigor afterward, the active group reported themselves as being more lively, mentally alert and full of pep than the seat-warmers.

If you feel vigorous, you feel good about yourself. Self-image is important to our health as well as to our emotions. People who *think* of themselves as healthy invariably *act* healthier than those who don't, regardless of what's actually going on in their bodies. And exercise boosts our self-image.

While exercise can give you a healthy "high," it also can provide you with a healthy way of calming yourself when you feel keyed up, anxious and agitated. Physical educators and physiologists have long been in on the secret that exercise is a tension reliever—that it relaxes tense muscles and evaporates anxiety without nasty side effects. Herbert A. deVries, Ph.D., while director of the mobile laboratory for physiology of exercise and aging research at the University of Southern California, ran a unique and highly effective training program for

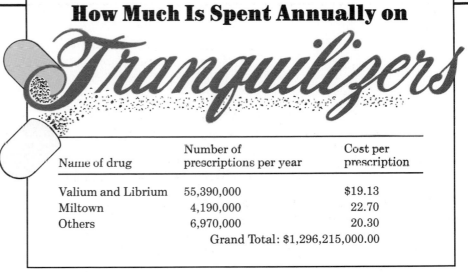
older adults. Along with the remarkable rejuvenating effect on body organs, Dr. deVries saw "improved ability to relax" as one of the most important benefits of the program for many older people. In his book, *Fitness after 50* (Charles Scribner's Sons, 1982), he tells of a typical example—a 68-year-old man who had spent all his adult life in a high-pressure occupation, had always been sedentary, and who, in retirement, was still unable to relax. His unease showed itself in severe tension headaches. After five months of physical conditioning, his headaches disappeared. When he stopped exercising while on a short vacation, they returned; when he resumed exercising they disappeared again.

It even may be that a sedentary life itself *adds* tension and anxiety to our lives. Researchers at the University of Florida found that only 10 percent of a group of people who exercised regularly—walking briskly or jogging at least 15 minutes a day—had anxiety, compared to 40 percent in another group that didn't exercise.

"Lack of exercise," the researchers conclude, "is associated with anxiety and numerous medical problems."

Start out wisely, start out sanely. Don't be like the middle-aged man who hasn't lifted himself off his duff all year and suddenly gets out there to shovel the snow from his driveway after winter's first storm. Instead, take the time to warm up. Athletes know the technique. You'll never see a baseball player get out on the field for a game without fielding

In a survey of 400 doctors, walking, swimming, golf and bowling were recommended to release tension—not tranquilizers.

balls or taking batting practice. Athletes know what's good for their systems, and we *all* can learn from them. Their technique breaks down into two categories—warm-ups and cool-downs.

Warm-ups, which can last 5 to 15 minutes or longer, are mini-exercises. They prepare your muscles, joints, heart and other organs for the more strenuous activity to follow. (Please see specific exercises on the opposite page.)

If you haven't been exercising regularly, take it easy even after the warm-ups. Start the main activity s-l-o-w-l-y. Begin with short periods, then gradually increase the effort. And listen to your body. The National Institute on Aging advises, "If you feel much discomfort, you are trying to do too much. Although most people will have no problems if they start exercising slowly, be alert for unusual symptoms such as chest pain, breathlessness, joint discomfort or muscle cramps. Call your doctor if any of these occur."

Once the exercise is over, it's time to come down from that high you've worked yourself into. But don't suddenly flop into a chair after having engaged in a lot of exertion. And don't rush right into the shower to wash off the sweat you've built up. While you might *want* a seat or a shower— you'll simply have to wait. Your heart is still beating hard and you're breathing hard, too. Your whole system is still primed for heavy activity; you need to wind down. That's where the cool-down exercises come in. Take advantage of them, because there are hazards if you don't: You could easily feel lightheaded, chilled—or even faint. (You'll find cooling down exercises on the opposite page, also.)

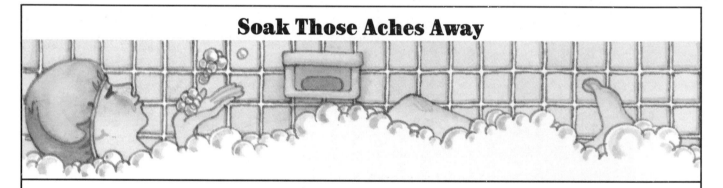

Soak Those Aches Away

If you haven't worked out for a long time and then start an exercise routine, sure as Charley had a horse, you'll be sore and stiff the next day. Your muscles will be little hard balls of pain—*unless* you take some preventive measures. And the measures to take are absolutely delightful.

First off, after you finish your exercise session, take some time to cool down. Drink a little water to replace the amount you sweated away. Do your cooling-off stretches. Walk around for a few minutes. Then head for the nearest bathtub, or better yet, a hot tub. Sink into the steaming water and let yourself completely r-e-l-a-x. The heat of the water will open up your blood vessels. Your muscles will begin to stretch out. (Goodbye tight little knots of pain!) If you're in really hot water (more than 100° F), limit your soak to no more than 5 minutes— build up the amount of soaking time in the same way you build up your exercise time.

Many people enjoy the addition of a home whirlpool attachment—which offers gentle massage along with the benefits of heat. Some people also like to take a relaxing bath *before* exercising—and if not a bath, then a hot shower using a massage shower head. It's a well-known fact that relaxed muscles are less frequently injured than tense ones, so a hot soak makes perfect sense.

Warming-Up/Cooling-Down Exercises

Before any vigorous exercise, it's absolutely necessary to first slowly warm your muscles. First, lie on the floor on your back with both knees bent. Close your eyes, take a deep breath and slowly exhale. Slide one knee forward till your leg is flat. Breathe deeply. Then bend it again. Repeat movement with other leg. Tighten both fists, then let go. Next, take a deep breath. Exhale slowly. Then shrug as you inhale and relax your shoulders as you exhale. Roll your head slowly from side to side.

Still lying down with knees flexed, slowly bring your right knee as close to your chest as you can. Put your foot on the floor and slide your leg flat. Return to flexed position. Now repeat with the other leg.

Lie on your right side with your head on your arm. Keep both knees flexed and hips loose. Slide your left knee as close to your head as comfortably possible, then slowly extend the leg until it is completely straight. Repeat twice, then turn to your left side and do the exercise with your right leg.

Kneel, resting on your hands and knees. Arch your back and drop your head at the same time. Then reverse the arch by bringing your head up and forming a U with your spine.

On all fours, move your hands 12 inches forward. At the same time, move your hips back, thus lowering your head and shoulders. Your pectoral muscles will stretch as your chest moves closer to the floor.

Lie on your back, both knees flexed. Bring your left knee up to your chest. Extend your leg, pointing the toe. Keep your knee locked. Lower this straight leg to the floor, then slide it back to a bent position. Repeat for the right leg. Do the exercise again, this time pointing the toe toward your head.

Stand with feet together. Relax by inhaling and exhaling deeply. Drop your head, shoulders and back gradually. Let gravity help you. Bend your knees and return to standing position. Repeat 2 or 3 times.

Stretching

A century ago people *lived* their stretching exercises. They split wood, shoveled coal, washed clothes on a scrub board. With our labor-saving devices and largely sedentary way of life, we lose the opportunity to work out as we work, and it shows.

With the exercises that follow, you can do stretches regularly, spread out throughout the day. Begin carefully — stop when a stretch begins to hurt; try it again next time. Do your stretches slowly, without jerky movements. You'll soon move in an easier, freer and more supple way.

Calf Stretch

Sitting on the floor, with your feet about a foot apart, place a towel around the ball of your foot. Without locking your knee, but holding it straight and steady, pull the towel toward you by leaning back. When you feel the stretch in the calf muscle, hold it for about 15 seconds. If it hurts, let up, or don't hold it as long. Alternate feet for 2 to 4 stretches. Gradually work up to 30-second stretches.

Wall Lean

Move on to the wall lean for further stretching of the calves after you have mastered the towel stretch. With your feet 2 to 3 inches apart, stand 3 to 5 feet from the wall. Put your hands on the wall directly in front of you and bend your elbows until your forearms are resting against the wall. Your feet should be positioned as far as possible from the wall with your heels on the floor and your legs straight. After holding the position for 10 to 15 seconds, walk toward the wall and relax. The wall lean is fairly tough, so repeat it only 3 or 4 times. Over time you may build up to stretches as long as a minute.

Bath Stretch

One relaxing way to stretch tired legs is in a bathtub full of warm water. Sitting in the tub with your legs straight, bend forward slowly until you feel the stretch in the muscles at the back of your legs. Relax, keep breathing normally and hold the stretch for at least 50 or 60 seconds.

Back Stretch

Sit in an armless chair with your feet about a foot apart. Bend forward, bringing your arms and shoulders between your knees. Lean forward as if you were going to put your elbows on the floor. Repeat the stretch several times and gradually build up your holding time.

Inner Thigh Stretch

For this stretch, you need an empty wall about 6 feet wide. Lie on your back with your legs stretched against the wall, at a 90-degree angle to your body. Your buttocks and heels should be touching the wall. With your knees slightly bent, open your legs as far as they will go. Let gravity do most of the work of pulling your legs down. Hold that position as long as you feel comfortable, up to 5 minutes at a time.

Side Stretch

Sit in a chair with your feet 12 inches apart and bend your body to the right, imagining as you do that you are lifting upward against the bend. Don't hold this stretch, just repeat on the left side, then go back to the right. Bend 5 times on each side. As the stretch becomes easier, add more weight to it by holding your hands behind your head as you bend. For even more weight later on, hold your hands above your head as you bend.

Neck Stretch

While either sitting or standing, clasp your hands behind your neck and let your head fall forward. Hold that position for 10 to 15 seconds, then raise your head and rest. Repeat the stretch, only this time hold your hands an inch higher at the base of your skull. That is the maximum stretch, and should be done only if it is comfortable.

Yoga Stretches

Asana 1

Lie face down, chin resting on floor, feet stretched out and together, arms relaxed at the sides. Clasp your hands behind your back, take a deep breath and exhale as you lift the upper torso high off the floor. Keep buttocks tightened as you come up. Tilt your head back and pull down strongly with the clasped hands so that the stretch is felt from your neck down to your shoulders and right into the small of your back. Hold this position without breathing for a few seconds, then breathe out and slowly lower your torso and head to the starting position. Release your hands from the clasped position, turn your head sideways and rest your cheek on the floor. Repeat 3 times.

Asana 2

From a face-down position, with your forehead resting on the floor, stretch your arms far in front of your head. Take a deep breath and lift your torso, head and arms high off the floor. Do not allow your head or chin to drop. Keep buttocks tightened. Hold this position briefly and then lower your arms and torso to the floor on an exhaled breath. Relax and repeat this exercise once more.

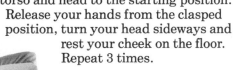

Both of these yoga stretches are difficult. If you have high blood pressure, peptic ulcer, hernia or hyperthyroid, consult your physician before you begin.

Exercise throughout the Day

We tend to think of exercise as something planned and formal, but movement is a part of our lives. And all movement is exercise. The more strenuous activities—heavy household chores like scrubbing floors, washing windows or digging in the garden—can be a real workout for our cardiovascular systems, too.

Daily activities burn calories, and with a little planning, can go a long way to help keep us fit.

Most people doing vigorous housecleaning know they're working hard. What they may not know is that mopping the floor consumes more calories per hour than chopping wood. Walking behind a shopping cart, pushing a vacuum—these and other chores need doing and can benefit our bodies as well as our homes.

Painting a Wall

Did you know that painting for an hour burns anywhere from 165 to 210 calories, depending on your weight? (The more you weigh, the more calories you burn.) Why, that's a better rate than driving a truck (115 to 145 an hour) or even hard labor like bricklaying (160 to 205). When you paint, *do* think exercise. Reach for the ceiling, stretch to the side and bend toward the floor.

Fixing Dinner

Bet you'd never guess that preparing a meal can burn up as many calories as spending the same time farming with modern equipment. If you're a woman of average weight, you'll cook off 105 calories; if you're an average-size man, 135.

Washing Windows

The person who announces, "I don't do windows," is missing out on good exercise. Washing windows, mopping floors and the like burn up 195 to 250 calories an hour. Robert Taylor, M.D., says that maybe it's the exercise provided by housework that enables women to outlive men. So shine those panes. And enjoy the job as well as the results.

Old-Fashioned Baking

Remember Grandma's baking day? From early morning until dinner time, she mixed and kneaded dough. She covered it like a baby and tucked it into a warm place to rise. Baking bread took all day, and cake batter was hand mixed, too.

So next time you bake, do it Grandma's way for a good workout. You'll burn up 130 to 165 calories, and develop a very strong forearm and wrist.

Hand Carpentry

Find the old crosscut saw and get it sharpened. Next time you plan to install a set of shelves, do the sawing by hand. Take frequent breaks so your muscles don't knot. To keep your shoulders loose, extend your arms to the side and make circles. Hand sawing consumes 305 to 390 calories an hour—the same as pitching a couple of innings.

Wash Day Workout

Laundering clothing in an automatic washer and dryer is almost no work at all. But you can achieve a certain amount of exercise by using your solar dryer. (You know, the washline in your backyard!) Hanging clothes on the line gets you outdoors, and gets you bending and stretching. Breathe deeply as you hang each item. This job uses up 190 to 245 calories an hour.

Gardening

This lovely, fruitful hobby is also a fine exercise. Weeding, hoeing, digging and spading will burn up 305 calories an hour for an average-size woman and 390 calories an hour for a man. To prevent sore muscles, alternate activities and change positions often. Stretch frequently to stay supple and unknotted.

Mowing the Lawn

If you're looking for exercise, lawn mowing gives you lots of options. Steering a ride-on mower around the yard burns up only 145 calories an hour; using a self-drive mower uses 250; a power mower you must push runs on 270 of your calories. But an old-fashioned (motorless) mower burns up a solid 460 calories an hour.

Walking for Health

"Walking," said the Greek physician Hippocrates over 2,000 years ago, "is man's best medicine." Hippocrates is best known for the Hippocratic Oath, to which doctors still give allegiance before beginning to practice medicine. He was, it seems, as astute about walking as he was about medical ethics. And modern physicians agree. For example, Albert Marchetti, M.D., author of *Dr. Marchetti's Walking Book* (Stein & Day, 1980), calls walking "terrific, and its time has come."

Not that the nearly 35 million adult Americans who take good brisk walks every day need any convincing. And it's a perfect exercise for people of any age; not surprisingly, a survey found that men 65 and older comprise the highest percentage of regular walkers in this country.

Walking doesn't require much exertion, yet provides many of the benefits that more arduous sports do.

Walking has many other virtues. You don't need any equipment (except a good pair of walking shoes). You can walk with friends or alone, as your mood dictates. You can go at your own pace, for as long as you wish, wherever you want.

As for the medical benefits, the list is impressive.

Walking helps you get a good night's sleep. When medical experts rated a number of exercises for the President's Council on Physical Fitness and Sports, they gave walking higher marks as a good sleep promoter than they did basketball, handball, squash, tennis, downhill skiing and calisthenics.

Walking reduces stress and tension. When feeling tense or angry, many people take a long walk to simmer down or cool off. They know, instinctively, what's good for them. The medical profession confirms their good instincts.

Walking helps you take off excess weight. When you walk you use up calories. How many depends on how fast and how long you walk. Robert Buxbaum, M.D., and Lyle J. Micheli, M.D., authors of *Sports for Life* (Beacon Press, 1979), calculated the energy consumption of a nice, leisurely stroll, one in which you cover a mile in an hour, at 35 calories per hour. Speeding things up a little—to 2 miles an hour—will cost you 200 calories per hour. A brisk walk—that's 3½ miles an hour—burns up 330 calories an hour. If you speed up to 4 miles an hour (not quite in the jogging category), the energy expenditure goes up to 400 calories per hour.

If you're thinking about embarking on a walking program in order to lose weight, here are some figures for you. To lose 1 pound, you need to burn up 3,500 calories. If you walk at a speed of only 2 miles per hour for an hour each day, you'll lose 200 calories that day. In a month you will have burned 6,000 calories—for a loss of 1.7 pounds. If that amount seems like too little, it's more impressive when you figure that you'll have lost 20½ pounds for the year.

Walking improves circulation and helps the heart stay fit. Michael Pollock, Ph.D., director of the car-

12-Week Walking Program

"To favorably alter cholesterol, to lower sugar, insulin and triglycerides and to lose weight, walking will do it," says Dan Streja, M.D., California body chemistry specialist. Plan to walk at least 3 times a week. Below is our program for getting started at an easy pace.

Week	Minutes/Day	Week	Minutes/Day
1	10, 10, 10	7	35, 35, 50
2	12, 12, 16	8	40, 40, 60
3	15, 15, 20	9	45, 45, 60
4	15, 20, 25	10	45, 45, 70
5	20, 25, 35	11	45, 45, 80
6	30, 25, 45	12	45, 45, 90

diac rehabilitation program at Mt. Sinai Medical Center in Milwaukee and a pioneer researcher in this field, put 16 sedentary middle-aged men on a 20-week walking program. Each man walked for roughly 40 minutes four times a week, gradually increasing the tempo from a base of 2½ miles per session to 3¼ miles. At the conclusion of the experiment, all of the subjects' resting heart rates had dropped a few points, signifying a clear improvement in the way their cardiovascular systems functioned.

Walking offers other important physiological benefits. Studies show that a brisk walk allows more oxygen to reach all the tissues of the body. A sustained program of walking also considerably improves the body's ability to take in oxygen; this improvement is especially marked in sedentary people. Walking regularly is a fine exercise for older persons who want to keep their bones strong.

To walk healthfully, keep these tips in mind. Be sure your shoes are comfortable and provide good support. Walk with your head erect and your tummy in; let your arms swing freely. Walk on your whole foot; if you "toe-walk" you put too much strain on your calves and ankles. Don't go on a brisk walk right after

Cardiac care patients often find the best place to walk is in the local mall—it's air-conditioned in summer and warm in winter.

eating; avoid brisk walks when it's very hot or cold. If you haven't been walking much, start out with a 15- or 20-minute walk. Don't just poke along, because ambling is not the tonic your heart and other organs need. Walk at a slow pace for the first several minutes as a warm-up. Some physicians recommend a pace of 3 miles per hour, even if you keep it up for only 20 minutes. Others suggest speed is less important than regular, sustained walking—putting in, say, 3 miles three times a week.

How to Buy Running Shoes

For jogging or running, look for the best running shoes you can afford. While they are costly, the expense is a good investment. After all, when you run you subject your feet to a force equal to 3 times your body weight. Without good shoes, you won't get very far down the road before you run into an injury.

Shop for running shoes in a store that specializes in running equipment, and that has a large supply of shoes and a knowledgeable staff. Choose shoes about ¼ inch longer than your longest toe. (Your toes should have room to wiggle.) Be sure the sole is flexible. It should bend easily along the area under the ball of the foot. However, the heel "counter"—the part of the shoe that wraps around the back of your heel—should be firm to protect your Achilles tendon and the rear of your foot.

Water Exercise

Playing in water is both relaxing and invigorating—whether we're seriously doing laps or just bobbing along with the tide. It's fun to exercise in water, too, because it allows us to do tricks we could never do on dry land. That buoyant feeling we get comes from the fact that our bodies are many times lighter in water, and for those of us with arthritis or orthopedic problems, that extra support is what makes exercise possible at all.

But the benefits are for everyone. While water exercises enhance muscle strength and tone, as well as overall stamina, they're particularly effective in promoting flexibility, coordination and circulation. And they're fun, too.

1 Scissors Split

(a) Float on your stomach, holding on to the side of the pool, your legs apart. (b) Bring your legs together like a pair of scissors, making them overlap before spreading them again. Keep your legs straight. Repeat 10 times; work up to 25. The splits are good for your thighs, hips and lower back.

2 Ballet Stretch

(a) Stand at a right angle to the pool side, holding on to the edge, both arms extended. (b) Bring your leg up to meet your hand. (c) Bring your arm over your head to the side of the pool. (d) Bring your leg down. Repeat 10 times, then switch sides. This exercise can be enhanced by using floats around your ankles to give your lower anatomy a more demanding workout.

3 Praying Mantis

(a) Stand in the middle of the pool where your swinging arms won't slug anyone. Keep your arms straight out to the sides. (b) Bring your arms down into the water until your hands touch your thighs. (c) Bring your hands out in front of you, lifting your arms to the surface. Repeat 10 times; work up to 25. For best results, keep your arms straight, and wear floats around your wrists. This strengthens your arms and upper back muscles.

4 Twister

(a) With your back to the pool wall, reach back and hold the rim. Let your legs stretch out in front. (b) Keeping your legs together, rotate them from side to side like a reversible drill with the hiccups. Repeat 10 times; work up to 40. This firms your waist, hips and thighs.

Dancing

As you trip the light fantastic, or go do-si-do-ing at a Saturday night square dance, the last thing you may think about is exercise. The fact is, though, that most dances really are exercise. They require some exertion. Your breathing deepens. Your heart beats faster. You use certain muscles in a way you ordinarily don't. If it's a vigorous dance—disco or square dancing—you work up a sweat. Square dancers, for instance, say their dancing is as good an exercise as jogging. Dancing regularly is a painless way to fill your "exercise quotient."

Whatever the dance, you improve your agility and coordination. You come away feeling good—feeling exhilarated. Even slow dances have these benefits, especially for the elderly. They get you up and moving in rhythm. As an 80-year-old woman wrote to a medical journal, "The advantages are obvious—gentle and well-controlled exercise which is suitable for everyone."

Fox Trotting

Fox trotting and other ballroom dances are a great way to get up and move without overdoing it. At the same time, you get wonderfully refreshing exercise and rewarding social contact.

As long as you can stand up and take a few steps, you can dance. Even if the hard rhythms of rock and roll or the energetic motion of aerobic dance put you off, you'll find little to intimidate you on the ballroom floor. The music and beat are friendly and so is the atmosphere. While many of the more modern rock dances focus on the individual doing his or her "own thing," ballroom dances emphasize togetherness. They produce a feeling of reassuring community.

Square Dancing

"As far as I'm concerned, square dancing is as good as jogging," says Danny Thibault, caller for the T-Bow Twirlers of Whitehall, Pennsylvania. "Physically it's excellent. Mentally, you've got to be alert; you're always listening to the caller. There are a lot of older people who do this."

One square dancer in New York is said to have attached a pedometer to his leg and clocked 8 miles in one average 2½-hour evening of dancing. All those dancing miles add up to a lot of burned calories.

84

Aerobic Dancing

There's nothing mysterious about aerobic exercise. It simply refers to the kind and level of physical effort that increases the body's consumption of oxygen. In fact, aerobic means "needing oxygen in order to live." When we exercise enough to need more oxygen, our heart and lungs are forced to work harder to provide it. When they work harder, a host of good things happen. The heart is conditioned to beat more strongly. As a result, it pumps more oxygenated blood to all our tissues, nourishing them better. Though we gain a faster heart rate during the exercise, the heart returns to its resting state quickly. In other words, it works much more efficiently. (These benefits translate into more protection against heart attacks.) Our capacity to take in oxygen and discharge carbon dioxide also improves; our lungs become better conditioned. As we gain in physical fitness, we become able to engage in more strenuous activity over a greater length of time with less fatigue.

There's confusion in some people's minds about what constitutes an aerobic exercise and what does not. Jogging is definitely aerobic. So are swimming, brisk walking and bicycling, as well as aerobic dancing. Tennis is not always an aerobic exercise because it isn't continuous. But, played vigorously, it provides aerobic benefits. Bowling and golf are not aerobic. In order for an activity to qualify as aerobic, it has to be somewhat vigorous and sustained, maybe 15 minutes or a half hour, at least 3 or 4 times a week. Improvement in fitness comes over time, not overnight.

To warm up for aerobic dancing, extend your arms. Make big circles, keeping your head centered between them. Reach toward the floor and to the ceiling. Keep your lower body still. Breathe deeply.

During this aerobic move, quickly shift your weight from one leg to the other. The movement is light and bouncy. Arms swing in same direction as weight change.

Jog forward 3 steps, then, with hands on hips, bring one knee up. Jog back 3 steps, then bring the other knee up. Alternate the starting leg.

Calisthenics

Stomach and Hip Twist

(Lie down, resting on elbows.)

1. Bring both feet toward hips.

2. Raise your knees toward your chest and twist them to the left.

3. Return your feet to the floor and straighten your legs.

4. Repeat and twist to the right.

5. Repeat Steps 1-4 from 2-10 times.

Calisthenics aren't aerobic exercises. They're not meant to strengthen your heart or give you more lung power. They *are* designed to build up your muscle strength and endurance—a goal as important as conditioning your cardiovascular system. The astronauts demonstrated this need for endurance and strength. After a month or so in a space capsule, they returned to earth (and gravity) physically weak, like patients who had been bedridden. You see, unused muscles deteriorate simply from lack of movement. In the more recent space flights, astronauts performed strength and endurance exercises that helped them come back fit.

Calisthenic exercises strengthen your muscles, give you staying power and help you to become flexible. In order for them to benefit you, however, you must do them regularly. Go through the sequence slowly; don't use jerky movements because they will defeat your purpose. Straining tells you you've gone beyond the point where they're good for you. Breathe deeply; avoid holding your breath while you're doing the calisthenics.

Begin this program by doing each exercise 4 times only. There are many in the sequence, and each will be done twice (the second time, do the sequence in reverse order), so it's wise to start on a modest level. Add 2 repetitions a week and before you know it, you'll be bending, twisting and moving all the parts of your body more than 400 times! (Do remember to warm up and cool down.)

For the Total Hip

(Lie down, resting on elbows.)

1. While keeping the left leg as straight as possible, raise and lower it 4-20 times.

2. Roll to the right side and continue to raise and lower the left leg 4-20 times.

3. Roll over on your stomach and continue to raise and lower the left leg 4-20 times.

4. Repeat in reverse for the right leg, 4-20 times.

For the Hips

(Get down on all fours.)

1. Raise your right knee to the side (hip height) 4-20 times.

2. Lower your knee to the floor.

3. Raise your left knee to the side (hip height) 4-20 times.

4. Lower it to the floor.

As the exercise becomes easier, extend your leg out and then return before lowering it.

Stomach and Hip Flexers

(Lie down, resting on elbows.)

1. Bring both feet toward hips.

2. Raise your knees toward your chest while bringing your feet off the floor.

3. Return your feet to the floor and straighten your legs.

4. Repeat 4-20 times.

As the exercise becomes easier, try to keep your feet off the floor for the entire set.

For the Stomach and Buttocks

(Still on all fours.)

1. Raise your right knee to your chest.

2. Swing your right leg back and lift.

3. Repeat 4-20 times.

4. Repeat Steps 1-3 with the left leg.

For the Stomach

(Lie on your back with knees bent and your feet securely tucked under a chair. Extend your arms over your head.)

1. Swing your arms up and toward your knees while raising your head and shoulders off the floor.

2. Touch your hands to your knees (right-right, left-left).

3. Lower your head and shoulders to the floor as you return your arms to the starting position.

4. Repeat Steps 1-3 and twist to the left.

5. Repeat Steps 1-3 and twist to the right.

6. Repeat Steps 1-5 from 2-10 times.

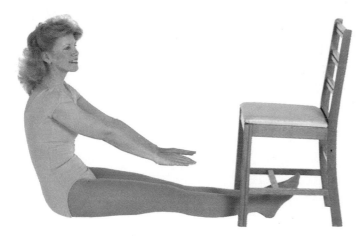

For the Middle and Upper Back

.(Lie on your stomach with a pillow under your hips, hands behind your head and your feet under a chair.)

1. Slowly raise your head, shoulders and chest as high as possible and then lower them immediately. (Slow, even motion.)

2. Repeat Step 1 and twist to the left.

3. Repeat Step 1 and twist to the right.

4. Repeat Steps 1-3 from 2-10 times.

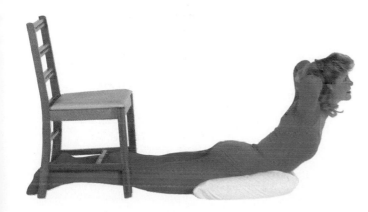

Bicycling

Think of a mode of locomotion other than walking that's quiet, fairly inexpensive, a real fuel saver, nonpolluting, fun and, most important of all, good for your health. Bicycling, of course, is what comes to mind.

Life insurance statistics show that nearly half of all Americans bike. By 1979, bicycles were actually outselling passenger cars in our suddenly bike-crazy country. Now, the Metropolitan Life Insurance Company tells us, there's one bicycle for every two registered passenger cars.

You don't have to convince Virginia Phelan of the rewards of bicycling. At 53, this mother of six commutes 15 miles a day—even in the dead of winter—to her job at the League of American Wheelmen (LAW). This 103-year-old organization, located in Baltimore, Maryland, holds rallies and lobbies on behalf of bicyclists. Virginia also loves to go camping—sometimes biking into the country alone, sometimes with friends.

"When I bicycle I feel totally free," Virginia says. "I don't have to depend on the car or others to get me where I want to go, because when I want to go I just go on my bike." But

Stationary Bikes: What's New

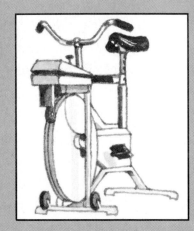

A bike is a bike, right? Not anymore. There are indoor bikes that calibrate not only your mileage, but also how many calories you burn along the way; bikes with built-in pulse monitors; machines equipped with fans to cool even the most ardent exercise enthusiast.

We scrutinized several bikes in a wide price range. One of the most reasonably priced is the Fitness Bicycle, distributed by Montgomery Ward. Basically, it's a coaster brake type with a luggage rack that swings down under the bike's rear wheel. It also has a lever that controls how hard you have to pedal. It's a simple bike best suited to someone on a limited budget.

On the other hand, the Monark Ergometer 868 is an investment in the future. Sturdily built, this brand has been used in Rodale Press fitness programs for several years without one major mechanical problem. This model has a sensitively calibrated device to measure your workload.

The Pulse-Data by Huffy uses sensors in the handgrips to monitor your pulse and gives a constant digital readout on a console. This is a convenience for those concerned with maintaining a specific pulse rate that signifies a good workout.

The Air-Dyne by Schwinn has a front "flywheel" that is actually a fan. It provides a stiff, cooling breeze as you ride. The handlebars are levers that move back and forth to give the upper body a workout, too.

The Ergo Metronic 35, distributed by Kiper-Dynavit, does everything—from keeping computerized count of your rotations per minute and heart rate to recording your time, mileage and work output.

a feeling of independence is just one aspect of her love for bicycling. "It gives me physical benefits in the sense that when I bike I feel great, I don't feel tired and worn out—it just renews me," she says enthusiastically. "Spiritually, too, it just renews my whole spirit, my outlook, my whole life. . . ."

Most interesting of all, maybe, is that Virginia calls herself a "late-bloomer"—she didn't begin to bike until she was 46 and never owned a bike until then. Pointing to a 1978 survey that showed 24 percent of the LAW membership as being 50 or over, Virginia says, "You could be 12 and you could be 98; as long as you learn to feel confident with your machine, age is no barrier."

Fun. Freedom. The open road. All contribute to the popularity of the bike. But the really big benefit is better health. For one thing, you can increase your lung capacity—one of the best signs of fitness. Champion riders have twice the lung capacity of ordinary people, which means their bodies get twice as much cell-nourishing oxygen. While most of us aren't in that class and have no intention of trying to be, it does show the potential this form of exercise has. Even bicyclists who stick to slow pedaling and level stretches of road benefit, in time, from improved respiration.

Blood circulation improves, too. In time, with regular outings on a bike, the heart muscle strengthens, goes longer without tiring and returns more rapidly to its resting state. Oxygen-rich blood is more effectively pumped to all the tissues that need it.

The wonders that bicycling can perform for our bodies were borne out in a study conducted by the Human Performance Laboratory at the University of California at Davis. Thirty-eight sedentary middle-aged men were randomly assigned to one of four groups. The first group was to bicycle, the second to jog, the third to play tennis and the fourth to do nothing extra at all. After a 20-week conditioning program the men who bicycled and jogged increased their oxygen intake significantly; the

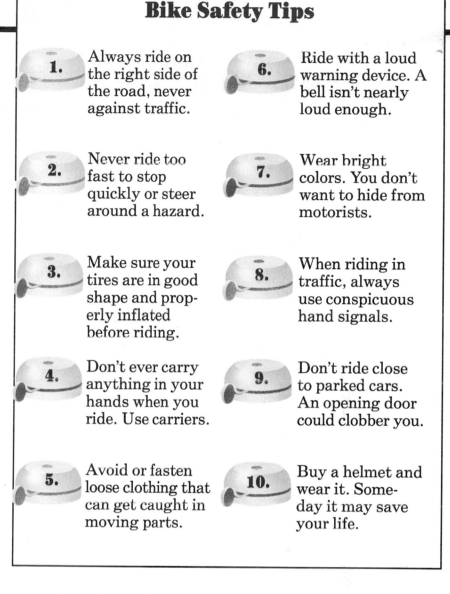

Bike Safety Tips

1. Always ride on the right side of the road, never against traffic.

2. Never ride too fast to stop quickly or steer around a hazard.

3. Make sure your tires are in good shape and properly inflated before riding.

4. Don't ever carry anything in your hands when you ride. Use carriers.

5. Avoid or fasten loose clothing that can get caught in moving parts.

6. Ride with a loud warning device. A bell isn't nearly loud enough.

7. Wear bright colors. You don't want to hide from motorists.

8. When riding in traffic, always use conspicuous hand signals.

9. Don't ride close to parked cars. An opening door could clobber you.

10. Buy a helmet and wear it. Someday it may save your life.

tennis players, less so; the nonexercise group, not at all.

People inclined to weigh more than they should love biking because it's a pleasurable, effective way of burning calories. Imagine yourself out in the country for an hour, pedaling along a river path at a fairly leisurely 6 miles an hour—and having the satisfaction of knowing you're burning up 270 calories an hour. If you go somewhat faster—10 miles an hour—you'll consume 400 calories per hour.

If outdoor bicycling isn't for you, try a stationary bike. You can use it any hour of the day or night, in privacy. Some even come equipped with a rack that lets you read your favorite magazine while you pedal. Pump and read or pump and see the sights—but do consider bicycling as the way to achieve fitness.

Competitive Sports

Essential to any successful exercise program is enjoyment. If you don't like what you're doing, chances are you won't do it for long. That's why, for many people, competitive sports can be just what the doctor ordered.

Take Jack Keough, for example. If you were to drop by the Y in Westfield, New Jersey, some morning, you'd see him playing in a rousing game of racquetball or else you might see him teaching other people how to play the game. What's so remarkable about that? Nothing—except that Jack is 76 years old and most of the people he plays with—or teaches—are decades younger.

Granted, these sports aren't for everyone. You've got to be in pretty good physical shape, Dr. Zebulon Kendrick says. Also, check with your doctor before you begin.

240 CALORIES PER HOUR
Golf

Golf is invigorating. People of all ages enjoy dropping a high-flying white ball into 18 scattered holes.

If you want to get the most exercise while golfing, you should walk from hole to hole and carry your own golf bag. Walking while carrying a golf bag is excellent for your leg and arm muscles, as well as your heart and lungs.

Swinging a golf club is also good exercise and it helps develop your hand-eye coordination. But before playing your first hole, do some gentle warm-up stretching. You'll be less likely to hurt yourself as you try to blast the ball down the fairway.

270 CALORIES PER HOUR
Ping-Pong

Ping-Pong is an indoor sport that requires very little strength to enjoy. The racquets are small pieces of plywood covered with rubber. The small, plastic ball weighs less that 1/10 ounce. So even if you can't lift a baseball bat, you can still aid your range of motion by swatting Ping-Pong balls.

An important nuance of the game is the spin you get on the ball with a twist of the wrist. (These spins make the ball do confusing bounces.) As a result, Ping-Pong players keep their wrist muscles and joints strong and fluid through constant use.

310 CALORIES PER HOUR
Badminton

A lot of people don't take badminton seriously (perhaps because you play with a "birdie" instead of a ball).

But a serious game of singles badminton is nothing to sneer at. A couple of good whacks with the racquet can really get the birdie migrating all over the court—and chasing that sneaky little shuttlecock can become a full-fledged aerobic workout.

A game of badminton is as close as your backyard. All you need is a net strung between the trees. The soft grass surface of the yard is perfect, since it lessens the wear and tear on your legs. An additional benefit is that the entire badminton set, including net, poles, racquets and birdies, is quite inexpensive.

180 CALORIES PER HOUR
Bowling

Bowling is good exercise and a great way to socialize. It's also one of the few sports you can play without buying any equipment. Everything you need is at the alley!

Here are some tips for selecting the right ball for you: Your thumb should be loose enough to rotate in the hole without friction. With your thumb in the ball, lay the 2 middle fingers flat over their holes. The second knuckle of each finger should go about ¼ inch past the near edge of the holes.

700 CALORIES PER HOUR
Racquetball

Racquetball is one of the fastest-growing sports around, because it's fun and easy to learn.

Aerobically, it can be top notch if you pick a partner close to your own level of ability. In fact, with the right partner, you can play racquetball at almost any age or state of physical fitness. Each of you will be able to match the other's pace.

When you play, be sure to protect your eyes against both the ball (which can travel at 127 miles per hour) and a moving racquet by wearing a protective guard. The very best is made with a one-piece nonhinged frame and polycarbonate lenses.

380 CALORIES PER HOUR
Tennis

While tennis is not in the same class with top-notch aerobic sports such as jogging or biking, it nevertheless serves the heart and lungs well.

According to a study at the University of California at Davis, a group of middle-aged, sedentary volunteers using tennis as an exercise increased both their endurance and their oxygen consumption.

Moreover, if you play regularly, the size of your muscles, bones and ligaments actually will increase.

Tennis also flexes your upper body as you stroke the ball.

310 CALORIES PER HOUR
Volleyball

Volleyball is a good "entry-level" sport because it mixes team play with individual effort. Moreover, it's fun—and often coed.

Although the game officially calls for 6 players on each side of the net, it's possible to play with any number from 2 to 9. Of course, the fewer the players on each side, the more of a workout you get as you scramble about trying to punch or slap the ball over the net before it hits the ground. If you participate in the sport regularly, you can expect several benefits. Played on a vigorous level, volleyball is an aerobic exercise that will strengthen your heart and lungs. Played on a more modest level, the game still burns up some calories, improves agility and sharpens hand-eye coordination. Moreover, serving and especially volleying provide a good workout for the shoulder joints.

5

Tips for Beauty and Fitness

Want to keep your youthful glow, shining hair, winning smile? Sure you do! Here's how.

Yes, aging is real. But there are many ways to keep ourselves looking and feeling young. The changes in the way we look—the wrinkles, the receding hairline, the "liver spots," the bent back, in fact, the entire catalog of age-related developments—can be prevented or ameliorated by taking certain steps.

While something like liver spots is not life-threatening, it *is* demoralizing, and for that reason, it's worth treating, rather than simply dismissing with a sigh. Yet, it's a very common practice to adopt a kind of caste system with regard to our bodies. We might be health-conscious in terms of doing what we can to protect ourselves from serious threats like heart attacks or cancer. A heart problem causes even the most careless of us to sit up, take notice and do what's required. But in this mental caste system, it becomes easy to push aside other, lesser problems, unaware that they can have serious consequences. The man who notices blood on his toothbrush might shrug off an evident gum problem, not realizing that he's in danger of losing his teeth. The woman who has occasional trouble urinating might ignore it, hoping it will disappear and not knowing, perhaps, that there are things she can do to check a potentially serious condition and to prevent a recurrence. There's no end of important examples.

It's these lesser problems—which can turn out to be not so lesser—that we also need to solve. And the solutions are practical. From the way to drive that's best for your back to what can be done about liver spots, you'll be getting the experts' advice on what to do and what not to do, on how to prevent problems from worsening and how to keep them from occurring in the first place.

Blueprint for Reading

When people are reading, they tend to slump, stick the neck too far forward and generally make every postural mistake in the book. After some time, a crick in the neck, stiff shoulders and a sore back can develop.

To avoid these problems, you should be seated at a desk in a comfortable chair that supports the lower back. It should permit the feet to be flat on the floor; if they don't touch, put a footrest under them.

Keep your reading material on a waist-high desk right in front of you. Don't lay the book down flat. Instead, prop it at a 20-degree angle, if possible. If you hold your reading matter, don't let it lie in your lap. Rather, hold it parallel to your face.

BE GOOD TO YOUR BACK

More often than most people might suspect, "Oh, my aching back" really translates to, "Oh, my lousy mattress." It may be new, it may be a mattress that took a hefty chunk out of your bank account—the fact remains that your back could sue this mattress for nonsupport. Or perhaps your mattress has seen better days. If the springs are nudging you here and there and there's a sag that propels you toward the middle, take it for granted that this mattress is bad for you. If you wake up stiff and achy, if your back feels as if it's been working on a road gang all night long, there's the reason: your mattress.

That's hardly surprising. As Lionel A. Walpin, M.D., clinical director of physical medicine and rehabilitation at Cedars-Sinai Medical Center in Los Angeles points out, for almost all of us sleep is the longest single postural activity.

If the mattress is too soft, or too hard, or as lumpy as a badly made pudding, our muscles work overtime, and are badly shortchanged of the rest they need.

The good mattress is the one that's ideal for our bodies. But what's ideal? Robert G. Addison, M.D., associate professor of orthopedic surgery at Northwestern University Medical School, has the answer: "The ideal mattress should cradle the spine in the same position as if you were standing with good posture," he says.

In a study conducted by researchers at the division of orthopedics and rehabilitation, University of California at San Diego, volunteers with chronic low back pain tested four different types of beds. All of them preferred an orthopedic (hard) bed or a water bed as the most comfortable. In another study the same researchers found that this was no figment of back sufferers' imaginations—the hard bed and the water bed distributed weight more evenly over the entire body than did the other beds.

Their conclusion: A hard, orthopedic bed is still the first choice, especially for low back pain sufferers. A good alternative is the water bed.

Now that you know what a good mattress is and isn't, here are some guidelines for when you go shopping for one. Don't rely on a label—such as "super-firm" or "ortho-firm"—no matter how medically impressive it may sound; there are no industry-wide standards and the name may simply reflect an ad agency's creative genius. When trying out a mattress, you need to lie on it for at least ten minutes to get the real feel of it, Dr. Addison advises. While you're lying there, ask yourself some specific questions: Do you feel your buttocks supported? Can you lie comfortably on your stomach without unnaturally arching your back? When you're on your side, do your shoulder and hip sink in slightly so that your spine settles in a horizontal rather than a curved position? If the answer to these questions is yes, you've found the mattress of your dreams.

Now that you have the right mattress on your bed, don't waste the money you've spent on it by sleeping in the wrong position. A straight spine imposes the least strain. Alternatively, if you suffer from low back pain, try sleeping like a baby—on your side, curled up in a semifetal position. For people who insist they can only sleep on their stomachs, placing a pillow under the pelvis will relieve lower back sag.

Of course, we don't spend all our time in bed—just a third of it. We spend a lot of time sitting, too, even when we don't have a desk job. Being a good "sitter," therefore, is another important way of being good to your back.

At this point, a little mathematics is in order. If your weight is average and you're lying flat on your back, you're putting roughly 100 pounds of pressure per square inch on the spinal disks in your back. When you're standing, it's 200 pounds. But when you're sitting, it's 300 pounds of pressure that push against these disks. So, whether or not you suffer from low back pain, you should learn to sit properly to ease that strain.

The first order of business in sitting properly is not to remain glued to a chair for long periods. Periodically, get up, stretch, walk around.

Sitting for long periods also can be bad news for your veins. The name of that bad news: phlebitis, an inflammation of a vein, usually one in the leg. Of every ten cases of phlebitis, seven are apt to occur in women, simply because more women than men have varicose veins, a condition that increases the risk of phlebitis. Usually phlebitis isn't dangerous—just annoying and maybe a little painful. Thrombophlebitis is something else again: In this version a blood clot accompanies phlebitis, and it can break free, lodge in the lungs and possibly cause death. To avoid phlebitis, the best advice is to avoid sitting for more than three or four hours at a time. Also avoid sitting with your knees bent, a position that aggravates or invites phlebitis by constricting the veins

Dos & Don'ts of Lifting

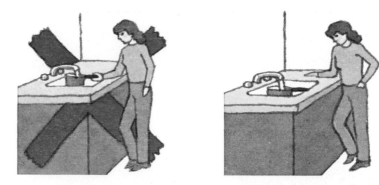

A pot of water is heavy, and you can hurt your back if you hold the pot in front of you while it fills.

Let the sink do the work. Simply set the pot in the sink while filling it.

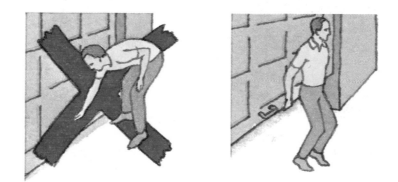

Overhead sliding garage doors should be easy to move up and down; however, the spring may fatigue or the door jam—and you may have to pull hard to lift it.

To minimize back strain, don't pull the door up in front of you. Instead, turn your back to the door and lift it behind you.

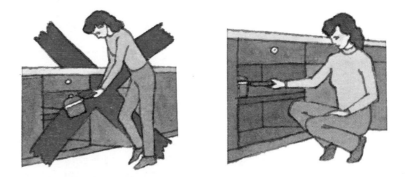

Don't bend over to get pots and pans out of low cabinets. Instead, keep your back straight and bend your knees.

Or, if you do bend over, support your back by leaning on the cabinet door.

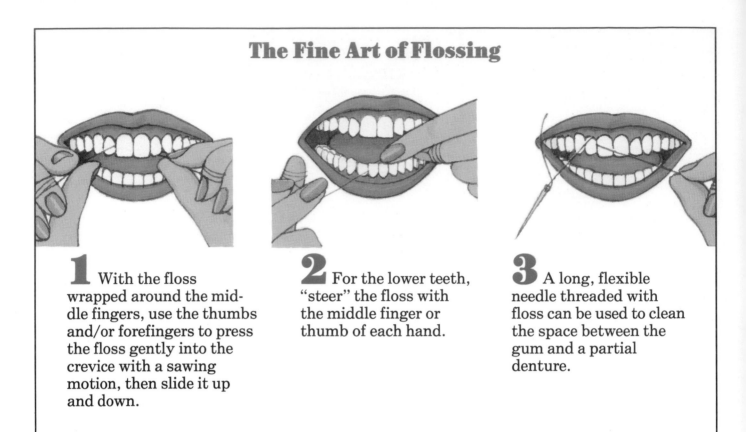

The Fine Art of Flossing

1 With the floss wrapped around the middle fingers, use the thumbs and/or forefingers to press the floss gently into the crevice with a sawing motion, then slide it up and down.

2 For the lower teeth, "steer" the floss with the middle finger or thumb of each hand.

3 A long, flexible needle threaded with floss can be used to clean the space between the gum and a partial denture.

underneath the knees.

If you do sit for long stretches, protect your leg veins by doing isometric exercises—tensing and relaxing specific muscle groups such as those in your thigh or calf. Whenever possible, too, put your feet up.

A WINNING SMILE

"If you want to keep your teeth, take care of your gums."

Most dentists wish all of us would live by this slogan. But most of us don't, and we're subject to periodontal disease, which in turn leads to loose teeth, teeth that fall out and the need for dentures.

The whole progression begins with gingivitis, when our gums redden, bleed and swell. Plaque—an invisible film of decomposed food and millions of live bacteria that coats our teeth and gums—is responsible for this mayhem. Left unchecked, the plaque hardens and periodontal

disease sets in—eating away at the gums and the adjacent bone.

You can, however, adopt a preventive program to keep this process from beginning, or to control it once it has begun. Brush your teeth with a good soft toothbrush at least once daily or, better yet, after every meal. Floss nightly to remove the debris the toothbrush misses and to discourage more plaque from forming.

Some of us are more susceptible to plaque than others, and nutrient deficiency may be the cause. Vitamin C is a prominent example. A growing body of clinical evidence suggests a relationship between a vitamin C deficiency and unhealthy gums. It seems that this deficiency allows bacterial toxins to penetrate the collagen (a protein that builds tissue), helping create the damage. It's true of the gums as of all other tissues— vitamin C is essential to their healthy maintenance.

There's more. Periodontal disease is like "osteoporosis of the mouth," in that this disease causes bone loss.

But more than a neat turn of a phrase is involved, because the jawbone, especially its crest, degenerates. Our teeth are anchored in the jawbone and when that anchorage becomes porous, the teeth loosen. As with all osteoporotic conditions, more calcium in the diet, including calcium supplements, has been shown to help. In a Cornell University study, for instance, giving supplements to calcium-deficient patients with periodontitis caused a striking reversal of the disease. Not only that, new bone formed in jaws where it had eroded.

Give your teeth a chance to live as long as you do.

THICK, LUSTROUS HAIR

"Hair today, gone tomorrow" may be a feeble joke among those with a full head of hair—but it's bound to produce little more than a wry smile when tomorrow becomes today. Female or male, we prize the hair on our heads; when it grays or whitens, when it falls out, most of us grieve a bit no matter how attractive people say we are.

To ward off grayness—or at least postpone it—relax. Ease up. Don't let tension overwhelm you. Chronic stress is a shock to all our bodily systems, including our hair. There are stories of people who have gone through dreadful experiences whose hair turned gray (or white) overnight; for most of us, stress does lead to gray hair, but much more slowly.

Certain nutrients help both the nerves and the hair. In one striking experiment, researchers put black rats on a diet deficient in the B vitamins. Soon their hair turned white. Then they were given the B vitamins they lacked. What happened? Their hair turned black again. This makes marvelous sense. The B's are the stress vitamins. They soothe the nerves—and are used up much faster when we're under stress. As an antidote to stress-related grayness, make sure your body has a good stock of the B's. A good way to ensure this is to take a B complex supplement or a tablespoon of brewer's yeast mixed with your morning juice.

Feeding Your Hair

Here's a hair "tonic" that you might think about taking on a daily basis. It contains virtually everything a head of hair could ask for. Whipped up in a blender, the cocktail can serve as a nutritious breakfast or a hearty nightcap. Be warned, however, that it's high in calories.

Makes 2½ cups

1 cup plain yogurt
1 banana
½ cup strawberries
3 tablespoons wheat germ
2 tablespoons brewer's yeast
1 tablespoon lecithin granules
1 teaspoon vitamin C crystals
1 raw egg yolk
1 envelope (1 tablespoon) unflavored gelatin
honey to taste (optional)

Combine all ingredients and blend until smooth.

Call zinc an all-purpose mineral. Every time a new zinc-related study turns up, it seems that it's good for something else that ails us. Quite possibly, zinc is good for baldness. Baldness is hardly an ailment, but since many of us are unhappy about it, that's what counts. In one laboratory experiment, rats lost most of their hair when they were given a zinc-deficient diet. Could such a deficiency be a possible explanation for some cases of baldness in humans? It certainly could. At a conference on trace element metabolism in West Germany, two American researchers presented a paper on this experiment—one that confirmed the equation: A deficiency of zinc drastically reduces hair growth.

A zinc deficiency may cause hair to fall out (or new hair not to grow back in); other nutritional deficiencies also play a role in hair loss. Irwin I. Lubowe, M.D., clinical professor emeritus of dermatology, New York

Sleep without Sheep

"Many poor sleepers are more aroused than good sleepers," writes sleep specialist Richard R. Bootzin, Ph.D., of Northwestern University. It means the insomniac's autonomic nervous system prepares him perfectly for dodging rush-hour traffic—but not for sleep.

A good way to send ourselves quickly to sleep, researchers are finding, is to learn the simple skill of muscle relaxation.

Lie flat on your back and close your eyes.

Working from feet to head, tense the muscles in each part of the body, then relax them. Now go to sleep.

Medical College, suggests that you make sure your intake of protein is adequate and take a vitamin B complex supplement to make sure you're getting enough of these important vitamins.

None of these vitamins and minerals will suddenly cover a bald spot or fill in a receding hairline, because the most common kind of baldness is caused by both heredity and hormonal factors. But if you make sure you're not deficient in them, you'll also be making sure you're not contributing to a loss of hair. Note, too, that crash dieting can bring on hair loss.

If you're a woman who's losing hair, you may be contributing to the problem by the way you care for it. One type of baldness (called traction alopecia) results when there's too much pull on the hair. Tight braiding, pulling the hair back in a pony tail, setting it with tight rollers or pin curls—any of these can bring on baldness. Avoid perms, too, if your hair is already falling out. If you use

a stiff-bristled brush, be gentle— don't brush too vigorously.

RESTFUL SLEEP

"Oh sleep! It is a gentle thing. Beloved from pole to pole."

For many of us, those words of Coleridge's from *The Rime of the Ancient Mariner* are fraught with irony. There's nothing gentle about sleep for us. We struggle unsuccessfully to slip into slumber. Or we awaken at 2, 3 or 4 each morning and spend the rest of our sleeptime tossing fitfully. We've got it: insomnia.

Age and sleep are intimately related. The older we become, the more troubled with insomnia we seem to be.

But sometimes we only *think* we have a problem sleeping when what's happened is that our sleep needs have changed and we're not aware of it. Many older people need only 4½ to 6½ hours daily. Our sleep is also lighter than it was. If we haven't adjusted to this changed sleep pattern—by going to bed later or getting up earlier—we're apt to toss and turn and tire ourselves out from sheer frustration.

Of course, those changed sleep patterns are averages; some older people do require as much sleep as ever. What they experience when they can't sleep *is* insomnia. It can be brought on by worry, depression, pain, the use of drugs that alleviate depression or some other tangible cause. Fortunately, there are many effective drug-free ways of getting a good and healthful night's sleep.

Eat foods high in tryptophan. This essential amino acid is a safe, natural mood changer. It calms, relaxes— and, when taken in sufficient amounts, often increases drowsiness and sometimes even lifts the depression that's associated with insomnia. Foods high in tryptophan include eggs, meats and certain fish—bluefish and salmon, in particular. Carbohydrates give tryptophan speedy passage to the brain. If you've been eating tryptophan-high foods during the day, try eating some whole wheat toast or a banana just before bed. You also can be sure of getting enough tryptophan by taking 1 gram as a supplement.

Remove caffeine-high foods from your diet. That means coffee, tea, chocolate and cola drinks, which cause sleep disturbances in many people.

Keep physically active. For sound sleep, time your exercises to give you the most nighttime benefit. Do your stuff sometime between 4 P.M. and 8 P.M.; that's the most effective time.

Stop smoking. After comparing 50 nonsmokers with 50 smokers— those who smoked a pack a day— researchers at Pennsylvania State University found that smokers had more trouble falling asleep. When they stopped smoking, though, sleep came easier.

More hints. Don't take bottled-up problems to bed; spill them out with someone before retiring. Try to go to bed at the same time each night. And forget the nightcap, because alcohol in immoderate doses keeps you from restful sleep. Don't nap during the day. And, of course, there's always the timeless remedy—a cup of warm milk at bedtime.

complications often can be avoided. Those telltale bluish, protruding blood vessels are not always visible before the condition has become serious. According to Howard C. Baron, M.D., a specialist in the detection and treatment of varicose veins, the most common early symptom is a tired or achy feeling or a feeling of fullness in the legs. It shows up after a prolonged period of standing or sitting, and it grows worse as the day progresses.

Give your legs enough exercise. You can jog or run or cycle or swim—or walk. The point is to give your legs a good, regular workout. If you don't have varicose veins, exercise helps ward them off. If the problem exists, exercise can improve circulation and ease discomfort. Going barefoot at home is also a help, because it strengthens the foot muscles and improves blood flow.

Go on a high-fiber diet. The eminent British clinician, Denis Burkitt, M.D., has been making a strong case for a connection between a low-fiber diet and the onset of varicose veins. According to Dr. Burkitt, a diet that's low in fiber

VICTORY OVER VARICOSE VEINS

Varicose veins. Bluish, swollen, cordlike veins. Tenderness, soreness, swelling and night cramps. Nobody wants to endure those symptoms, but millions of Americans—most of them women—do. Women, obese persons, people who have to stand a lot, or those who have parents or grandparents with varicose veins—are all at high risk in terms of varicose veins. So are all of us as we age; the fact that veins become less elastic and supporting muscles less strong is what does it.

Varicose veins occur when their walls are weak or their tiny, delicate valves, which regulate the flow of blood back to the heart, malfunction. The best approach to dealing with them is to keep them from worsening, or, better yet, from forming in the first place. Here's what to do:

Don't neglect the symptoms. If varicose veins are detected early enough, more serious symptoms and

How Veins Become Varicose

Arteries carry blood away from the heart, while veins carry the "used" blood back for oxygenation. The trip from your feet to your heart and lungs—against the force of gravity—is not an easy one. Veins achieve this task mainly with one-way valves that let the blood move up, but not down. These valves must hold tight, or the blood will flood lower compartments.

Should leg muscles fail or backflow occur, the veins become stretched and bloated.

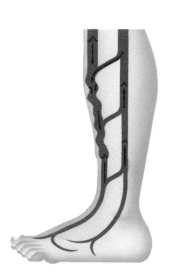

The Cranberry Cure

Doctors in general practice know that one of the most common (and frustrating) complaints made by their women patients concerns painful urination. But the cure may be right in a bottle of cranberry juice. D. V. Moen, M.D., of Shell Lake, Wisconsin, reported success with cranberry juice more than 20 years ago. He recommended drinking 2 6-ounce glasses daily.

Leo Galland, M.D., previously assistant clinical professor of medicine at the University of Connecticut, said the key to cranberry juice's power is a component called hippuric acid, which inhibits the growth of bacteria.

In addition to drinking cranberry juice, doctors also recommend drinking 8 glasses of water a day and supplementing the diet with vitamin C.

But, if the self-help remedies don't relieve symptoms in 24 hours, it's time to see your doctor.

---

results in constipation that causes straining. This straining triggers a chain reaction that puts a lot of pressure on the leg veins, eventually weakening the valves. Switching to a high-fiber diet—which means plenty of whole grains, bran, wheat germ, fresh fruits and salads—won't make varicose veins disappear. But it can keep the condition from occurring and from worsening once it's present.

More hints. Avoid sitting or standing for long periods; if you must do so, flex your leg muscles and wriggle your toes from time to time. Avoid crossing your legs. Tight garments—knee-high boots, panty hose that bind at the waist, girdles, belts that fit too tightly—are a no-no. Wear elastic stockings; they prevent swelling, act as a support for the veins, and encourage good pumping action for proper circulation.

URINARY TRACT PROBLEMS

They're not something most of us like to talk about, dealing, as they do, with such a private part of ourselves. But urinary problems do happen to quite a few of us as we grow older. Fortunately, we can take measures to prevent or alleviate them.

Urinary tract infections are a case in point. Symptoms like frequent, painful urination, or a need to void even though the bladder is empty, show up singly or in combination. Lots of people over 65 know all about those symptoms; in fact, urinary tract infections are second only to pulmonary (lung) disease as the main cause of fever in that age group. Women become more vulnerable to these infections after menopause. In men inflammation of the prostate, a fairly common condition, can lead to infections.

While antibiotics can clear up the condition, prevention obviously is better.

Drink plenty of liquids daily and urinate frequently. That's the only conclusion of a study of 23 women with recurrent urinary tract infections at Beth Israel Hospital in Boston. What these women had in common was a lower fluid intake and fewer trips to the bathroom than another group of women without recurrent infections. But when the infection-prone women drank at least eight glasses of water a day and urinated every two hours, they had noticeably fewer infections.

Prostate trouble, too, is pretty firmly tied up with what we take into our bodies. Generally the size of a walnut, the prostate can grow to the size of an orange when enlarged. There are other disorders of the prostate—prostatitis, an infection of the prostate, and prostate cancer. The symptoms, however, are the same in all three cases: increased need to urinate, burning pain, dribbling and inability to urinate.

All of these problems are treatable, but prevention is obviously the best course. Prevention means, first of all, keeping to a low-fat diet, because high cholesterol levels are associated with enlarged prostates.

Zinc, too, is a necessary ingredient for the health of the prostate. In the early 1970s researchers in Chicago found that patients with chronic prostatitis generally had low levels of zinc in their prostate and semen. When a group of those patients received oral zinc therapy, their symptoms generally eased.

Yes to zinc, no to fatty foods— that's the correct prescription for the good of the prostate.

FOR BEAUTIFUL SKIN

To be an older person and to have beautiful skin—now, *that* seems like a contradiction. We know that a life of smiling and frowning leaves its mark. But is our only recourse to shrug and—pardon the pun—put a good face to it? Fortunately, no. There are many things we can do to reduce those bad effects and keep our skin beautiful.

Take liver spots, for example. These flat brown spots that often make their unwelcome appearance as we grow into our fifties and beyond are thoroughly misnamed. In fact, they have nothing to do with the liver. It's the sun that causes this spotting. Explains Albert Kligman, M.D., Ph.D., professor of dermatology at the University of Pennsylvania Medical School, "At one time they were thought to be due to liver disease, but they're not. They are areas of skin where the pigment cells are overproducing pigment. And

they're entirely due to sunlight. You'll never find an age spot in the armpit."

Liver spots don't itch, don't hurt and aren't a potential medical menace—but you probably still wish they'd disappear. So what's to be done?

One likely remedy would seem to be an over-the-counter "fade cream." But it's considered best to keep away from skin bleaches, no matter how the ads for them tempt. There's too low a concentration of bleaching agent for them to be effective. Furthermore, as a medical panel reported to the FDA, stronger concentrations over longer periods of time "may produce disfiguring effects." Instead, try an old folk remedy that some women find very helpful. Lemon juice, applied daily to the spots, lightens them somewhat. Be aware that the process does take time. In conjunction with the juice, stay out of the sun as much as possible, or at least use a protective sunscreen. Most brands are labeled with a number from 2 to 15. The higher the number, the greater the protection.

Are you bathing too much? Some dermatologists say we overdo it in the United States, especially if we have dry skin. The more we bathe, the more we wash off the essential oils that keep the skin pliable. Avoid very hot water. Use a bath oil. A deficiency of oils in the diet, notes Leo Roy, M.D., a Toronto physician, is the main problem of persons with dry skin. Dr. Kligman reminds us that harsh cleansers and astringents should be avoided. A mild soap for washing the face, followed by a moisturizer, may be the best prescription.

Special care is definitely needed in winter, when the harsh cold tends to turn even normal skin dry and flaky. A number of Canadian dermatologists, practicing where winters are brutal, make sure their patients get enough vitamins A and D. Calgary's Max Vogel, M.D., advises patients to take vitamins A and D in a halibut-liver or cod-liver oil capsule. His advice is supported by Gerald Green, M.D., a Toronto doctor who says the oil not only provides nutrients, but also lubricates the skin.

SOD— No Cure for Wrinkles

Maybe you've seen it on the shelf at the health food store. It's labeled SOD, or superoxide dismutase, for long. It's rumored to be the latest weapon against age.

Sound too good to be true? Well, it probably is.

Superoxide dismutase is a water-soluble protein found in liver, red blood cells and other tissues.

Irwin Fridovich, Ph.D., a scientist who has studied and written about SOD, says, "There is no data to support the theory that it works as an antiaging, antiwrinkle or even as an anticancer substance."

Moreover, he says, even if SOD did have some of these properties, taking it in pill form is a complete waste of money. As an enzyme, it is totally destroyed by digestive juices.

6

The Mastermind

The mind stays bright and clear all life long. As we age, we grow smarter, learning from experience.

No doubt about it, there are some of us who do fear the aging process. Caught up by our prejudice against old people, we view with dismay the signs that tell us we're growing older. We speculate about what's in store for us. We wonder whether our zest and vitality will slip, whether we'll develop a major illness, whether we'll be confined to a nursing home. But what we fear most—if we dare think about it—is mental deterioration. Our concern about the effects of aging on our brains is understandable. Throughout the ages the litany has been repeated time and again: To grow old is to become mentally enfeebled, to lose one's memory, to behave incompetently. Shakespeare wrote in *Hamlet,* "They say an old man is twice a child." Vergil, the classical Roman poet, wrote, "Age carries all things away, even the mind." It's almost as if we're born with this message imprinted on our minds. And that imprint becomes larger and sharper, of course, when we're exposed to the tragic consequences of what's generally (if erroneously) called senility—when dear friends or relatives go through the devastating experience of losing touch with reality and no longer are able to care for themselves.

It happens—but it *doesn't* happen to most of us. We possess brains of astonishing virtuosity, and as neuroscientists perform the difficult, painstaking experiments that let us know more about its workings, they become still more astonishing. For a long time it was believed, for example, that the brain is one of the few organs of the body without the capacity to repair itself. New research shows that this is not the case—that in at least one of its parts the brain compensates for the loss of cells that normally occurs. In fact, based on their work at the Gerontology Research Center, scientists report that, "in the absence of disease, trauma or overwhelming stress, the aging brain does not become exhausted." It seems to be that when we're young and something goes wrong, it's called "illness," but when we're older it's called "aging." But this is a vast oversimplification and often—as in the commonplace view of the brain—just plain wrong.

This chapter deals with the workings of the brain; with memory and how to keep it functioning properly; with the facts and myths surrounding senility; and with the way older people, by the conduct of their lives, disprove the widespread belief that aging has to mean mental deterioration. The news with regard to the aging brain is—and should be—upbeat.

That 3-pound jellylike mass we call the brain is awfully demanding. It's only 2½ percent of our total body weight, but it requires 15 percent of our blood and 25 percent of the oxygen our bodies consume. It's fragile, too. It has rigidly precise requirements for food and oxygen. A few moments without the latter, for instance, and we faint; a few minutes more, and we become paralyzed; a few more minutes, we die. But while our brain asks a lot, it also gives a lot.

Everything we are, everything we feel, everything we think, every one of our reactions, everything we

Left- and Right-Hemisphere Brain Functions

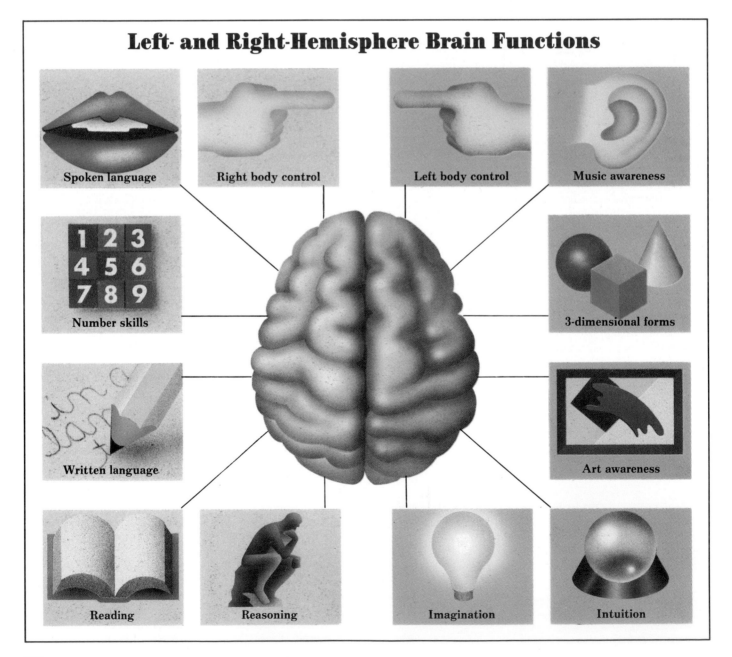

Spoken language

Right body control

Left body control

Music awareness

Number skills

3-dimensional forms

Written language

Art awareness

Reading

Reasoning

Imagination

Intuition

do—all, all begin or center in the brain. It's via the brain that we see and hear, laugh or weep, experience sexual arousal and sexual release. It's the brain that triggers our body's emergency systems to work instantaneously when necessary. And it's through our brains that we make the decisions to lead lives characterized by health or self-destructiveness.

Even the most sophisticated computer can't remotely approximate the functions the brain handles with ease every moment of the day. Much remains unknown. In honoring three pioneering brain researchers, recipients of a Nobel Prize in medicine and physiology, the *Journal of the American Medical Association* rightly called the brain, "the most complex mechanism in the universe."

Inside this "mechanism" resides a system of dazzling intricacy: billions, possibly as many as one trillion, nerve cells (neurons) connected to each other—sometimes thousands of times—by spidery little fibers called dendrites and long single fibers called axons. The neurons don't actually touch; it's in the gaps between them, the synapses, that communication between the cells takes place. Signals zip along the axon, across those gaps from cell to cell at speeds of up to 300 feet per second. The process is both chemical and electrical, with electrical impulses causing the release of chemical substances called neurotransmitters. In a split second, neurons can be recharged to begin the process anew. It has been said, with good reason, that the brain is both a computer and a chemical factory, one with a remarkable capacity for work, processing millions of impulses from all parts of the body.

Of the brain's main parts, it's the cerebrum that most makes us what we are—human. All animals have brains of sorts, even the smallest insects, but our highly developed cerebrum sets us apart and makes us special. Here's where information is interpreted and processed and emotions are experienced. Not surprisingly, the cerebrum takes up the largest portion of the brain—by weight, about 85 percent of it.

Another part of the brain, the cerebellum, integrates the data it

Neurotransmitters: The Brain's Messengers

Our brains contain anywhere from 10 billion to 1 trillion cells called neurons, which communicate with each other via electrochemical messengers.

Here's how the process works. A neuron sends an impulse down its long, thin "tail" (axon). When the impulse reaches the very end of the tail, it causes the neuron to release a chemical called a neurotransmitter. The chemical jumps the gap (synapse) between brain cells, carrying a message from one to another, and eventually to billions of them. Certain neurotransmitters excite brain activity, while others inhibit it. Not surprisingly, there is a direct relationship between nutrition and many chemicals of the brain. For instance, studies have shown that when choline is added to the diet the amount of the neurotransmitter acetylcholine in the brain also increases. Similarly, the neurotransmitter serotonin can be increased by the consumption of the amino acid tryptophan. Doctors writing in *Contemporary Nutrition* say that "tryptophan administration can reverse insomnia and . . . has also been used to treat depression successfully in some patients."

Foods rich in choline include liver, eggs and fish, while those high in protein are good sources of tryptophan.

needs to keep our bodies in balance and our muscles coordinated. The brain stem, shaped like a stalk, connects the higher part of the brain (cerebrum) to the spinal cord; it's involved in many vital functions such as breathing, heartbeat and growth, by regulating hormone flow. But it's the cerebrum that's the most interesting, because so many aspects of our basic selves are centered in its two hemispheres.

Those hemispheres have lately fascinated not only medical scien-

EASY MEMORY TRICKS!

Remembering Lists

Ever wonder how some folks with a flair for showmanship can rattle off a long shopping list or a column of statistics? Actually, the feat is quite easy.

Take the simple trick of memorizing a shopping list. Construct mental images to connect each item on the list with the one that follows. The more preposterous and vivid the images, the easier they are to recall.

Let's say the first 4 items on your list are eggs, apples, toothpaste and milk. If you are sure you'll remember eggs, picture a hen laying an apple. To get to toothpaste, you might visualize someone peeling an apple with her teeth. And for the final link between toothpaste and milk, picture a cow brushing her teeth. Once you've fashioned all the visual links in your memory chain, you can spout off long lists with ease.

Remembering Names

There's nothing more embarrassing than forgetting the name of someone to whom you've just been introduced. And yet, even at the most crowded gathering, there's always someone who can reel off both first and last names of everyone in the room—even if they've met only once. Again, the trick lies in vivid mental imagery. Let's say you've been introduced to Mr. Harper, who's a plumber. Would you still remember his name weeks from now if you saw him on the street? Yes, if at your initial meeting you had visualized a strong associative image—say, an angel strumming a harp in a bathtub. Or if the new baker's name is Robinson, you might picture a robin perched on a gigantic loaf of bread.

PLUMBER = HARPER   BAKER = ROBINSON

Remembering Phone Numbers

Even a long string of numbers isn't difficult to remember if you apply the following technique. Say you want to remember a 7-digit phone number. Simply assign each digit an alphabetical equivalent. It's generally more useful to use only consonants. For example, 1=b, 2=d, 3=f, 4=l, 5=m, 6=n, 7=r, 8=s, 9=t, 0=w. Take some time to thoroughly memorize the equivalents. (Use some form of visual association to help you. For instance, for the b representing 1 think of a single bed; the d representing 2 can stand for a double bed. Three in a bed would make the bed too full, and there's your f! You get the idea.) Just convert each digit to its corresponding letter of the alphabet, then use your imagination to fill in the gaps to build a word phrase. For example, the number 498-7517 converts to LTS-RMBR or LeTS-ReMemBeR.

Now you're ready for license plates, Social Security numbers—whatever!

1=b, 2=d, 3=f, 4=l, 5=m, 6=n, 7=r, 8=s, 9=t, 0=w

NUMBER IS 498-7517

LTS-RMBR

LeTS-ReMemBeR

tists, but also psychologists and philosophers, since it was discovered that the brain is, in fact, really *two* brains, with each hemisphere capable of functioning separately in certain ways. The left hemisphere originates speech, along with handwriting, reading and math. The right hemisphere could be called the artistic, creative brain—the one that gives us the capacity to play and enjoy. The left brain organizes experience and joins past to present, making sense out of them; the right takes fragments of information and builds them into a coherent pattern.

A growing number of brain researchers feel we've placed far too much emphasis on left-hemisphere functioning—and that, in our daily lives, we're not integrating the two hemispheres properly. As a result, we isolate the heart from the mind. Some researchers are attempting to work out ways in which we can train ourselves to better utilize *both* hemispheres for a richness of recall, logic, intuition and learning capacity beyond anything most of us experience.

MEMORY

Like all body parts, the brain ages, too. In fact, most of us associate forgetfulness with the aging of our brains. We don't recall things as keenly as we used to, and the gradual awareness that our memory isn't what it used to be can be shocking. But while we may connect memory loss to growing older, forgetting is actually a *lifelong* process that just seems to accelerate as we grow older. Observes Sandra Weintraub, Ph.D., of Beth Israel Hospital in Boston, "After age 50 almost everybody loses some ability to remember names. This is normal. Still, up until the seventies, memory shouldn't deteriorate very much. Between 70 and 80 some people show signs of memory failure, and after the age of 80 almost everybody does."

Yet to refer to loss of "memory" as such is to oversimplify. There are, in fact, two kinds of memory. Long-term memory comprises what you remember from the past, mostly because of repetition—like the phone number you know by heart—or

because the event was dramatic. The second kind of memory is short term. Say you get a phone number from the operator and dial it a moment later from memory—that's short-term memory. In a minute or less it will probably be forgotten.

As we grow older both kinds of memory slip a bit—though some studies show that we are much better at long-term memory. Thus it is that some people can tell a lot of wonderfully detailed stories about the past but can't remember where they put their glasses or what day of the week it is. That's understandable: They've repeated those stories many times; they're reinforced in the mind. We don't usually have the benefit of reinforcement with new information.

But does the brain *inevitably* age to the point where forgetting is the norm? At one time scientists would have answered a matter-of-fact yes. Now there's some controversy. As we grow older there is a perceptible slowdown in our ability to learn and problem-solve. But we make up for that slowdown by becoming more persistent and careful than younger folks; we compensate with our accumulated store of knowledge and experience. Also, while many older people do complain of having poorer memories, others remain keen, incisive, retentive. Scientists know that as we grow older the brain shrinks in size. (There's a 5 percent loss by the time we reach our seventies.) But new research has prompted at least a few scientists to question what was once assumed to be an established fact: that over the years we lose so many brain cells that significant loss of cognitive function is inevitable. Neuroscientists are finding—much to their surprise—that the brain may compensate for lost cells by making new cell connections, that parts of the brain may not lose cells at all and that certain dendrites, which connect nerve cells, grow well into old age.

Older people who volunteer for aging studies also tell us that growing old needn't defeat the brain. When the Duke University Center for the Study of Aging and Human Development examined about 800 people between the ages of 60 and 90, their scientists came up with some happy news—namely, that a healthy older person's capacity to respond to I.Q. tests remains stable over time. Other research has turned up similar results.

Then why does some people's ability to remember slip—sometimes drastically—as they grow older? One National Institute on Aging study suggested that not remembering things as we age may be less a matter of forgetfulness than of failing to concentrate on what we're doing. The study further suggested that not paying close attention is usually the cause of forgetfulness when the tasks involved are simple ones.

"Concentration plays a big part in memory," agrees Nancy J. Treat, Ph.D., assistant professor of human development at Pennsylvania State University. "If you don't get it in, you can't get it out."

It also may be that we exaggerate our forgetfulness—a conclusion drawn from a widely cited study by Robert L. Kahn, Ph.D., of the University of Chicago. Dr. Kahn found that many older people complain of having a poor memory—but that their complaints don't jibe with their actual performance on memory tests. We may have a better memory than we think, but downgrade our abilities because we're so worried about losing the memory that we overreact to any little slip.

Many people in Dr. Kahn's study suffered from emotional depression, a very common problem among some older people. Bereavement, illness, loneliness, economic worries—all can contribute to a chronic case of the blues that can wipe out the memory. Many of the 153 people in the study experienced two unfortunate things. One was that, feeling so down, they did have some memory loss. The second was that when they forgot something as people *normally* do, they saw it as proof of their mental deterioration—which made them all the more depressed. Quite a trap, and one that's very easy to fall into.

A dull life easily can lead to depression and to mental deterioration. It's not only true for humans but also—to prove this human point —for animals. Studies at the Jackson Laboratory for Genetic Research in Maine showed that mice in a stimulating environment, one that offered daily learning skills, exercise and the like, kept their capacities for learning and memory. In fact, most did almost as well when they were old as when they were young. But mice deprived of an enriching environment quickly grew fat and dull, and soon lost the ability to learn. Moral: If you want to keep your memory keen, exercise your mind as well as your body. Spice up your life with interesting, challenging things to see, do and think about.

To enhance your memory, also eat the right "brain food." New, if preliminary, research shows that choline, a vitaminlike substance, may be a key to good brain function. In a study carried out under the auspices of the National Institute of Mental Health, normal, healthy volunteers who took just one 10-gram dose of choline were able to memorize a sequence of unrelated words more quickly than normal. What's more, the people whose memories were poorest were those most helped by choline. In unrelated studies, patients suffering from Alzheimer's disease, a type of senility, had improved memories when treated with choline.

Here's the reason scientists think choline enhances memory: extra levels of it in the diet result in increased levels in the brain of the neurotransmitter acetylcholine, which is essential for the smooth flow of nerve impulses. (Foods that provide choline include soybean lecithin, beef liver, eggs and fish.)

Deficiencies of certain B vitamins also cause disturbances in brain function. For example, just a mild thiamine deficiency can bring about memory disturbances, inability to concentrate, insomnia and lack of initiative—symptoms doctors can mistake for senility. Elderly people sometimes are diagnosed as senile when all they have is a thiamine deficiency. Beef kidney, brewer's yeast, sunflower seeds, dried soybeans, kidney and other beans all contain thiamine. Probably the surest way to guarantee adequate amounts of this brain food is to take a B complex supplement.

But all the right foods won't help your memory if you drink too much, smoke cigarettes or take

The Importance of an Enriched Environment

Many people believe that as we grow old our minds become dull. It would seem that we lose the capacity for growth, that our natural curiosity is gone, that the sharp eye has been replaced by a vacant stare.

But the brain seems to have a mind of its own. Bored, it just shuts off. Stimulated, it flashes with brilliance, regardless of age.

Marian C. Diamond, Ph.D., a California neuroanatomist, challenges some of the myths regarding the aging brain in a search for its true potential. The brain's decline may be the result of the bland and boring lives some older people lead.

Getting out, going to see a good film, visiting the museum or just playing a sharp bridge game—all create the same sense of expectation and vitality we knew when we were kids.

certain drugs. It's a well-established fact that heavy drinkers suffer from memory loss. Now it seems that even moderate drinking (2 ounces of alcohol a day) can affect our ability to remember. This finding emerged from a study at the University of Oklahoma Health Sciences Center in Oklahoma City. When researchers there tested the memories of young and middle-aged women volunteers, they found that an alcohol-induced memory impairment may become greater as a woman ages—and remain even when she's not drinking.

Researchers at the University of

California at Los Angeles discovered that smoking also cripples our memories. They divided 23 confirmed cigarette smokers into two groups. One group was asked to smoke a typical cigarette, the other a nicotine-free type. Both groups were then given a memory test. The results? After three trials, the nonnicotine group recalled an average of 24 percent more than the nicotine group did.

Finally, some drugs—including a number of tranquilizers, along with heart and blood pressure medications—cause memory problems. If you are taking these drugs and find that memory problems occur, check with your doctor.

FEAR OF SENILITY

Carl S., 72, was a widower. As far as his son and daughter were concerned, he was rapidly deteriorating. Sometimes his voice trailed off and he looked at them blankly, losing his train of thought. Sometimes, when he did talk, what he said didn't make much sense. Forgetfulness became more and more of a problem. For instance, his daughter would visit in the late afternoon while he was watching soap operas, see an uneaten sandwich lying on a plate in the kitchen and ask Carl whether he'd eaten lunch. He'd sheepishly reply, "Oh, I forgot."

A terrible day finally came, a day when Carl was found wandering the streets of his hometown, confused and disoriented—he'd forgotten where he lived. Carl's doctor pronounced him senile and urged placement in a nursing home. Luckily, a close and perceptive friend of the family suggested Carl first be given a thorough physical examination. It soon was discovered that he'd suffered a very mild stroke, whose symptoms mimicked what's customarily called senile behavior. Carl's diet, inadequate in certain vital nutrients, was also found to contribute to his mental problems.

Senility, the deterioration of our mental faculties, is one of the most feared diseases of aging. It's a catch-all term for a host of symptoms—mental confusion and disorientation, the inability to make judgments, extreme forgetfulness, impaired intellectual functioning, inability to take care of oneself and so on. Yet, the physical problems causing these symptoms can be quite different. For example, one type of senility is triggered by a series of minor strokes. Another is Alzheimer's disease, in which the brain literally wastes away. Although 1.5 million Americans suffer from these diseases, it's important to understand that this is *not* the fate most of us can expect.

Much of what passes for senile dementia—and is now called "pseudodementia" to distinguish it from the real thing—is brought on by other, *curable* causes. In fact, perhaps as many as 30 percent of the older people diagnosed by their doctors as senile may, in fact, be suffering from some other problems that mimic senility.

For example, anemia can cause mental confusion and disorientation. Mild strokes also can produce senility-like symptoms. Unrecognized depression is a major cause of misdiagnosis

---

Maybe It's Just "the Blues"

Occasionally, a person is misdiagnosed as senile when the real problem is depression.

The behavioral differences between the two are subtle. For example, a person suffering from senility often will try to hide his memory loss, while a person suffering from depression will express anguish over his forgetfulness.

Additionally, the depressed person commonly will answer questions with an apathetic "don't know," while a senile person may volunteer answers that are wrong. Similarly, a depressed person frequently is so apathetic that he makes very little effort to perform tasks, whereas the senile person will struggle to do well.

A final clue to the difference between depression and senility lies in the way their symptoms develop. The person who is depressed most likely succumbed to that feeling rapidly. On the other hand, the symptoms of senility begin slowly and progress insidiously.

because the people involved can act in a lethargic, apathetic, hopeless way reminiscent of actual senile dementia. The institutionalization of depressed aged people is all the more tragic because proper treatment can cause dramatic improvement.

As a host of research studies has proven, nutritional deficiencies can produce the mirror image of true senility. For instance, in a study of ten elderly patients whose behavior showed them to be mentally confused, investigators found that they really had a deficiency of folate, one of the most important members of the B vitamin family. Other studies revealed that elderly people with mental problems were found to have striking deficiencies of certain B vitamins— B_6, niacin, folate and B_{12} were the most common.

A deficiency of zinc also may be a factor in the onset of genetically based senility, according to a report in the *Lancet,* an English medical journal. Possibly, this paper says, zinc supplementation could "delay or prevent" the onset of dementia (senility) in people who are "genetically at risk."

It's clear: Rob the brain of the nutrients it needs, and you rob the brain's power.

In addition, certain drugs can—and all too often do—cause reactions that create a mistaken impression of senility. The danger is real because statistics show that the older we are, the more drugs we take. Nearly one-fourth of all medications in this country are consumed by older people. On the average, older persons take five to six drugs (prescription and nonprescription) at the same time. And the hazard doesn't just lie with taking these drugs. With age, the body often absorbs, distributes, metabolizes and excretes drugs differently than is the case with younger adults and children. (See "Drugs That Cause Confusion" for some specific drugs.)

Depression, anemia, heart disease, nutritional deficiencies, inappropriate drug intake—all such conditions are treatable, the symptoms reversible. A single doctor's diagnosis of "senility" should never be taken as the final opinion.

"A person should have an inten-sive workup before he's labeled senile," says Jacob Brody, M.D., at the National Institute on Aging. "And even if the person is diagnosed as having senile dementia, you should get a second opinion from someone who specializes in the medical care of older people— a geriatrician."

He adds, "Senility should always be considered a disease—not the natural consequence of growing old."

OLDER MAY BE BETTER

We are valuable resources. Our accumulated years provide us with a broad base of knowledge. We know more. We've acquired priceless experiences—both the joyful and the painful leaven our maturity. We are more self-confident, more insightful, and better able to learn from our mistakes. We bring a wisdom and sensitivity to our lives we couldn't possibly have had when we were younger. Our experiences add depth to our judgment, the decisions we make, the conclusions we come to. Yes, if we choose to view it as such, age is a precious commodity.

Viewed with this attitude, even one of those dry, statistical federal reports, the U.S. Bureau of the Census's "Social and Economic Characteristics of Americans during Midlife," suggests optimism. If we look at its numerous tables and graphs with a human rather than a statistical eye, there's cause for a reasonable amount of self-congratulation.

Those of us in midlife are, in financial and career terms, at our peak. This is especially true of men, most of whom have reached the highest point in their careers when they reach their middle fifties. They've accumulated a substantial amount of seniority or professional standing, not in small part due to those "older" brains of theirs. In fact, the Census Bureau report indicates, "incomes of families maintained by men 45 to 54 and [incomes] of women 55 to 64 are higher than for adjacent younger or older groups. For many Americans, midlife represents years of plenty after years of relatively modest circumstances."

Drugs That Cause Confusion

Unfortunately, a person may *seem* to be suffering from senility when the symptoms are really side effects of certain drugs, including:

Psychoactives
sedative-hypnotics
tranquilizers
lithium

Antihypertensives
methyldopa
clonidine
betablockers

Anticonvulsants
phenytoin
barbiturates

Anticholinergics
atropine
antispasmodics

Others
narcotics
steroids
digitalis
diuretics
anti-inflammatories
disulfiram

Bill and Mary A. are the statistics come to life. At a time when about 10 percent of the working population was unemployed, Bill's gross salary was $43,500 in 1982, a $4,500 jump from the year before. A school administrator, Bill had been promoted to principal of a fairly large high school in the suburban Chicago area. His wife, Mary, a legal secretary, earned $21,000 a year. Prudent investments gave them another $5,000 or so, bringing their total pretax earnings to $69,500. "That may not sound like much to people earning those ultra-high salaries you read about, but it's more money than we ever had before and we really do feel we're at a peak," says Bill, who's 57.

Bill and Mary own their own home, which they bought for under $50,000, and which is now worth roughly three times that much.

Expenses? Both their children are in college, but with partial scholarships and parttime jobs they defray a considerable amount of the cost; Bill and Mary kick in $9,000 a year. They contribute $2,000 a year to help maintain Bill's ailing father—who had a crippling stroke—in a good private nursing home. They have no other extraordinary expenses and they live well.

As if spying on this family, the census report states, "Consequently, for many persons in husband-wife families, midlife is a time of increasing personal and financial freedom, a time for travel, and a time to catch up on the myriad activities that have been postponed or denied altogether." The report does caution, however, that this good fortune applies only to intact households, those in which husband and wife live together. Families headed by women with dependent children have incomes less than half those of husband-wife families with children.

Those of us in midlife are in our most stable and dependable years. Age seasons us, gives us a maturity and stability we couldn't have had before. Looking at ourselves this way (doing left-hemisphere reasoning), we can congratulate ourselves on how far we've come.

Take rootlessness vs. stability. What social commentator Vance Packard has called the "increasingly rootless nature of Americans" doesn't apply to us. We have too much of an investment in staying put. Like plants whose roots have grown strong and deep in a favorable environment, people in midlife are, the Census Bureau report says, "less likely to move because they have a considerable emotional and financial investment in their present location." The statistics prove it: between 1975 and 1979 only about 23 percent of 45- to 64-year-olds moved—in contrast to 65 percent of 25- to 34-year-olds.

Stability also shows up in a low rate of absenteeism at work. In a study sponsored by the Corporate Committee for Retirement Planning, personnel directors of the Fortune 1,000 companies were asked whether older or younger workers had the better attendance record. No contest —an overwhelming majority of the personnel directors said that older workers have a lower absenteeism record and fewer on-the-job accidents. As for job satisfaction, older workers seem content. When asked whether older workers were generally more satisfied in their jobs, a vast majority of those personnel directors (74 percent) said yes, they were generally more satisfied.

Those of us in midlife are far better able to handle many life changes. Bernice L. Neugarten, Ph.D., of the University of Chicago, has devoted much of her professional life to the study of the psychology, and sociology of aging and what happens to people throughout their life cycles. It's in the middle years, she finds, that we become more preoccupied with the inner life. We still have a lot to do in life—we may still be filled with a passion to fulfill goals, to realize cherished plans, to turn dreams into reality—but we're changing significantly as well. One such change is the way we measure our time on earth. We no longer just count forward, taking life and time for granted; now we count backward, too, seeing an end point ahead. As Dr. Neugarten says, there comes upon us "an awareness that time is finite."

Do we fall apart in the face of this high drama that punctuates the continuity of our lives? Do we become inevitable victims of the oft-mentioned "midlife crisis"? Happily, most of us do not.

As Dr. Neugarten writes in *Growing Old in America* (Beth B. Hess, ed.; Transaction Books, 1976), "the normal, expectable life events do not themselves constitute crises, nor are they trauma producing." Yes, they make us view ourselves differently, but most of us neither suffer greatly nor fall apart as we encounter these turning points. In other words the idea of a midlife *crisis* is vastly overblown.

Many of us retain our goals, plans and enthusiasms well past middle age. This is important to note and to celebrate. Those midlife studies usually deal with a 45- to 55-year-old group, or, if more generous, with 45- to 64-year-olds. But what happens afterward? Do we simply pull the covers over our heads or retire to our rocking chairs? Most of us definitely do not. In a *Newsweek* cover story entitled, "Growing Old, Feeling Young," the focus was on the vitality that older people have and on the persistent myth that they lack it. Most of the older persons quoted in the article—their ages in the seventies and eighties—live vital lives.

The new reality for many of us is that we will live to a ripe old age. A few years ago Paul T. Costa, Ph.D., psychologist then at the University of Chicago, analyzed the results of a study done on people 100 and older. The results astonished him. Rather than being past-oriented, 80 percent had projects and plans. In some cases they were very ambitious, like the centenarian in Vermont, who was 103 and wanted to get a bank loan to enlarge the private telephone company he'd bought at 90. He got it, too.

Dr. Costa says, marveling, "All those future plans. It was remarkable." And it is remarkable how many of us are putting those plans into action and living satisfying lives.

TWO MASTERS

Child psychologists often talk about the importance of "proper role models" for children. That is, if they're to grow into healthy, mature adults,

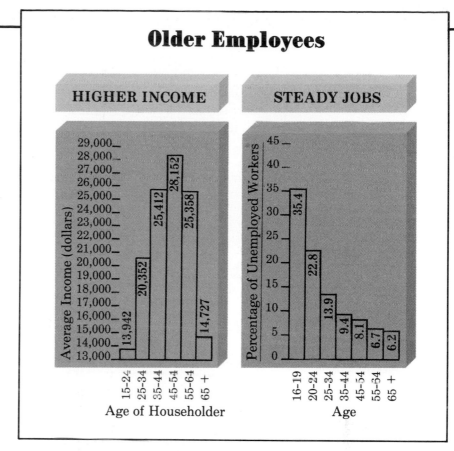

they need to observe healthy, mature adults.

We never really lose the need for role models in our lives—for people who, by their example, can show us possibilities for ourselves we may not have dreamt existed. Because the rocking chair image is still so firmly entrenched in this society's consciousness, we're very much in need of good models of what it's like to be a healthy, robust older adult.

Fortunately, there are many such role models at hand—older people from the past and the present whose lives can inspire and energize all of us. There's Michelangelo—the most towering figure of the Italian Renaissance—who was still creating triumphantly at 60, 70, and right up to his death at 88. He was already 75, in fact, when he began work on one of his greatest, most sensitive sculptures—the *Pietà*.

Other examples abound. Eubie Blake, the ragtime king, was still giving music to the world on his 100th birthday in 1983. John Kenneth Galbraith, the well-known economist, is still writing and lecturing in his midseventies. And Victor Borge, the Danish musical humorist, doesn't let his age—he was 74 in 1983

Statistics reveal that workers achieve peak income at about age 50. At the same time, older workers consistently have lower rates of unemployment (8% for a 50-year-old vs. 14% for a person half that age).

—dictate to him.

Let's stick with Victor Borge for a bit; he's an excellent example of the vital, active, alert, alive older person. Borge has impressed critics and delighted audiences all over the world with his performances. He has been knighted by four Scandinavian countries, has been honored by the United States Congress and the United Nations and has been called "the funniest man in the world" by the *New York Times*.

It all seems easy for him now, but in his early life he didn't escape pain and tragedy. He'd built a successful career in Denmark but was forced to escape to the United States because Hitler's Nazis, whom he'd satirized, threatened his life when they invaded Denmark. He left behind not only his career, but all his belongings. Fortunately, his success here came quickly, when shortly after his arrival he ascended to fame on the "Kraft Music Hall" radio show with Bing Crosby. In 1953 he opened a one-man Broadway show called "Comedy in Music." It still holds the record for number of performances.

Now in the seventh decade of his life, Borge is relaxed and urbane, his wit as sharp and his endurance as strong as ever, still giving 100 to 150 concerts a year all over the world.

What's the secret of his tremendous vitality? Borge points to his rugged constitution—which he maintains by taking care of himself. He has stopped smoking. He keeps physically alive. Each morning he exercises 20 minutes for his back, then often works out on a stationary bike, as well. An early riser, he walks a great deal in the parklike setting of his Connecticut community. "I love to walk—my physical existence demands it," Borge says. In addition, he considers his activity as a performer—and particularly as an orchestra conductor—the best form of exercise.

What about people whose attitude toward aging is negative, people who do live more in the past than in the present? Though he wouldn't presume to try to tell them what to do with their lives or how to live them, Borge says, he strongly feels their problem could be reduced by increased activity—mental and physical. Activity would widen a perhaps narrow, routine kind of life—a life that has become stagnant through inactivity. Borge's personal prescription for longevity: to be active and open to experiencing life's excitements. It's obvious from his busy schedule, his future plans —among them to do more serious conducting, which he loves—that this is exactly what keeps him vibrant and alert.

Borge is a performer who gives unstintingly of himself—not only in his performances but also as a human being. He does benefit performances, acts as a spokesman for charities, establishes scholarship funds. Maybe these heartwarming activities, too, help keep him young, although he puts it a little differently: "We 'celebrities' receive an awful lot of accolades and benefits from society—and I feel we're obliged to reciprocate. Also, I have lived through two world wars, through the holocaust, and I never received a scratch. I'm very fortunate, and I feel indebted. Life is like a bank, you know; if you want to take out, you have to put in."

The mischievous Borge twinkle in his eyes, he concludes, "Old age has never bothered me much because I have never been old before. I don't know what it is. Every new day is a new age. When I look into the mirror I must laugh because my mother couldn't possibly have recognized me. When I was 18 I wished I was 19, I couldn't wait—but now I'm going to wait."

HOBO TO PHILANTHROPIST

Half the world has heard of Victor Borge, but only in his own little community of Bethpage, Long Island, is Leo E. Schottland famous. Yet 83-year-old Leo, too, is a perfect model of the alert, active, energetic older person.

One could hardly call Leo's background conventional, either. He was raised in a Manhattan orphanage, which he left at 16. After that he worked in a bookstore, in a furniture factory, on a farm; he drove a horse and wagon for a textile firm, helped organize a Teamsters local, became a

Victor Borge, the talented humorist and musician, refuses to bow to age. He has the stamina and drive to give 100 or more concerts a year, traveling around the globe. How does a man in his seventh decade keep such a grueling schedule? He exercises daily, taking long walks, working out on a stationary bicycle and doing special exercises for his back. In addition, he indulges in lots and lots of fun. His prescription for longevity: Be active, open, outgoing, experience life's excitements and live intensely.

bus driver; he drove a taxicab and an ice cream truck and signed on as a cook's helper in a Maine lumber camp—all before he was 23.

Then he became a hobo, one of those men now celebrated in song and story who rode the rails in the West and Midwest in the early years of the Depression. More often than not he was broke and hungry. More odd jobs followed, then a stint in the Air Force. He married, raised a family and took over a hardware store, which he ran successfully for 25 years. Eventually he retired, at the age of 75.

You wouldn't expect a man with Leo Schottland's background to fade quietly into his retirement—and there's the point of it. Like Victor Borge, he still celebrates life by embracing its excitements. Most of his activities have to do with community affairs. In fact, Leo's list of achievements is so impressive that on the occasion of his eighty-third birthday the Bethpage Rotary Club honored him with a fellowship award and the local library announced that its auditorium would henceforth be named the Leo E. Schottland Auditorium.

What has Leo done? He set up the first blood bank in Bethpage. He organizes fund-raising events and community clean-up campaigns. He started—against some community opposition—the first senior citizens' center in Bethpage and he's a founding member of a boys' shelter in the area.

Enough? No. Once he was instrumental in helping the local Rotary Club collect trees from all over the world—including the Soviet Union— and plant them in one of the local school yards. When a hurricane devastated the northeast coast, he gathered toys, food and clothing, then arranged for their transportation and distribution to an "adopted" Connecticut community.

In the midst of all this community activity he has found time to write nine books of poetry. "Most deal with my early life, my love of nature and of animals, and my concern for the environment," he says. He writes a weekly column— "Leo's Lines"—for the local newspaper, as well. He also finds time to give poetry readings to children, school groups, church groups and senior citizens' centers.

To be with Leo—as with Victor Borge—is to be with a living refutation of all those myths about the aging brain. He's trim and healthy; he has the face of a man 20 years younger. His mind is obviously as sharp as ever and one can't help but be struck by his remarkable memory for names, dates, events of all kinds, both recent and those going back 60 or 70 years.

What gives Leo his tremendous energy? Several important factors. For one, he's health minded. "I eat a nourishing breakfast—juice, oatmeal, wheat germ," he says. "If I eat a substantial supper I have a very light lunch, and vice versa. I don't eat red meats, but I like chicken and fish. I love vegetables, fruits and salads. I eat whole grain breads and take a multivitamin tablet every day."

Exercise is as important to him as to Borge. He swims daily in the local pool and takes lots of walks. "I walk and walk and walk," Leo says. "Up the hills, down the road, for hours. Sometimes I walk with a friend, sometimes alone. Sometimes I meditate, soliloquize, think; sometimes I walk with an empty head. I look for little animals; I consider them my friends."

It's from his good works, however, and from working closely with people that Leo is most nourished. Basically, he remains active by keeping active. Quite simply, he has things to do. He has goals to accomplish. And he conserves energy by dismissing destructive emotions like anger.

"I've known hunger and poverty," he says, referring to his early life, "but I'm not bitter. I don't eat my heart out hating anybody. And I can give. I'm retired and in a position to give." Pausing, Leo smiles slightly, then adds, "This is what I say to myself, and this is what I'd say to other people: As long as you can walk, and as long as you feel well enough, get occupied. Get involved in your community and your neighborhood. Give of yourself and you'll find it easier to sleep at night—and you'll last longer."

Leo E. Schottland is 83 and very, very happy. Once a hobo who rode out the Depression on the railroad tracks of the West, he is now a community activist in his Long Island town. Raised in an orphanage, he helped found the town's first boys' shelter—and its first senior citizens' center. In addition, Leo writes a column for the local newspaper and—even more important to him— books of poetry that express his love of nature.

Jim Herron

Jim Herron, artist, worked for the Cleveland Press until 4 years before it, like so many other afternoon papers, folded in June of 1982. At 76 he has every reason to sit back, put his feet up and simply retire. But there's a hitch. Herron loves to draw and paint. He's working with 2 small advertising agencies, developing business logos. He's learning calligraphy and the technique of painting with acrylics. And he's free-lancing the caricatures for which he's famous.

His favorites include Katharine Hepburn and George Burns, but over the years he's portrayed the comic likeness of almost every big star. His most famous is of Ed Wynne, which was purchased by the Cleveland Art Museum and displayed often.

"My favorite caricature of all time was the drawing I did of Ethel Merman as she appeared in *Gypsy.* Remember the song 'Everything's Coming Up Roses'? I used that as the basis of my sketch, drawing leaves coming up from a flower pot, and Ethel coming out of the leaves. Merman liked it so much she put it on the cover of the *Playbill* that was used all over the country!"

Robert Redford is the
reat Jay Gatsby

HELLO

"They're great retirement gifts. I do a caricature of the person, then surround it with his life's highlights. Often, everyone at work signs it. It makes a nice memento.

"Some people are difficult to draw. They look so normal it's like doing a caricature of an egg. On the other hand, I don't like to do people who are too obvious, either. They're natural caricatures!"

MACBETH
By William Shakespeare; Prod

Herron says, "So many retired people are throwing their lives away. My advice? Stay well dressed. Shine your shoes. If you don't have an avocation, get one!"

Herron's work appeared in the entertainment section of the Cleveland Press for 59 years. His illustrations span the period from the golden age of movies to the situation comedies of the 70s —as represented by "The Fonz," portrayed by Henry Winkler.

7

Life's Personal Changes

Kids grow, retirement calls; life changes but still goes on.

One of those discoveries we universally make as we grow older is that age is very relative. As adolescents, we thought 40 was positively ancient. In our thirties, we regard 50-year-olds as over the hill. But when we ourselves are in our fifties, it's the 70-year-olds we consider truly "old." Yet many 70-year-olds, as vital and alert and active as they ever were, either think of themselves as middle-aged or they no longer make age distinctions, realizing it is irrelevant.

Nevertheless, age-related events do occur. The middle years, in particular the years between 50 and 65, are fraught with major changes that can have a powerful emotional impact. For instance: The last of our children leaves home and the relationship between spouses takes on a new dimension. Some of us divorce—more all the time. Many of us subsequently find new mates and build new lives. Our parents die, and we are no longer anyone's child. At some point we decide to retire—or are forced to do so by the rules of the companies that employ us. As we grow older, death becomes less and less of an abstraction. Friends and relatives pass away, and some of us must face the cruel fact of life that we're now widows or widowers.

Changes mean adjustments. Major changes require major adjustments. Most of us handle these adjustments extremely well, but in the process we must sometimes grapple with very contradictory, difficult feelings. Furthermore, the life changes that occur alter the way we relate to others, particularly members of our immediate family. You may happily wave goodbye to your son or daughter as they set off on their own, only to find loneliness and loss behind the closed door.

This chapter and the ones that follow will discuss these transitions in our later years and how best to deal with them.

Time spent together, (preferably alone together) just having fun adds richness to a marriage and simultaneously reduces the strain as well.

THE MERITS OF MARRIAGE

If you're married you are statistically ahead of the game. It means you're happier: Happiness studies show that married people are more content than single people. It means you're healthier: Longevity studies show that married people generally outlive single people, particularly lonely singles.

Each marriage, whether brand new or seasoned by decades, is, of course, a unique relationship. Richard and Betty T., in their late sixties, are a storybook couple—the kind honeymooners hope to be when they're in their vintage years. They never walk down the street without holding hands; they still preface remarks to each other with terms of endearment (and mean them); and, when they're apart for a day, they still miss each other. Saul and Esther W. had such a marriage once, they say, but there were too many quarrels, too many differences in the way they looked at things, too many of

life's problems they couldn't jointly resolve. They stay together still, because it's easier to be together than alone. If we look at these two couples as extremes of sorts, then most couples in and past middle age fall somewhere in between.

Studies on marital satisfaction don't all reach the same conclusion. Some say married people become less pleased with their marriages over time, while other studies sound a much more optimistic note. Despite present-day cynicism about lasting, loving relationships, the vast majority of the senior citizens interviewed for a study published in the *Journal of Marriage and the Family* were generally pleased with their marriages. Even more interesting, they said their marital relationships had gotten better over the years.

We don't lead our marital lives in a vacuum, isolated from other aspects of life. As we enter and leave our fifties, sixties and beyond, we become participants in some emotionally powerful events. Menopause is an event—even if it isn't necessarily a traumatic one. The children leave home—or, as is increasingly happening, unexpectedly come back again. We retire. Some of us sell our homes and move, perhaps to a warmer climate, perhaps to a retirement community. We become grandparents. We make our adjustments to our aging selves. We encounter some illness. Some friends and some relatives die . . .

All these events and others that normally occur in the unfolding of our later years affect not only us as individuals but our marriages as well. Sometimes the impact is very strong. For instance: Psychotherapist Muriel Reid, who has worked with many older couples, tells of a husband who looked forward eagerly to his wife's retirement so that they could travel to the countries they'd always dreamt of visiting. But when she left her job she plunged into a long, deep depression. Their travel plans had to be shelved. Another example: A husband and wife in their seventies were barely speaking to each other, a situation that had existed for many years. Like many a younger couple, they were leading largely separate lives—albeit under the same roof. Then the husband had a massive heart attack, which he barely survived. Unexpectedly, his wife nursed him devotedly, making an emotional connection with him that hadn't existed for years.

Holger Stub, Ph.D., of Temple University, a researcher in the field of social gerontology, points out that married couples today are in a different situation than those of earlier generations. We live longer. As a result, we live with our marriage partners longer—up to 50 years or so if our marriages remain intact. Such a long relationship can mean spending a quarter of a century together after the kids have grown. It is, in fact, a whole new stage of marriage.

WHAT MAKES IT WORK

Good marriages, Ms. Reid and other experts say, have certain characteristics in common. The partners involved are aware of each other's needs and try to meet them. They admire each other; there are more things each likes than dislikes about the other. They're fairly open about their feelings; they work at—or work out—their problems. They know that perfection is impossible and have come to terms with unrealized expectations about the marriage. They aren't stuck in the power struggles so common to newlyweds. They have a sense of commitment to the marriage.

"It's so easy for couples to let their differences become more important than what they have in common, so easy to let quarrels and disagreements, boredom and loss of interest, anger and disappointments take over and allow marital partners to grow apart," Ms. Reid says. "It becomes their style, so that by the time the last child has left home they're in some ways strangers to each other. But what I so often find is that beneath those disagreements both partners often really want the same things. They want to be loved, respected, appreciated and treated with consideration. When couples seem angry or act like strangers to each other, it helps if they can bring their minds and feelings back to their early days together. What attracted

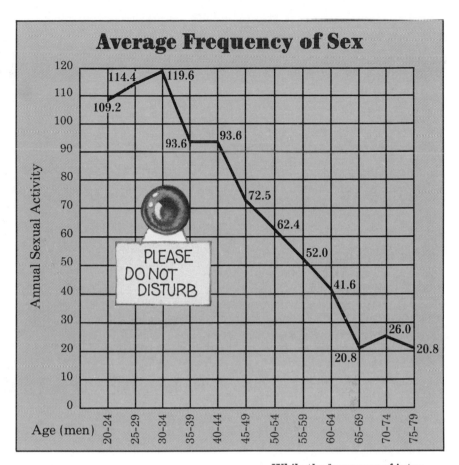

them? What made them fall in love? It helps in making stronger connections now if they remember the past—if they get in touch emotionally with the closeness they experienced then. It's a golden opportunity to strengthen the marriage."

In these later stages of a marriage, when both you and your spouse are defining yourselves in new ways, the changes in your lives may make you anxious, even angry. It's easy to displace that anger onto your partner, but doing so cuts you off from a potential source of comfort and support. Draw on your shared history, on the affection between you. You've gone through changes and crises successfully before. Only this time you have the advantage of more experience, wisdom and sensitivity.

WHAT ABOUT SEX?

As many reassuring studies show, age needn't—and for large numbers

While the frequency of intercourse may diminish with time, the love, pleasure and satisfaction each romantic interlude brings continue unabated throughout life.

A second marriage is often the marriage of two entire families. Here the children serve as attendants in their parents' wedding ceremony.

of people, doesn't—stop sexual activity or enjoyment. Nevertheless, we do go through some changes as we grow older. It's helpful to know about those changes—so they don't surprise or frighten us.

If you're a man, be aware that when you're older you're not nearly as much in a state of sexual readiness as when you were younger. Men are at their sexual peak during adolescence, after which they begin to slow down. Just looking at a woman or thinking about sex won't do it anymore. As you grow older, you may not always experience full sexual arousal. Desire may suddenly, unexpectedly wane on occasion; it may return in minutes—or it may not. Also, there may be times when you think you want sex, but find that body and mind are not on the same wavelength.

In adolescence, desire came quickly—but so did the sexual climax. As a man grows older, it takes him longer to reach that climax. Far from seeing it as a problem, many older men are delighted with this change. Another possible change: Not every act of sexual intercourse may lead to a climax; sometimes a man may find himself perfectly content making love without an orgasm. This is perfectly

normal. Normal, as well, is a delay in a return to sexual readiness after climax.

Women also go through sexual changes in their mature years, though these changes aren't as dramatic or as visible as those for a man. The postmenopausal woman may feel some discomfort during intercourse—a sense of scratchiness or irritation in the vagina. She's apt to be slower in her sexual arousal and her orgasms may not be quite as strong as before. However, Masters and Johnson are quick to say, "the levels of sensual pleasure" she derives from sexual intercourse "usually continue unabated."

These descriptions are general; they take no account of individual differences, but such differences obviously occur. Nor do they take into account serious illnesses and the use of medications that might interfere with desire. About half of all men with diabetes, for example, are impotent. A convalescing heart patient may not be able to resume sexual activity for a short while; for most such patients no restrictions are necessary once the convalescent period is over. Hysterectomies, common to older women, have no physical effect on desire. Emotional depression, however, usually has a strong negative effect.

The sexual revolution has influenced people in their seventies as it has people in their thirties. After interviewing 800 older people for their book, *The Starr-Weiner Report on Sex & Sexuality in the Mature Years* (Stein & Day, 1981), Bernard D. Starr, Ph.D., and Marcella B. Weiner, Ed.D., conclude, "But contrary to the fears and apprehensions of young and middle-aged adults about the status of sex in the later years, a significant 75 percent of our respondents said that sex is the same or better now compared with when they were younger."

The changes that occur are important to understand because they can bring on the worry that can have an inhibiting effect on sex. Both sexes go through those changes; both need understanding, encouragement and support from their partners. If a man reacts to an unexpected loss of desire with shock and shame, he's apt to trigger a cycle of anxiety that can result in impotence. Also, "some women immediately think they're less wanted or loved; they don't realize that it simply happens at times, as a normal consequence of aging," notes psychotherapist Reid. She stresses that blaming is harmful both to the overall relationship and to sexual functioning.

Humor can help in these situations. People often take sex too seriously anyway, and a bit of laughter, a shrug, an attitude of, "Well, that's the way it sometimes happens" when things go wrong can do a lot to defuse the situation. Besides, intercourse isn't the only way to enjoy sensuality. Simple touching and caressing can be a pleasure in itself, rather than a means to an end.

What's sometimes called sexual boredom is another area of conflict with some older couples. "Well, we've been together for 30 years," the refrain goes. "There are no surprises left; the excitement went long ago." Many people are convinced that sex is not exciting after a lifelong marriage, yet other couples find sex an ever-deepening, ever more pleasurable experience.

Sometimes sexual boredom is a reflection of other tensions in the relationship—accumulated resentments, unspoken anger, problems that haven't been resolved but that have a corrosive effect on a couple's intimate life. These need to be faced if the couple's lovemaking is to improve.

In many other cases, though, boredom has much simpler causes— sex has become routine, predictable, a matter not so much of knowing each other well as of only doing the things one knows well. The age-old advice— "vary the routine"—is as sound today as it ever was. Bring each other little, unexpected presents. Share your fantasies with each other, but don't put pressure on yourself or each other by insisting that the fantasy be realized. Remember, sex ought to be fun.

On a physical level, sex both relaxes and energizes; it's also physical exercise. On an emotional level, it's a powerful way of showing love and caring. For all its positive aspects,

Living Together

As much as anyone, older people are beneficiaries of the 70s human potential movement and the opening up of lifestyle options. A few take the unorthodox course of pairing and not marrying. Even Social Security sometimes works in favor of an unmarried couple, with the single person's allotment 50 percent greater than a spouse's would be.

however, it's not something every older person *must* engage in. There are people for whom sex isn't that important—perhaps never was. Such persons simply feel more comfortable having sex infrequently or not at all. To have sex or to abstain from it are equally healthy choices—depending on our backgrounds, our needs and the circumstances.

A TIME TO REMARRY

Unfortunately, marriage doesn't always work out. Divorce, common enough among younger people, is becoming more commonplace in the later years, as well. Divorces among middle-aged American couples have approximately doubled in the past couple of decades. "Longevity has added as much as a quarter of a century of close living to many marriages," Dr. Stub points out. "This alone exposes marriage to a phenomenal increase in disruptive influences and culminates in higher divorce and separation rates."

Divorce at any age is a personal crisis of immense proportions. On a scale of traumatic life events used by psychiatrists, it ranks second, just below the death of a spouse.

All of us who experience divorce also experience—to a greater or lesser degree—pain, grief, anger, loneliness and fear of managing alone. We also may have a sense of loss, failure and rejection.

Alex R., 63, divorced about six months, says, "Funny, I wanted to

Divorce and Social Security

Divorce or remarry and you transform more than your lifestyle; you change your Social Security coverage, too. Here are a few basic rules:

- You're a 62-year-old woman, divorced after at least 10 years of marriage, who has not remarried. If you never worked outside the home, you still can receive Social Security benefits based on your former husband's work record.
- You're a man or woman who has earned coverage on your own. Claim the benefit for a single person.
- You're a 65-year-old man divorced after at least 10 years of marriage. Your former wife never remarried, but you did. Both your present and former wives can receive Social Security benefits based on your working income.

split; I pushed for a divorce against Helen's resistance. There were all these things I was going to do, but I sit in my room a lot, wondering what life is all about, anyway."

The intense stress generated by divorce makes us more vulnerable to illness. Domeena C. Renshaw, M.D., professor in the department of psychiatry at Loyola University Medical Center in Illinois, has listed some of the symptoms that appear in women: rapid heartbeat, hyperventilation (abnormal breathing), insomnia, vaginal discharge in the absence of a true infection, pelvic pain with no abnormality to cause it, tension headaches and the like.

"Women under the pressure that follows divorce often have back and neck pains, abdominal tension, spastic colon and irritable colon," Dr. Renshaw advises physicians in *The Female Patient,* a medical journal.

Some of these symptoms also show up in men, of course. The physical manifestations of depression —sleep disturbance and lack of concentration, for instance—are common to both sexes.

For whom is it harder, this dramatic change from married to single life? That's not so easy to say. Both share the pain, the fear. If there are children living at home, the woman is usually tied down with them. The man, usually the partner needing to establish himself in unfamiliar surroundings, has it harder in the sense of having to take care of himself alone, something he may not have been used to doing.

We can help protect our health and our psyches, too, by reaching out to others: to friends, to relatives, to our children. It's important to let in those who are close to us—to give vent to our feelings and accept the help and concern offered us.

So, slowly we begin to make adjustments. We have a better grasp of our capabilities. We may engage in a personal search that is best done alone.

Kathy F. is such a person. Like so many other women, she regarded her identity as based almost exclusively on her housewife-mother roles. When her husband left her, shortly after her fiftieth birthday, she felt shattered. But in slowly reassembling the pieces of her life, she came to realize certain things. "I've grown a lot," she says now, three years later. "I felt very intimidated by my husband. Now I no longer see myself as an extension of somebody else but as a person in my own right . . ."

The wounds do heal—at least to some extent. In time many of us do become dating singles—divorced men seem to begin the dating process sooner than divorced women do—and some of us then think about remarriage. U.S. Bureau of the Census figures show that, in the 40 to 60 age group, 82 percent of the men and 74 percent of the women marry a second time.

Some of those second marriages also end in divorce, but being older gives us some pluses. We're more mature. We're better able to share of ourselves. We're not as frantic as when we were younger. All this predisposes us to successful second marriages.

It predisposes us, but doesn't guarantee that the outcome will be successful. Much depends on the circumstances of the first marriage, and, in particular, on what we've learned from the dissolution of that relationship and how we use that knowledge in the new marriage. Do we understand what went wrong with the first marriage? Have we learned from our mistakes? Can we say, with some degree of certainty, that we're not likely to repeat those mistakes? (It's easy to fall back into old, destructive patterns if one isn't careful!) As for new relationships, those that have the best chance of succeeding are those in which we have slowly gotten to know the new person in our lives and have spent time with him or her in a variety of circumstances, and in which we leave our shared experiences feeling positive and comfortable.

People who rush into remarriage take the biggest risk. Very risky, too, are divorced persons who remain bitter about their former spouses. As Jim Hobday of the Family and Children's Service of Minneapolis points out, such people haven't cut off from their ex-mates. They're still tied to them emotionally—in a negative way—and many transfer some of that rage to their new partners. Also at risk are persons at the other extreme—those who have nothing but praise for their former spouses—because, Hobday says, they haven't separated emotionally, either, and resent the new partners for not being the old ones.

What's least risky, most hopeful? A balanced attitude toward that ex-husband or ex-wife. We accept our share of the responsibility for the breakup of our marriage and we look forward to the blossoming of the new tie with a feeling of ease and optimism.

THE DEATH OF A SPOUSE

The loss of a spouse is quite possibly the greatest test of emotional endurance that many of us ever face. And though it may seem impossible to envision in the early stages of our pain and grief, some of us emerge from the ordeal not only having found the strength we needed, but stronger than we were before.

Doctors have established that grief is experienced in several stages, which are the same for all of us. We deny the reality of our spouse's death for as long as we can. We're angry at the unkind fates, and maybe even at the mate who has gone and left us alone. We experience feelings of guilt if, for instance, in the period of mourning, we allow ourselves to laugh. When we finally accept the reality of our loss, depression becomes an ever-present companion for some of us.

In the first year, we sense our dead mate everywhere. A widower comes home, starts to call out his wife's name—and then stops himself, confused as he realizes what he was doing. "Bereavement dreams"— dreams about the dead spouse so vivid they seem more like reality— are common.

What's especially hard to deal

Divorce Rates

Midlife is our time of tempest, when our marriages, careers and even identities come due for evaluation. If you are between the ages of 30 and 44, you are most vulnerable to divorce, or so the U.S. Bureau of the Census indicates.

People 45 to 54 years old also suffer relatively high rates of divorce: Out of 5.8 million divorced women, a little over a million are 45 to 54; among divorced men, 740,000 out of 3.8 million fall in that age group.

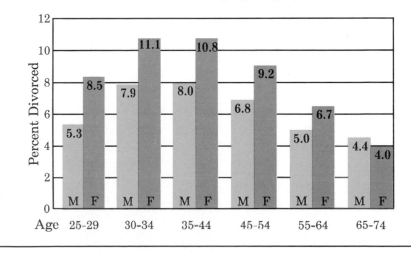

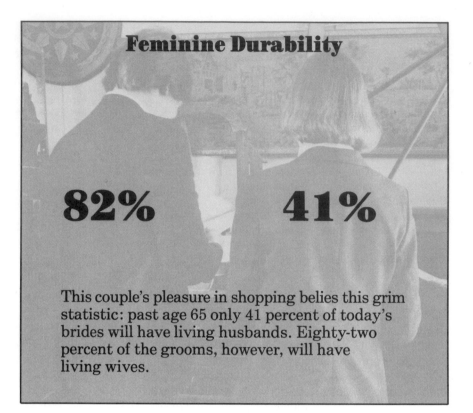

Feminine Durability

82%   41%

This couple's pleasure in shopping belies this grim statistic: past age 65 only 41 percent of today's brides will have living husbands. Eighty-two percent of the grooms, however, will have living wives.

with is the day when the involvement stops. The difficulty is particularly acute in cases where there was prolonged illness: So much of our time and energy was spent in talking to doctors, visiting the hospital, making arrangements, answering questions. But one day that's over. We ask ourselves, "What shall I do?" It's as if our own whole life has stopped after we've been so busy, so electric with energy we didn't know we possessed. That's when we know we have to begin to think of ourselves in a different way. On some unconscious level we decide that we want to make our lives better.

"It's so bewildering," observes Lilly Singer, coordinator of services for the bereaved at the Westchester Jewish Community Services in White Plains, New York. "You'll find somebody who's had a good day or week or month who'll say, 'I'm feeling better.' And then it will hit again."

Ms. Singer, who leads groups of older widows and widowers at the agency, says another unexpected and difficult feeling is that of being overwhelmed. "The remaining partner has to take on roles he or she has never before been responsible for,"

she explains. "It can be overwhelming for a woman to have to learn about insurance, about the car, about the bills. It can be overwhelming for a man to have to worry about the marketing and the cooking and the dishes and the laundry. At a certain point they feel so helpless they want to say, 'I've had it.'"

But we don't give up, of course, and if we're wise we intuitively take Ms. Singer's counsel, which is to set priorities for ourselves when we're feeling inundated—not to tackle everything at once, but to do the important things first, organize ourselves to conserve our energy. And we call for help from anyone who can help us—the neighbor who knows about the workings of the furnace, the friend who will come when the car breaks down.

Time *will* heal, but meanwhile our bodies crack a bit under the strain. Many of us evidence physical manifestations of our psychic stress. "Grief will make you sick" is an old folk saying with just enough truth to it to make us wary. That is, we should be wary. Studies show that the bereaved make more trips to the doctor than do other people.

Healthy grieving demands that we acknowledge and find acceptable all of our feelings, the ones society has decreed not so nice as well as the others. They are all acceptable. They are all normal. Healthy grieving demands that we make a conscious attempt to shake ourselves out of our sorrow at a certain point—the point varies for each of us—and notice with the beginnings of renewed pleasure that there's a real world around us. If we can't overcome our grief, the wisest course might be to seek professional counseling.

Soon we become less dependent on those around us—learning to do the income tax or host a party, for example. We become active in a variety of ways, and at a certain point—unthinkable at first—we're apt to seek companions of the opposite sex. "One of the things that has surprised me is how actively a lot of widowed people seek new relationships," Ms. Singer remarks. In myriad ways, including some we're unaware of, we grow stronger than ever, and this is so even though we still sometimes listen for the footsteps that aren't there.

Freda Tucker still finds herself listening for those footsteps. It's exactly a year since the death of her husband, Louis, the childhood sweetheart to whom she was married 46 years. "It's been the hardest year of my life," she says. "Being without him has been so difficult because we'd shared so many wonderful things—we were sightseers, we loved trips; he was a wonderful tennis player, swimmer and photographer and he loved classical music. I have beautiful photo albums of our whole life. I look at them sometimes and even laugh out loud. I've such good memories. I wish I could have more."

The transition was brutally harsh for this 68-year-old woman. One day he was alive, with her; the next day he was dead of a heart attack.

"The hardest part is accepting the reality and finality of death," Freda says in her engagingly emphatic way. "I couldn't believe that Louis wasn't coming back. I could almost feel that there was someone in the bed beside me. Many times when I lifted my head from the pillow I could swear he was walking around . . . That was very hard, accepting the fact that he will never come back again, that it was forever. I'm not 100 percent sure I've accepted it still, but I'm much better."

Social scientists say numbness is the very first reaction to the death of a loved one; the mind refuses to comprehend it. It takes time; so it was with Freda. "I spent the first week with my older daughter," she recalls. "I don't think I shed one tear in that whole time; it was so bottled up it was unbelievable. But once I got back to my apartment I wondered how my routine would change. I love an orderly place; my husband was like that, too. You know, I picked up where I left off, with the neatness and the arranging, just like he was still there. I changed the linens on his side of the bed just as though he were coming back to sleep. But the healing didn't start until I started to cry. I did that all alone. Nobody knew."

Almost immediately, Freda says, she started to do things for herself— "it was either sink or swim." She didn't isolate herself, didn't turn down invitations. She accepted the comfort of her close-knit family. She enrolled in a French language course because she loves languages. She goes to lots of places alone and with friends. She is optimistic about the future. She loves life and thinks she's doing well on the whole.

A few days after the anniversary of Louis's death she talked about driving to places where she'd always hesitated to go alone for fear of getting lost, and she said, "Sometimes I say to him, 'Boy, would you be proud of me. You'd be so proud of what I'm doing!' And he would!"

AN EMPTY NEST

The "empty nest syndrome"? What's that? It used to be—or so mental health experts thought—the reactions of a woman who'd invested herself completely in being a housewife and mother, the reactions of a person who felt confused, lost, terribly useless and lonely when the last child left home. The syndrome depicted the two parents alone for the first time in 20 or 25 years, now strangers in a sense, with little to talk about without child-rearing matters to discuss.

Today social scientists are discovering that the empty nest syndrome has been exaggerated— especially since women now have so many options for self-realization outside the home. It does affect some middle-aged couples, according to psychologist David Chiriboga, Ph.D., who is with the human development and aging program at the University of California at San Francisco, but probably no more than 5 percent or so.

Increasingly, studies and observations of midlife couples show that, far from being a crisis, this transition period in the lives of women and men is liberating. In a landmark study of 54 parents by Marjorie Fiske Lowenthal and Dr. Chiriboga, none of those studied felt threatened by the emptying of their nests. They felt they'd be able to relax more and do more things together. It's not hard to find wives and mothers who blossom

"The hardest part is accepting the reality and finality of [my husband's] death. I couldn't believe that Louis wasn't coming back . . . I wondered how my routine would change . . . You know, I picked up where I left off . . . Sometimes I say to him, 'Boy, would you be proud of me. You'd be so proud of what I'm doing!' And he would!"
—Freda Tucker.

after the last child has gone.

Ruth M., a 58-year-old book-keeper, is typical of today's midlife woman in that she didn't say anything about feeling depressed when her youngest daughter left for college. "Oh, sure, Tom and I felt some pangs," she says. "The silence was a little strange—the kids always had their friends dropping by. But we were eating dinner a week after she left, and Tom and I looked at each other and just laughed. Each of us knew exactly what the other was laughing at—what a relief! It was *quiet*!"

Laurie V., 59 and the manager of a large florist's shop, recalls how much better she feels today than she did a few years ago. After her last child departed, when she was 49, she went back to school and studied business administration. After a couple of years she began to work, first as the assistant manager of a boutique, then at her present job. She loves it.

"I've matured," Laurie says. "I used to see everything that happened, every problem, from the perspective of how it would affect my family. Now I'm much more of a person in my own right. My husband says it's only now he realizes how exciting I can be."

Small wonder, given reactions such as these, that a nationwide "quality of life" study conducted by researchers at the University of Michigan found that women with children over 17 are the second happiest group of women in the country. (Happiest of all are young married women without children.) When Compton Advertising, Inc., talked with panels of women who were 50 and older, the same theme emerged. For the first time since their marriages they weren't simply somebody's "wife or mother." They might have enjoyed those roles, but they also were limited. Now they were standing on their own, discovering new hobbies, interests, courses, jobs and volunteer work—and delighted with it all.

That doesn't mean there aren't any problems. At the very first many couples are a bit lonely for their children, and some wives may become a bit fearful and depressed wondering what they're going to do with their lives. Sometimes when wives go back to school, begin careers or start businesses, their husbands are disturbed at first. Often they have mixed feelings: It should be the woman's right—but they miss not having her around as usual. "Such feelings are perfectly normal," psychotherapist Muriel Reid says. "We always mourn what we lose, and there's always a tug to stay in the same place—we resist change." With enough caring, patience and understanding on the part of both partners, such conflicts usually work themselves out.

The empty nest adjustment is generally most difficult for parents who don't have a good marital relationship or who have tied their children too closely to them in an emotional sense. Many couples, though, experience that sense of relief and the happy feeling that life is more open, less restricted and more fun than it was before.

Daddy's Empty Nest

When the last child clears out of the home, everyone knows it's Mom who suffers the loss.

But recent studies suggest at least as many fathers as mothers feel pangs of loneliness and regret.

HOMING PIGEONS

Discovering how nice life can be when the last child leaves home doesn't mean that the parents involved don't love their children. They do. It simply means that they've largely completed the vital task of child-rearing and now can go on to yet another phase of their lives.

However, not all mothers and fathers go through this transition period. Some children never leave home. Mostly these are troubled children—too dependent or unstable to be on their own. Increasingly, another phenomenon is taking place: the children leave, but then return.

They have been returning home in ever greater numbers from failed marriages, as dropouts from college or the military—but most of all because of economics. In a time of high unemployment and inflation, they're unable to make it financially on their own. The parents, though they welcome their children back, often have mixed emotions.

Feelings of ambivalence are common, predictable—and under-standable. The relaxed time is gone. The parents can't move about their own home as freely as they did. They might have thought of selling the big family house and moving to smaller, more manageable quarters, but now they have to stay put for a while.

Parent-child conflicts are common when adult children move back in, and it's not just parental resent-ments that precipitate tension. The adult children *are* adults and expect to lead as independent lives as when they were on their own. Often the parents forget that those offspring are now adults and treat them like much younger children—wanting to know where they're going, when they're coming home or why they came home so late. Children often feel an enormous amount of resent-ment. Tension also arises around such issues as chores and what financial contribution (if any) the child is expected to make.

Things work out best when arrangements are discussed ahead of time and a verbal "contract" is arrived at. The more things that are spelled out, the less chance there is

Redoing the Spare Room

Once the last child has vacated the premises, you *should* have an extra room for your own use. But often the former resident simply becomes an in-visible guest. Clothes, posters, books and furni-ture remain as they always were. The bedroom, in fact, becomes a kind of shrine. However, most families don't have a home so large they can allow a room to remain unused.

Consider the best use for your

new room—a study, guest room, art studio or office are possible con-versions for most bedrooms. Begin by removing *everything* from the old room (memorabilia can be stored else-where). Unlike your first time decorating it— when you aimed for cute and cozy, with yellow ducks and washable wall-paper—this time aim for function, convenience and style. You'll never believe it's the same room!

Along with productivity, companionship and health, involvement in stimulating, challenging activities can be a key factor in enjoying later life.

for misunderstanding. There are also clashes around values. For instance, the adult child may want to sleep with a lover in the parents' home. Mental health experts say that if this situation conflicts with the family values, the parents should say no—it still is their home.

THE END OF THE BEGINNING

Over and over again people are discovering this happy fact: The fear is worse than the reality. That is, we face a stressful event, view it with dismay or even dread and when it's upon us, it doesn't turn out to be as difficult or as painful as we imagined.

So it is with aging and the events surrounding it. Some people dread growing older. They notice every little creak in the joints, every new gray hair, every laugh line that's grown a little deeper. They mark the passing of the years with ever-greater concern. Happily, they're in the minority. Most of us cope. We see ourselves in life's

mirror—more mature, more aware, more philosophical. We've had a long, rich history and are now able to take advantage of this accumulation of experience to stand back and see the big picture of our lives—and truly make a golden time for ourselves.

Thus it turns out that so many of the supposedly stressful events of later life aren't the crises they have often been made out to be. Until recently, these predictions had been based on the experiences of only a few severely affected patients. Now that studies of a broader population have come out, it's become clear that most people handle these life events much more positively than was originally thought.

"If we expect an extreme reaction, we're apt to weave the kind of emotional atmosphere in which it's much more likely to happen," explains New York City psychotherapist Ellen Mendel. "For instance, women who think that menopause is a great trial are more prone to be sensitive to any discomfort that actually does occur. Women who don't think negatively about menopause are more inclined to shrug off their symptoms." What Ms. Mendel is talking about is that old truism, the power of positive thinking. And it *is* a power. People who enjoy their later years—who really do make them into golden years—can't help but see them positively.

The good, solid, healthy older life also requires companionship, for both emotional and physical well-being. Many important studies bear this out. For instance, a British study of psychiatric disturbance in English women found that, as the *American Journal of Medicine* put it, "having an intimate and confiding (but not necessarily sexual) relationship with a husband or boyfriend reduced the likelihood of depressive symptoms in the presence of life stress ordinarily provocative of such symptoms." Another British study concluded that having friends—especially confidants—results in fewer physical problems.

American studies have come to the same conclusion. In a clever and significant piece of research whose findings are important to all older people, Lisa Berkman, Ph.D., and S. Leonard Syme, Ph.D., looked at the relationship between social contact and health based on a study of 4,725 Americans living in Alameda County, California. These people had been extensively interviewed about their social relationships and other aspects of their lives, thus providing a wealth of material about their friendships. Matching this information with death records for the same large group, the doctors found that those who had lived isolated lives had death rates two to three times higher than those whose lifestyles incorporated good friendships.

This is of special significance for older people who live alone. It's vitally important to our health to reach out to others, to share ourselves and our feelings.

For example, traditional Japanese society places great value on close social networks, while Western society stresses individualism. One study showed that Japanese men who led a fast-paced life, smoked, ate fatty foods and had high blood pressure, but who retained social ties, had a lower incidence of heart disease than those who became Westernized.

What is there about the human psyche that makes us so vulnerable to disease when we are isolated from others? Nobody knows why human connectedness is such a powerful medicine that can color our late years golden, but the fact that it does wouldn't surprise Irene Nechas. She knows the value of friends and relatives, and it's a knowledge that obviously has served her well. At 72, Irene has gone through her share of change and trouble, but still retains the spunk that has always been a key factor in her personality.

Her most difficult time began when she was 55 and her 28-year marriage ended. And it ended not with a whimper but with a bang.

"Here I was, with just two or three thousand dollars and no Social Security because, even though it was a lengthy marriage, I didn't qualify," she explains.

Quite sensibly, she reviewed her precarious situation without panicking. She determined to use any and all resources at hand to turn a probable disaster into a secure retirement.

First the good news. Irene decided to start fresh by moving to Florida, where her sister lived. Next, the bad news. Although Irene was an experienced hairdresser, she lacked the license necessary to operate in Florida. While she tackled the state's bureaucracy, she took an interim job selling swamp land and another as a motel desk clerk.

"It was a difficult time, but I got a lot of emotional support from my sister and her husband," says Irene. "It's good to have a family you can lean on. But you can lean only to a point and after that you've got to stand on your own two feet."

She did just that. Hairdressing license finally in hand, she found a job, made friends and established herself in the community. She carefully invested her money so that it snowballed into a comfortable cushion for retirement.

Once established, Irene felt free to pursue another love—traveling. While it might seem improbable (if not downright imprudent) for a single woman in her sixties to go trotting around the globe, Irene toured Europe several times and visited other continents as well. Her secret? Networking. She travels with a close group of friends. "We not only travel, we also go to the theater, movies and concerts," she says, "and we check on one another to make sure we're all right."

Despite a heart attack at age 60, Irene has always continued to work—putting in five or six vigorous hours a day in the beauty shop.

Irene's advice for other older people is the same advice she follows herself: "First, you've got to keep looking good," says this woman who had a facelift at age 70. What else? "Get out of the house, whether it's to a job or some other place. Get in with people—and not just people your own age, but *all* age groups. And be interested in what's going on—nationally, locally. There's so much fun you can have, there's not enough time to do it all."

"Here I was, with just 2 or 3 thousand dollars and no Social Security because even though it was a lengthy marriage I didn't qualify. . . . It was a difficult time but I got a lot of emotional support from my sister and her husband . . . It's good to have a family you can lean on. But . . . you've got to stand on your own two feet . . . Get in with people. And be interested in what's going on, nationally, locally. There's so much fun you can have, there's not enough time to do it all."
—Irene Nechas.

8

Retirement: A Golden Chance

"Be Prepared" is the motto
of all successful retirees.
Financial planning is the key.

Retirement is one of the major events of our lives. No matter how smoothly we may think we're going to make the transition from working to not working, we're bound to have some contradictory feelings about it. We may love the idea of leisure, then unexpectedly experience a sense of loss, as well. We may dread the whole idea of retirement, then come to love it. In retirement we lose a special kind of structure, but we gain time to make our lives more fulfilling than ever before.

Retirement has, in the past, received poor notices. Studies showed retired people as suffering from loneliness, loss of purpose and failing health. Yet retirement does not always create these problems. In fact, life insurance statistics show that, in actuality, many people become healthier once they leave jobs that are stressful or that they dislike. Others rediscover mental acuity lost during years of performing boring or repetitive tasks. These days, many people truly enjoy their retirement years, as marked by a continuing trend to early retirement. In 1978, Congress passed a law prohibiting mandatory retirement, with few exceptions, until the age of 70. Are working people then clamoring to stay on the job until that time? Not at all, not even in economically troubled times. Most still retire at anywhere from 62 to 65.

But there are dangers in retirement. Too many people just slip into it without planning. They hope for the best, but flounder. They suddenly find their stretch of leisure time has become a barren desert. And, maybe, they go broke.

Our retirement years truly can be golden, but only if we make a deliberate effort to shape them to our needs. It's important to begin planning early—well before retirement age. And it's important to share the task of planning with your spouse.

FRAMING A PLAN

For George and Betty A., retirement is everything they hoped it would be—and more. They garden together, go swimming three times a week, do a lot of traveling. "I think I was ready to retire about five years before I finally did," grins George, who opted for early retirement and hasn't regretted a day of it.

For Stan and Georgia K., things haven't worked out that well. Sixty-seven and in good health, Stan misses his job and his friends at work. He watches television day and night and finds himself quarreling with Georgia, who doesn't seem to want him around. "Retirement is for the birds," he says.

Differences in temperament account for some of the differences between the attitudes toward retirement of these two couples. Planning and not planning for retirement account for the rest. Retirement experts emphasize that planning is crucial to successful retirement.

Men are the hardest hit, notes Linda Caigan, a retirement specialist with the Whitehill Counseling Service in Hartsdale, New York. "Men's identities are very much connected with their jobs, their earning power, their association with other people at work," she explains. "They base their sense of self on their work, not their personal relationships. When they retire, a lot of men have trouble with that." And so, more and more, do working women.

It's common for people facing retirement to deny the reality of their situation. They deny that a major adjustment has to be made. This refusal to face reality can lead to trouble.

"There's a lot of work to be done, otherwise the whole retirement experience becomes frightening," Ms. Caigan says. "And that's very understandable. Our parents got us ready for school. Many years went into preparing us for the world of work. Nothing prepares us to leave it."

The very fact that one is no longer working can be a very significant loss, especially if the retired person exercised some power on the job.

Another loss is the loss of structure. In certain professions and occupations, people are required to be self-starters. Free-lance writers and artists, for instance, don't punch a time clock and nobody looks over their shoulders; they're on their own. Most of us aren't like that—we need the structure of a nine-to-five job to keep us going. The absence of that structure can be extremely upsetting. When we think about it ahead of time, an unstructured life may seem wonderfully inviting, but waking up each day without a plan or a purpose spoils the dream. It's the basis for the old saying that hell is a perpetual holiday (meaning vacation).

"Boredom is one of the biggest fears retired—or retiring—people have," Ms. Caigan notes. "It's because people too often associate retirement with a retiring from life, rather than having a continued vision of life as growing."

Money problems may surface—and, if there's a reduction in income as a result of retirement, this also can be experienced as a very real

People are retiring earlier and living longer. In 4 decades, the average age of new Social Security applicants dropped by nearly 5 years, while the average life expectancy of people over 40 increased by a little more than 5 years. That's a dividend of 10 years to spend on ourselves, but supporting this extended retirement requires shrewd financial planning.

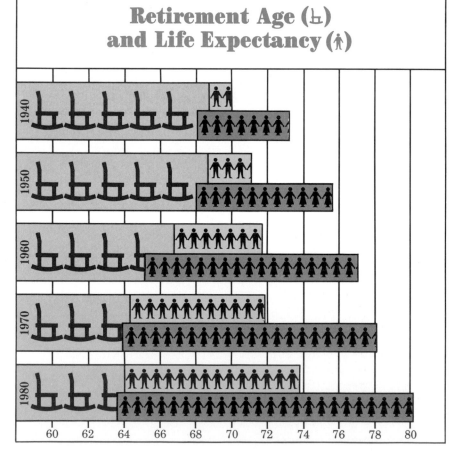

loss. People who aren't used to economizing may have to begin to do so for the first time in years. Here, too, preplanning is important. Retirement counselors say many people on the eve of retirement haven't even explored what health insurance they will have in the years ahead.

People facing retirement sometimes think they will spend a lot of time with their children and grandchildren. But sometimes their children are caught up in their own lives and may see this new interest as more of an intrusion than a help.

Often, at least in the initial stages of retirement, there is some stress between husband and wife. The life they share, the routine they've established over the decades, undergo a radical shift. It's a shift that affects both partners. Each has legitimate apprehensions to deal with and adjustments to make. Retirement is very much a family affair.

In the case of a traditional marriage, Ms. Caigan says, "For the past 30 years he's gotten up and taken the 7:30 train or driven off to work at 7:45. She's gotten up at 8:15 and had breakfast alone. She loved that. She talked to her friends on the phone, then went off to a course at 10:00, and had a bridge game at 1:00. She got back in time to do the grocery shopping and he walked in at 6:00 and dinner was ready. Now it's all different. Now he wants to have breakfast with her. Then he wants to know if she's going to be home for lunch. He feels lost and vulnerable in his new role. She may see him as vulnerable for the first time; she may not like that—it does change the balance of a relationship." If both partners work and would like to retire at the same time, but for financial reasons they can't, or if they want to spend their retirement time in different ways, other problems occur.

All the stresses to which newly retired people are subject can take their toll. Ms. Caigan sees the physical signs of stress in some of the preretirees she counsels—high blood pressure, more reliance on alcohol and drugs. Those who have trouble adjusting to their new life are those most susceptible to such

problems. Furthermore, according to research by Charles H. Hennekens, M.D., at the Harvard University School of Public Health, men who retire may have an increased risk of heart disease.

As in all stress-related situations, this is an especially important time to maintain a healthful diet to ensure good nutrition, to exercise regularly and to get sufficient sleep.

Most of us do find ourselves content in our retirement; we work through the initial stresses as we've coped with other stresses and crises. Obviously, though, the more physically fit we are, the better able we are to use our inner resources in planning wisely for and making a good adjustment to our retirement.

RETOOLING FOR RETIREMENT

"People ought to begin to plan for retirement at least five years before they actually do retire," says Julian Brodie, head of Retirement Program Services, an organization that develops and produces preretirement counseling programs for businesses. Brodie's firm reflects a trend; many corporations today offer retirement counseling, developed either in-house or through an outside service. He suggests that if you are employed and are a few years to a few months from retirement, you check with your employer's personnel office to see if such counseling is available.

Good preretirement planning, whether or not it involves outsiders, includes all areas of concern—financial, social and marital.

If your company doesn't offer retirement counseling, or if it's limited, consider enrolling in a retirement program. They're being offered in many parts of the country by universities, community colleges, high school adult education programs, labor unions and Y's, as well as some churches. Such programs cover every aspect of retirement, from what to do with your free time to how to apply for Social Security and Medicare.

The financial, insurance and housing aspects of retirement will be covered in the pages that follow. Right now we'll look at some of the other important issues that require

"People ought to begin to plan for retirement at least five years before they actually do retire . . . you must have a pretty clear idea of what's coming to you in order to plan your retirement budget. Some long-term employees get pensions as high as 70 or 80 percent of their earnings, while others receive 'peanuts.'"
—Julian Brodie.

your planning and careful thought.

Let's begin with early retirement, a significant trend that began a few years ago. While it has leveled off, largely because of the economy, many people still opt for it. For some, the loss of income is balanced by outside investments; for others, there are plans to start another career; and for still others, it's simply the desire to spend the rest of their lives pursuing activities they enjoy most.

Jim R. is an example. A foreman in a California wallet factory, Jim decided to quit work at 62. He loved to paint and decided that was how he wanted to occupy his time in his later years. He enrolled in painting courses at a nearby community college. Today he's happily engaged, five or six hours a day, creating oil paintings of local woodland scenes. The hours fly, and he finds his life more richly satisfying than ever.

"Because I retired early, I didn't get my full pension or full Social Security, and I would have had to pay for my own health insurance if

my wife couldn't carry me on hers," Jim says. "But ask me if I have any regrets and I'll tell you no. I worked because I liked the money, not the job, and I'm happier now than I ever was." It does help, he adds, that his wife, a teacher, backs him to the hilt and continues to work.

Whether early retirement is for you depends on many factors—your work situation, what you want to do in the postretirement years and, of course, your financial situation. As is the case with Jim, some people for whom early retirement has meant a drastic cut in income—perhaps 30 or 35 percent—say they're glad they made the decision anyway. They may have had trouble with their bosses. They may have been relegated to back-office jobs with younger employees taking over their former responsibilities. They may have been in high-pressure work situations and become tired of the rat race. They may have worked nonstop from the time they left high school or college and been just plain tired of working. They may be in ill health. All of these are reasons given by men and women who opt for early retirement.

Whether you retire early, at 65, or later, a prime consideration is what you will do with all that unstructured time. You might look forward to doing nothing, but that soon begins to pall. In fact, it becomes demoralizing. "We advise older people that they can work for pay or work for free, but work they must," Brodie says. If possible, treat yourself to something nice right after retiring. One man, for instance, saved to go on a two-week cruise with his wife. Afterward, he enrolled in classes and began teaching sports at his local Y. He knew that people who just sit around become depressed—that the secret of aging slowly is to remain vital, active, engaged.

It's never too early to think about how you might want to define "work" in your life once you're no longer an employee. If you have some absorbing interest or hobby, as Jim did with his painting, all to the good. You need to do things that stimulate your mind and provide you with satisfaction. Be on the alert for things that catch and hold your interest.

Retirement is a time for creative pursuits and learning new skills—not for time on your hands. If taking a sculpture course is something you always wanted to do, now's the time. Learning and creativity are not limited to youngsters. In addition to enjoying old pursuits, learn new skills, too.

Once you do find things you enjoy, don't close your mind to other possibilities. Review your activities every so often to see if you really still enjoy them or are just continuing them out of habit. Don't forget that no matter how old you are, you're still evolving. Don't forget, either, that these are *your* precious years to shape in the way that nourishes you most.

Ms. Caigan tells of a chemist, a highly intellectual man, who loved to teach his younger colleagues about sophisticated chemical reactions. When his retirement time came, he was in a panic. Chemistry had been his whole life—what was he going to do now? Aware of his love of teaching, Ms. Caigan encouraged him to become a tutor to high school students needing special help. She suggested courses and lecture series he could attend, as well as other cultural events he might just enjoy. Each summer he spends two or three weeks in an Elderhostel program—living in university dorms and taking courses. His life now is busier and more fulfilling than he had thought possible. Ms. Caigan points out, "He realized he had to structure his life; he couldn't just 'float around.'"

Ms. Caigan stresses, "The whole point of retirement planning is to get your feet wet, to test things out, if possible in some concrete way, or at least in your mind." Ms. Caigan has the members of her retirement counseling groups do a lot of imagining— "imaging," she calls it—of what life will be like in retirement. The more you imagine yourself in the situation —as well as explore it or try it out concretely—the more effectively you'll be able to plan.

The range of activities open to you is limited only by your imagination, your stamina and, depending on your finances, the cost.

Volunteer work is an obvious choice for many retired persons. The skills and talents you honed on the job may serve you well if you decide to do something in a volunteer capacity. Thousands of retired businessmen, accountants and management experts help other people of all ages who want to get started in business; they belong to a federally sponsored organization called SCORE

(Service Corps of Retired Executives). Others serve in another federal program, VISTA (Volunteers in Service to America), which is a kind of domestic Peace Corps—volunteers serve in areas of great poverty. Many (with or without special skills) are needed by schools, hospitals, libraries, conservation groups, nursing homes, humane societies and in the Foster Grandparent program. (More about volunteer work in the chapter to come.)

The more caught up a retired person is in the activities that interest him, the easier the marital adjustment to retirement is likely to be. This is especially true if the couple is used to a traditional way of life as described earlier—one in which the man has been working daily while his wife has had her days to herself.

Husband and wife need to plan for their retirement(s) together. They need to discuss what it is they individually want, expect and fear in this new stage in their lives. What do they want to do together? What do they want separately? What compromises will be needed?

If it's hard to talk about these things, Ms. Caigan suggests putting your expectations and fears on paper. After each of you does this, start talking about them with each other, sharing your anxieties, your trepidations. Don't think you have to solve everything in one evening's discussion; these are serious life issues that require a lot of thought and negotiation.

FINANCIAL PLANNING

A rule of thumb has it that after retirement your income (from pension, Social Security, investments, etc.) should be roughly 75 percent of what it was in order for you to live comfortably.

Because Social Security is very often the cornerstone of retirement incomes, let's look at it in some detail. The amount of your monthly Social Security check depends on your age, how many Social Security "work credits" you've earned and your actual earnings over a period of years. Being indexed to inflation,

Preparing for Retirement

Review, research, reexamine are the three R's of retirement. Review your financial situation, and keep a diary of *every* expense. Prepare a retirement budget. Research the benefits provided by Social Security, pension plans, IRAs, annuities, etc. Calculate your exact income. Review your housing needs. Reexamine your will and all insurance policies for possible revisions. One last R: register for Social Security 3 months *before* you retire.

Social Security benefits do keep rising, a feature of the troubled system that may change in time as reforms are considered. You don't have to stop working altogether to get full Social Security benefits, provided your outside earnings don't exceed a specified limit—$6,000 in 1983 for people 65 and over, $4,440 for people under 65. Pension money, dividends and interest, annuities and trust fund payments don't affect Social Security benefits.

You can begin to collect Social Security benefits when you're only 62, or anytime between 62 and 65, but there's a catch. If you retire early, your benefits will be permanently reduced. Should you start working again, and therefore stop collecting benefits, you can begin to collect again at 65—at the higher rate.

If you're married and you and your spouse have both worked over the years, and both qualify for Social Security benefits, you can claim them in one of two ways—as a worker with a dependent spouse or as two independent workers. Which is better? If both spouses have earned a great deal, it probably pays to collect separately. If one of you has earned much more than the other, filing as a worker with a dependent spouse will probably get you the best benefits. Figure out which is best for you.

Also think carefully about when exactly to commence your retirement, because of a first-year exemption that comes into play. If you retire at midyear and, during the year's remaining months, don't earn more than one-twelfth of the limit allowed for outside earnings, you can collect your full Social Security benefits for the rest of the year. So, if it's possible to arrange it, retire fairly early in that year and cram as much in earnings as you can into the months before retiring.

These facts and figures are merely an overview of Social Security and its benefits. It points up how important it is, as part of your retirement planning, to study Social Security provisions and changes in order to make them work best for you. Be sure to register for Social Security three months before you retire. As for determining what your Social Security earnings will be, get a "Request for Statement of Earnings" postcard from your nearest Social Security office. Fill it in, mail it off and the information will be sent to you.

What are you getting in the way of money from your company or from private pension plans, annuities and the like? Some long-term employees get pensions as high as 70 or 80 percent of their earnings, Julian Brodie says, while others, in his words, receive "peanuts." He adds that some workers, who have a great many years invested with a firm and are enrolled in a profit-sharing plan, "may have more money coming to them when they retire than they had in their entire lives. For instance, it's not unusual for a $15,000-a-year employee to receive $30,000 or more

The average annual earnings from Social Security are near the poverty level. The workers represented below were employed for the same number of years and earned the same salary. Despite identical income, individual benefits vary greatly.

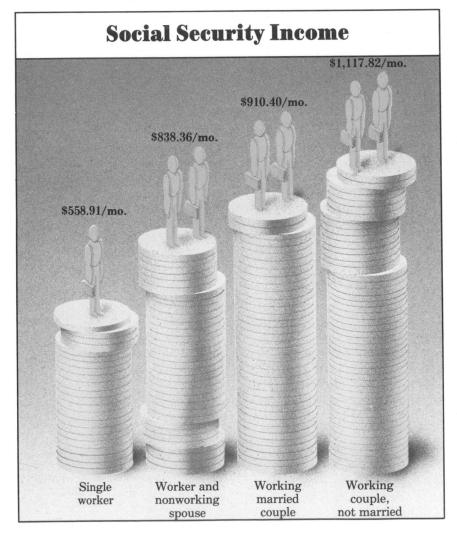

Social Security Income

$1,117.82/mo.

$910.40/mo.

$838.36/mo.

$558.91/mo.

| Single worker | Worker and nonworking spouse | Working married couple | Working couple, not married |

in a lump sum as his profit-sharing sum." Decisions have to be made about the investment of such money. An attorney, accountant or financial planner—in the event a very large sum is involved—can help.

Next, you need a budget for your retirement years. Let's assume you're not yet retired but are close to it. Figure out your present income. Next, calculate the income you expect once you're retired. Finally, add up your yearly expenditures. Be sure to include *all* outlays. And don't forget to add in the cost of gifts.

In all probability, there will be a discrepancy between your current income and your projected retirement income. This dilemma is what happened to Fred A., a draftsman, as he planned his retirement at 67. His pretax income, barely sufficient for his needs in a high inflationary period, was $32,000. His retirement income would come to nearly $9,600 less. Fred was dismayed. Actually, his reduction in income would amount to 30 percent—still within an expected and acceptable range.

Don't panic if you find a similar difference after you've made your calculations. Though you may have to economize, you'll have reduced expenses, as well. Lower income means lower income tax. Best, you get a second exemption when you reach 65. Also, you won't have any work-related expenses.

Take advantage of all the discounts a senior citizen is entitled to—whether going to the movies, buying airline tickets or using local transportation. Some restaurants offer discounts on certain days or at certain times of the day. A number of hotels and car rental agencies also offer discounts through retirement organizations.

Then there's life insurance. You may have taken out life insurance when you were much younger to protect your wife and children, to pay off the mortgage, for your children's education and as an endowment to provide income after you retire. But many of these reasons may no longer be valid. Though insurance broker Norman Finkelstein, of H & N Finkelstein Brokerage Corporation in New York City, stresses that each situation is differ-

Tax Benefits for Older Americans

People over 65 are entitled to a double exemption of $2,000. Certain types of income are nontaxable, including Social Security benefits, railroad retirement benefits, welfare, veterans' benefits, most medical compensations and certain types of gifts. Life insurance proceeds generally are not taxable, and some funds (such as IRAs), pensions and annuities *may* have special tax status. Up to $125,000 profit on the sale of your home is tax free. And finally, you may not need to file income tax at all, under a certain income. Many older Americans overpay their federal taxes. For information, write to the American Association of Retired Persons, 1909 K Street, NW, Washington, DC 20049.

ent, it's entirely possible you may not need a lot of life insurance now. Therefore, it's sometimes advisable to cash in a life insurance policy and put the money into a better income-producing form of investment, and, perhaps, to buy a small life insurance policy to cover estate expenses.

In considering your budget, be sure to take inflation into account. Let's say you need $15,000 in income when you first retire. With an inflation rate of about 8 percent a year, in less than nine years you'd need about $30,000 just to keep up with the effects of inflation.

Considering inflation, it's imperative that you increase your income to stay ahead in the coming years. Reducing your expenses is one way of reconciling any discrepancy between preretirement and postretirement income. Working, either part time or full time (or turning a hobby into income) is another. Brodie says that almost everywhere but in Florida, California and Arizona, with their high concentrations of older people, work is available for many qualified retirees.

A third way to increase income is to invest both prudently and with an eye to the best return—whether that means stocks and bonds, money market funds, mutual funds or other types of investments. In order to have more cash to invest, many people decide to sell other types of assets. Selling a house that's too big for just two people, investing the proceeds and moving into an apartment, a smaller house or a retirement community is one of many possibilities. The point here is not to suggest specific types of investment—that's beyond the purview of this book—but to point up the importance of sound financial planning for retirement. It's never too early.

HEALTH INSURANCE

Whether you're near retirement or already there, you may be looking to Medicare to provide all your post-65 health insurance needs. Warning: Don't! While most people 65 and older qualify for Medicare, this coverage simply isn't adequate protection against the cost of an illness, especially if it's a lengthy or serious one.

Also, as Bill and Alice T. found out the hard way, Medicare doesn't pay benefits to dependent spouses until they turn 65. Three months before he retired at 65, Bill registered for Social Security, which automatically enrolled him for Medicare. His company's health insurance coverage (which ended at 65) had covered Alice, too, and he assumed Medicare would do the same. He discovered how wrong he was when Alice, who was only 61, had to be hospitalized for a minor operation; they had to pay the cost, nearly $3,000, themselves.

Before retiring, the Health Insurance Institute advises, check your group health insurance plan, whether it's from your workplace or your professional or fraternal organization. A few plans now continue at least partial coverage after retirement. If you can continue that plan, or convert it for continued coverage, it might cover both you and your spouse and fill in Medicare's gaps.

Medicare is divided into two parts—A and B. Part A is the hospital coverage. It's free. After a deductible—$304 in 1983—which you pay, you're entitled to free full hospital care in a semiprivate room for a period of 60 days. For the next 30 days you pay flat per-day deductibles; Medicare pays the balance. After 90 days of hospitalization,

Costs of Coronary Bypass Surgery

The coronary bypass is becoming one of medicine's most-used procedures. For those without health insurance, picking up the tab is almost as painful as the operation itself.

Hospital Expenses					Physician Expenses	
Major		Minor				
Operating room	$ 2,919	Surgical supplies	$ 260		Surgeon	$3,193
Critical care	1,440	Blood	254		Anesthesiologist	927
Laboratory	1,276	Roentgenograms	245		Cardiologist	756
Pharmacy	1,273	Physical therapy	222		Radiologist	67
Room	993	Blood gas determinations	199		Pathologist	26
Cardiac catheterization	901	ECG	199			
Inhalation therapy	794	Recovery room	192			Total $4,969
Fluids	435	Anesthetic equipment	177			
Total $10,031		**Total $1,748**				

Grand Total $16,748

you're on your own insofar as that illness is concerned. Medicare also provides a 60-day "lifetime reserve"—free hospital days that you can draw on if you're hospitalized longer than 90 days. However, there's a per-day deductible; also, once you use up a reserve day, it's gone for life.

Medicare's Part B is strictly medical insurance—it pays an allowance on doctors' bills and on a variety of services: lab tests, ambulance service, prosthetic devices, chemotherapy and the like. Part B is optional and there's a moderate cost—$12.20 a month with a $75.00 yearly deductible (in early 1983), but almost everyone signs up for it. Despite its inadequacies, it's still a lot cheaper than private health insurance.

However, Part B is not without problems. For example, in all likelihood, you'll have to supplement the Medicare coverage because the doctors' fees and other expenses will exceed the Medicare allowance.

"Medicare's schedule for physicians' fees is years behind what doctors currently charge," says Norman Finkelstein. "The average person finds that the allowable benefit comes to approximately 40 to 60 percent of the actual bills. Not only is the reimbursement schedule antiquated, Medicare deducts 20 percent from the amount of the doctor's bill it approves for payment. And don't forget that yearly deductible."

Finkelstein offers an example of how Part B works. A man named Harry had a $2,000 eye operation. Medicare allowed only $1,000 for this operation, but it actually paid much less. Since this was Harry's first medical expense of the year, he had the $75 deductible to pay. (This is only paid once a year, however.) With $75 deducted from the $1,000 allowed for the operation, the balance was $925. But Medicare paid only 80 percent of that sum—a total of $740. Subtract $740 from $2,000, and the end result is that Harry was stuck with a $1,260 tab for his illness.

Because of gaps in Medicare coverage, many people buy supplemental health insurance if they can't continue their preretirement policy. Policies vary considerably, depend-

ing on the insurance company, the coverage it offers and the premiums it charges. One popular, relatively low-premium supplemental health insurance policy pays 20 percent over the amount that Medicare pays. In other words, it makes up for the 20 percent that Medicare automatically deducts. Many other policies, including those offered by Blue Cross, provide similar coverage.

Other policies offer other benefits. "You're dealing with an individual product," Finkelstein points out. "There's no standardization in the insurance industry. Every company markets a product it thinks is attractive."

Make sure the policy you get is really the most attractive in terms of your needs and pocketbook. Shop around. Keep in mind that a good supplemental policy pays a percentage of actual charges, rather than a fixed dollar amount. It fills in the important gaps in Medicare coverage, provides for private-duty nursing (which Medicare does not cover) and has a reasonable "preexisting conditions" clause. That is, while it may not immediately pay for a medical condition you already have, it won't eliminate that condition entirely from coverage and won't make you wait more than six months before coverage begins.

Finally, be cautious about buying any insurance policy. Check with the insurance department of your state to find out how many complaints have been filed against the companies in which you're interested.

You also might consider more specialized insurance policies. A "catastrophic" policy is a major medical plan with a very high limit—it's protection against a very long, expensive illness. Such policies do, however, have deductibles—in some cases as high as $25,000.

Finally, there's Medicaid, for people who don't qualify for Medicare or can't afford the premiums. Eligibility and programs can vary from state to state; local welfare offices have Medicaid information. As for Medicare information, your local Social Security office has a variety of material you should obtain and study—preferably before you retire.

What Medicare Covers

- Outpatient care
- Hospitalization
- Doctor services (not checkups)
- Rehabilitation care
- Home health care
- Hospice care
- Kidney dialysis
- X rays and lab tests
- Blood (after 3 pints)
- Oral surgery
- Psychiatric care
- Wheelchairs and some other home equipment

RETIREMENT COMMUNITIES

Beachfront condominiums are the popular conception of retirement communities. Yet, there is a great variety available—some in small towns, some right on golf courses. Shop around.

Residents enjoy outdoor activities, sports and games. But best of all, they enjoy having the time to socialize.

Most communities have activity rooms where residents enjoy card games, crafts and even little theater productions.

THE ADULT COMMUNITY

"We just enjoyed driving around, looking at model homes, but for a while we didn't really think seriously about buying one—and when we did, we made up our minds quite suddenly." That's how Gertrude Todd recalls the circumstances in which she and her husband, Fred, made one of the major moves of their lives—leaving the town of Cranford, New Jersey, where they'd lived for 36 years, and starting the next phase of their lives in a retirement community, Leisure Knoll, about an hour's drive away.

Why do people who have lived such a large chunk of their lives in one community decide to pack it in and move to another?

For the Todds, the move, made when Fred was 73 and Gertrude 61, made perfect sense. Their old house really was old—and would soon need repair; that was one consideration. They were also looking realistically at their own ages—and thinking ahead. The time might come when they would not be able (or want) to drive, restricting them considerably. In Leisure Knoll these problems would be easily solved. They would have a nice new house, with outside maintenance done by the community. A shopping bus, which shuttles regularly back and forth between the community and nearby towns, would solve any driving problems. And with all the activities available to them at Leisure Knoll—bowling, golf, card games, a pool room and special-interest clubs of all kinds—the community would become the focal point of their social life.

For the Todds, things worked out happily; they don't always. Relocation is a serious and dramatic life event; it's a complicated one that involves emotional as well as practical issues. Don't act too quickly, retirement counselors warn. Some newly retired couples make impulsive moves to the Sun Belt, for instance, without ever having been there. Once they're relocated, they find it isn't what they wanted.

Before deciding that relocation is for you, thoroughly investigate the areas where you think you might want to live. Talk to people who have been established there for a while. If possible, too, spend a week or more there, or visit for several long weekends. Get a personal feel of the place. Explore the climate, geography, taxes and other costs, the transportation, recreational facilities and other aspects important to you.

Retirement communities are

very popular, but homes are not cheap, often costing $50,000 to $100,000 and up. There are also monthly maintenance charges of $50 to $100 or more. A strong point of attraction—and of criticism, as well—is the fact that they're age-segregated to exclude younger people. Grandchildren usually can visit, though there will be restrictions on the length of time.

Another big attraction is security. The more posh retirement communities have gates and guards; visitors must always be announced. Many others have evening and night security patrols—a real comfort to people who, for fear of crime, were reluctant to go about after dark in their home communities.

But best of all for many is that somebody else takes care of the maintenance. Nobody is more delighted than Charles and Rosemary Foley. It's one of the main reasons they decided to buy a retirement home. Says Charles, "I had a house for some 30-odd years, and I was just getting tired of taking care of it, taking care of the lawns in summer and shoveling snow in winter."

Like the Todds, the Foleys talk enthusiastically about all the things their adult community offers. Their monthly maintenance charge—a nominal $54 in 1983—covers snow removal, mowing and fertilizing the lawns, periodic painting of the exterior of the house, as well as a seemingly endless variety of activities, including the use of a clubhouse and pool. Though they enjoy many of these activities, and the round of parties common to this adult community, the Foleys are aware, as are some retirement community dwellers elsewhere, that there can be too much of a good thing. "Sometimes you can get too caught up in things; you have to learn to say no sometimes," Rosemary says.

If you're wondering how you would fit in, consider certain aspects. Friendship is one. There's comfort and security in building a network of friends who all live in the same self-contained community—friends you see daily in the clubhouse, at the pool or wherever. But friendship doesn't happen automatically. You have to be outgoing, join the activi-

ties and make it clear that you want to participate in the community and make friends there. Also, things work out best when residents of roughly the same age group live in close proximity to each other. Fifty-five-year-olds and 75-year-olds don't necessarily have the same interests and concerns even though both qualify for an "adult" community.

Think about your own needs, your own personality. If you're inclined to stay by yourself and you don't enjoy a lot of activities, a retirement community might not be for you. (Besides, you'd be paying for services you wouldn't use.) If you like the sight and sound of laughing, playing children, adult communities are definitely not for you. If you value the friends you have where you live, moving to a retirement community will loosen the ties; soon you'll be caught up in the community's social life. If you don't like rules and regulations, you may not care for a retirement community; there are restrictions on children visiting, pets (most allow one or two) and perhaps the decorating, selling or subletting of your house.

All of the foregoing applies whether you're married or single. Many communities have a fair number of single residents, mostly women, but some men, too. And romances do blossom. Many widowed or divorced older women find retirement communities especially congenial—they make friends with other single women with whom they have much in common, and the setting provides an outlet for their energies and abilities.

By and large, retirement communities don't cater to people with significant health problems. ("Comprehensive life care communities"— often sponsored by church groups—are differently structured; they do provide comprehensive medical care.) In some adult communities a nurse and a first-aid station are on the premises and there are ramps for the handicapped, but in general, residents provide for their own health care.

The people who love living in a retirement village, people like the Todds and the Foleys, do so because they feel secure there, find the companionship of peers, and— thinking ahead—know that, as Rosemary Foley puts it, "if only one of us should be left, we know that one can stay there, maintain it, and have friends close by."

STAYING PUT

"We like it just where we are," say Jack and Edith Keough, who live in a charming, comfortably large split-level home in Westfield, New Jersey. It's not that this retired couple hasn't considered other options. They definitely have. They've visited a number of retirement communities and talked at length to friends who've happily settled in them. Yet each time they themselves have toyed with the idea of moving, a big "stop sign" pops up in their minds.

Their feelings on the subject are strong, well thought-out and based on practical, emotional and social considerations. Family is one of their major reasons for staying—one of their children and two of their grandchildren live in Westfield, a middle to upper middle-class town with a population of about 30,000. The Keoughs see them often and delight in watching their grandchildren grow up.

Then there are friends. The Keoughs are very active socially, giving dinner parties, visiting and traveling to places near and far with good friends. The warm way they talk about their friends makes it clear how important a factor they are in the Keoughs' decision not to move to a retirement home or community.

"It seems that people who live in retirement communities become totally absorbed by them," Jack explains. "They make friends there and engage in all the activities. It's not practical for them to maintain their previous ties. We didn't want that to happen with us and our friends."

Our Beautiful Home and

To Jack and Edith Keough, Westfield, New Jersey, has been and always will be Home, Sweet Home. After Jack's retirement, the couple opted to stay put. Rather than move to a warmer climate, they chose to bask in another kind of warmth: that of family and friends. They entertain often and enjoy community activities. And once a week they do volunteer work for the local Meals on Wheels program, delivering food to homebound people, most of whom are senior citizens.

Retirement communities offer a variety of activities, but Westfield also offers many. The local Y, high school and college all offer courses in a broad range of subjects. These activities tie in beautifully with this couple's philosophy about how to remain happily married throughout retirement. They were aware of the impact that retirement has on marriages and how it can have a destructive effect.

"Some of the men have a hard time adjusting and some of the wives are exasperated," Jack says. "They talk about it at dinner parties. They take their wives out shopping, because there's only one car in the family now; and when their wives go out by themselves they want to know where they're going and when they're coming back."

"I don't think they're being nosy," Edith adds, "but the wives can't stand it; they're not used to having their husbands underfoot."

The Keoughs' philosophy, simple but realistic, is based on a recognition that each partner is an individual as well as half of a couple. As Jack puts it, "We have separate projects and we have together projects." The separate projects include Jack's athletic interests, playing bridge and working part time. Edith enjoys doing volunteer work for her church and community. Their together projects include their extensive socializing and travel.

Some people would consider their decision to remain in their home as ridiculous, given the large size of the house. Edith and Jack agree that they could sell the house for a large profit, buy a smaller retirement home for half the sum and invest the rest. But among their other considerations is the fact that this isn't just a place they live in; it really is their home.

Our Friendly Community!

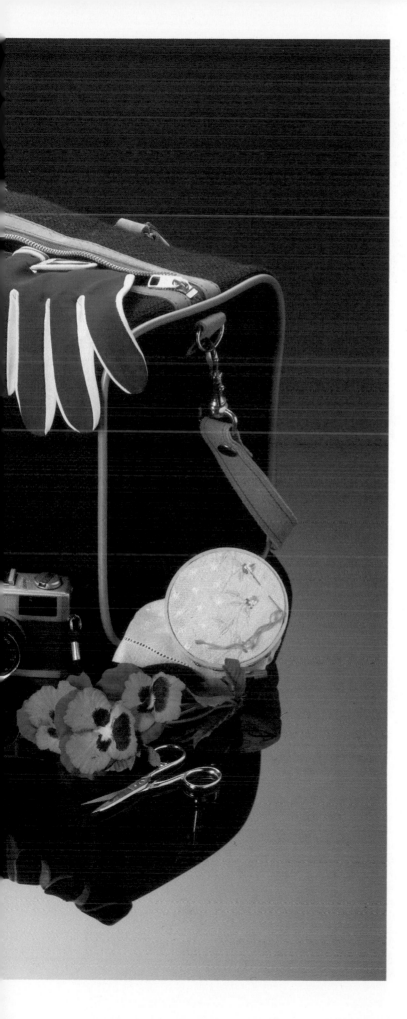

Action and Leisure

Retire to a full, satisfying life of fun, creativity and adventure.

Retirement implies a withdrawal from life. Yet this period of free, unfettered time can offer the chance you've long waited for—the chance to be *you,* to do what *you* want and to enjoy.

Experts at the Ethel Percy Andrus Gerontology Center of the University of Southern California make a thought-provoking point: Following retirement you can, on the average, count on at least 14 active years—a really impressive amount of leisure time considering how you will spend it.

Before you lies a smorgasbord of activities. The choice is your own—and the array of choices guarantees something for everyone. As this chapter details, you can work for pay or volunteer your services in some capacity that betters the life of others and brings commensurate satisfactions. You can dance your way through your community hospitals—as do the elderly residents of one Philadelphia housing project—or take walks on a deserted beach in winter. You can devote some of your energy to keeping pets (with some possibly unexpected rewards in terms of health); take a freighter to a far-away port; collect stamps or sign up for a summer session at a college or get a long-coveted graduate degree.

You can do one or some or all of those things; what rejuvenates you personally depends on your individual nature, but here's a tip from research studies: The more activities you engage in, the more likely it is you'll be well satisfied with your life.

However we define "action and leisure," we're all after the same thing—that involvement, that hobby or interest or pursuit that catches us up, that quickens the step and triggers healthy excitement in us.

"**An awful lot of artists live to be elderly, and some of their best work is done when they're older. Everything seems to come together then. The first thing you realize is that you could almost not live unless you were doing the thing that you want to do.**"
—**Gregorio Prestopino.**

INVOLVED IN LIFE

To discuss "aging slowly" is, from one very important perspective, to refer to a life that's *interesting*. All other things being equal, people who remain vital longest are those absorbed by one or more aspects of their lives. Boredom, at the other extreme, is corrosive to the spirit. A bored child or a bored adult reacts the same way—with a lack of freshness, of spontaneity, of verve. It's a depressed state. In fact, bored children and bored adults often look older than their actual years.

At the other extreme are what could be called the bright-faced people. Their faces *are* bright. Their eyes are clear, alert—and, most important, they radiate an expectant look. No matter how old they are, they still expect surprises, they still expect new and good and interesting things to happen to them. They still have a purpose in life. More accurately, they still find purposes in life; they make energetic contact between themselves and the world around them. In a sense, they view their lives the way a sculptor views a piece of clay—as something to mold, to fashion, to form, to shape. Just as the artist recognizes his power to work that unformed clay into a satisfying form, so these people sense their power to do good things, nourishing things, rejuvenating things, with their lives.

This book has offered dozens of examples of men and women in the elderly category, as society types us, who are amazingly active, productive and creative; some of them larger-than-life figures in this respect. A great proportion of these people, these examples and role models, have turned out to be artists—musicians, painters, sculptors, writers. That's probably no coincidence. Artists have—and retain—the most passionate connection to their work. It's a constant process, one might say, of reinvolvement and rejuvenation. And all of us, whether or not we're in artistic fields, can learn from them.

A few years ago *Prevention* magazine ran a remarkable interview with a remarkable man. Yes, he was an artist, and he eloquently proves these points. Gregorio Prestopino was 72 at the time, still as active as ever in his studio in Roosevelt, New Jersey, where the interview took place. He was successful, in demand, the winner of a prestigious artistic honor—yet there he was, spending his later years as he had his earlier ones, energetically creating, creating, creating. He worked every day, breaking off only for a vigorous swim in a local pool three times a week.

"Unfortunately, a lot of people think that once they're 60 or 65 they're supposed to do without creative activity," Prestopino said. "I *could* quit tomorrow and live well for the rest of my life, but I find myself in here working. Your psyche makes demands on you and you can't ignore them. You have to go on. As long as I find myself waking up in the morning, I find myself gravitating to the studio, and making another painting. I've done thousands, but that's the point.

"An awful lot of artists live to be elderly, and some of their best work is done when they're older. Everything seems to come together then. And if they're really devoted, this is what they're going to do all their lives. The first thing you realize is that you could almost not live unless you were doing the thing that you want to do."

If it seems Prestopino was addressing himself most forcefully and specifically to artists, his remarks nevertheless apply to all of us. It can "come together" for us all—if we let it, if we choose to live that way, leavened by our experience and maturity. We may not have a studio to rush to—we may not even want anything remotely suggesting an actual artist's studio, given the great diversity of individual preferences—but we all do need "studios" of whatever kind to draw us in.

This is a human discovery that we repeatedly make. We need to do things that stimulate our interests and imaginations, things that spark us into activity and thought. Things that will make us want to leap out of bed in the morning, put on our clothes and make exciting contact with the world. This "thing" may be work—paid or unpaid. It may be the energetic pursuit of sports or travel. It may be a hobby. Hobbies can be wonderfully constructive in this sense—but they may not be. A hobby shouldn't be a device for filling the hours but rather a way of being involved. Successful hobbyists enter into their pursuits with all their senses, their imaginations open.

"A man I know was an executive for the better part of his life," Prestopino said. "A few years back he started doing pottery. Now he's retired and is at the college three days a week going more and more in depth into pottery. And he is so exhilarated and so happy that he does pottery every day! He set himself up a pottery kiln and wheel in his garage and he hasn't missed one day. The man hasn't skipped one day since his retirement. It works!

"I always say to my two sons: 'Do whatever it is that makes you want to get up in the morning and do it again.' The most terrible thing that can happen to anybody is to get up in the morning and say, 'I have to go to that awful job again.' That is devastating. On the other hand, when you have something that keeps you going at it day after day, I don't believe that you remember how old you are any longer. You just keep doing what you want to do forever."

This may be a fitting time to recall again a group of very old people studied by Paul T. Costa, Jr., M.D., of the National Institute on Aging in Baltimore. Most were not only active, but maintaining their professional or other interests, keeping up with the literature in their fields. They nearly all had projects. They all had plans. They were all forward-looking.

Pondering his observations of these centenarians, Dr. Costa said, "Intuitively, I am convinced that having a reason for living is probably the most important concomitant of successful aging."

LEARNING NEW TRICKS

Cato the Elder was a Roman statesman who lived from 234 to 149 B.C. Among his accomplishments: When he was 80 years old, he started to learn Greek.

Greek at 80? Happily, despite the bad press the older brain has

---

Alternatives to Television

Watch too much television and life slows to the funeral pace of a soap opera and narrows to the scope of Archie Bunker's mind. So warn psychologists and the new breed of TV sociologists.

Joan Wilkins, who wrote *Breaking the TV Habit* (Charles Scribner's Sons, 1982) says more than 2 hours of television a day is too much. Yet Americans get an average dose of 2,300 TV hours a year.

Like other addictions, the TV habit can be tough to break. Probably the best way to stop is to start doing something else, something that exercises body and mind. Some ideas:

Volunteer for a social service or a political cause. Take a course toward a degree or a second career. Engage in a physical fitness program.

Try out for a community choir. Break up the week with visits to a museum, botanical garden or zoo. Tune in to short-wave radio. Start a small greenhouse, plant a Victory garden or adopt a pet.

The list ends only where imagination falters.

---

received, Cato was far from unusual. Millions of people are learning new things in their most senior of years. Currently, better than 3 percent are enrolled in some kind of adult education course in the United States. Mary T. is an example. She's 67 and thrilled with the weekly French impressionism course she's taking at an art museum in a nearby town. Though Mary has to travel 45 minutes each way by bus in order to get to the museum, she considers the trips well worth it. "I'm learning about things I've always wanted to learn. I never had the time before," the retired executive secretary says. "It's like discovering a new life."

(continued on page 154)

Leisurely Hobbies

During your working years, your job is one of the most important aspects of your life. But it's the hobbies you get involved in now, while you're still on the job, that can spell the difference between happy retirement years and misery.

And, according to E. W. Busse, M.D., founder of the Duke University Center for the Study of Aging and Human Development, "People should develop a *number* of interests before retirement. You might not be able to participate in one . . . [so] you'd better have some others in reserve that are fun to do."

Photography

Do your days pass faster and faster each year? Well, we have an easy way to make time stand still. Photography. It's a good way to take a little piece of your life and preserve it on glossy paper.

And photography is one area where modern technology has become our friend, making it easier than ever to take decent pictures. Automatic focus and automatic exposure devices are available on almost any size camera. That means all you have to do is aim your camera and shoot.

Have trouble keeping your hand steady while shooting? Then use a tripod for a firm grip. And to make it easier to look through your viewfinder, buy an inexpensive eyepiece that attaches to your camera.

Model Building

From a ship in a bottle to a miniature antique car, model building can be the pastime that provides pleasure that far exceeds your investment of time and money. It's a hobby that requires patience, precision and a steady hand. Perhaps this is why the rewards are so grand.

Imagine being able to build with your very own hands a tiny version of that dream machine you were never able to afford. You can re-create with great accuracy the world's most beautiful sailing ships, airplanes of World War I, the Brooklyn Bridge, Victorian mansions—almost any object that might strike your fancy.

Bird Watching

The best way to start bird watching is to join the Audubon Society. First of all, you'll meet other bird watchers. Second, you'll learn the ins and outs of birding from the Audubon expert who leads the bird watching walks.

Tools you'll need are a field guide to the birds (make sure you get the book that covers your neck of the woods) and a decent pair of binoculars.

If you want to bird watch in your own backyard, put in a birdbath and a feeder. A shallow basin set on the ground makes a good, inexpensive birdbath, or you can buy the kind that sits on a pedestal.

Collecting

Almost anything in the world can be collected. And it probably is. Insects, coins, stamps, seashells, baseball cards and matchbooks—you name it.

A large, complete collection of any kind of object can bring the satisfaction of a job well done.

In addition, collecting can be an educational experience as you learn more about the objects you collect. For example, an insect or rock collection can lead to a knowledge of entomology or geology.

And, who knows, you may strike it rich by collecting something that will explode in value.

Flower Arranging

You know you can't draw, hold a tune or find the C chord on a piano to save your life. Yet you know somewhere deep inside there is a hidden artistic talent just yearning to get out. Maybe a class in flower arranging can open the way.

This hobby requires an eye for color and balance along with creativity and a sense of design. A handful of wild flowers or twisted branches can be transformed into a lovely work of art.

To get started, seek out an adult education class in flower arranging.

Painting

"Painting," said Winston Churchill, "is a companion with whom one may hope to walk a great part of life's journey. Painting is a friend who makes no undue demands . . ." yet provides great satisfaction.

Churchill ought to have known; he took up painting late in life, as did Dwight Eisenhower and Grandma Moses. They all believed painting helped them enjoy their later years.

Courses for beginning artists are numerous. Or you can even learn out of a book, if you're more of a homebody. Either way, the joy of creativity can be yours, along with satisfaction from the final product.

Music

"If only I had some time to *practice,*" is a frequent lament of would-be musicians. Now, finally, the time has come. Get the piano tuned, restring the banjo and buy the sheet music.

For those who prefer to listen rather than perform, send for the printed listings from your town's national public radio station. Scan the newspaper for local concerts. Begin to build a library of records and tapes so the world's great musicians can perform in your home.

Active Hobbies

Abody in disuse, says gerontologist Walter M. Bortz, M.D., is a body growing old. "Use it or lose it," as the saying goes. And what better way is there to retain that youthful vigor than with the pursuit of a pleasurable hobby?

Vigorous activity is fun, satisfying and rewarding. And the best part is that there is such a wide variety of active hobbies to choose from.

Dancing

"Dancing," said writer/ physician Havelock Ellis at the turn of the century, "is the loftiest, the most moving, the most beautiful of the arts because it is no mere translation or abstraction from life; it is life itself." Seemingly Ellis knew quite well the benefits of dancing, for he lived to be 80.

The aerobic power of dancing is well documented. It keeps the heart pumping, the muscles flexible and vital capacity in top shape. Then there are the social advantages. Community, senior citizens' and other social groups often organize dances. Or you and your neighbors could get together and sponsor your own. You quite literally could have a ball!

Cycling

Bicycling is a good sport for the later years. You can take it easy and still get good exercise. There's also less wear and tear on joints and muscles than there is in activities like jogging or tennis.

Victor L. Hadlock took up the bicycle at 65. Now he says, "My blood pressure is under control. My health is excellent, not to mention my increased stamina and improved mental and emotional outlook."

And when you first start out, cautions Hadlock, "Don't overdo it. You could do more harm than good. Don't strain your lungs until you're gasping for breath. For the first few months, rest after each ride to let your body catch up. Act your age now, so you can act younger later."

Swimming

Scientists have found that people who have higher lung capacity—who can inhale and exhale large amounts of air—tend to live longer. "And when you swim regularly," says Paul Hutinger, Ph.D., professor at Western Illinois University, "you maintain lung capacity." In fact, he told us, swimming can restore parts of the lung that have weakened because of disuse.

Swimming's other characteristics also make it a favorite late-life activity. "Swimming is a non-weight-bearing sport," says Allen Richardson, M.D., chairman of the USA Swimming Sports Medicine Committee. "That's great for the joints, especially for people with ankle, shoulder or back problems."

Gardening

Gardening is one of the simpler joys of life—and one of the most rewarding, as well. Whether you're farming a country acre or growing violets on the windowsill of a big-city high-rise, playing a hand with nature can reap great pleasure. Imagine creating a blaze of color with one green thumb. Under your husbandry, a small packet of seedlings can grow, bud, sprout to maturity, flower and go back to seed again, giving you the chance to relive the incredible life cycle over and over again.

Each new project is bound to generate new ideas and good feelings. And the only obligation you really have is to enjoy the beauty of it all.

Carpentry

The creation of a useful and lasting piece of work can be one of life's truly satisfying experiences. Carpentry as a hobby presents just such an opportunity.

It is possible to retreat to that basement workbench and turn out everything from a simple set of bookends to an intricate corner cupboard. You can begin with a few inexpensive tools and gradually acquire more advanced equipment as your skill is polished.

If you enjoy working with your hands and creating everlasting things, this could be the pastime for you.

Sheep Raising

Alma M. Campbell is a senior citizen who has no problem finding things to keep her busy. After all, Alma started planning her retirement fun when she was 12, some 62 years ago.

Alma loves to spin yarn—yarn from the wool of the sheep she's been raising as a part-time hobby on her Bucks County, Pennsylvania, farm for a good part of her life. She used to shear the sheep, too. But retirement life has gotten too full for Alma and she farmed out the job a year or so ago.

Alma would rather be spinning the wool, dyeing it and wrapping it into skeins to give to her friends, or even sell, if the spirit moves her. At 74, Alma just can't seem to find enough hours in the day.

"My mother bought me my spinning wheel in 1922 at an auction for 50 cents. She thought I was crazy for wanting it," says Alma, a retired science teacher. "I knew I would use it some day. I had it in back of my head that I just might want to spin the wool from my sheep. When I retired in 1964 I found the time."

Alma admits that finding someone to teach such an unusual hobby wasn't easy. "I found people who knew how to spin, but they weren't willing to divulge the secrets of the trade," she says. "So I had to teach myself. I did it on a hit, miss and cuss basis.

"Raising sheep is a good hobby for a person—a person with a lot of energy," she emphasizes. "The raising is fun, the shearing is work and the spinning is sheer pleasure."

Alma admits to letting her sheep-raising hobby slip a little in the past few years. She used to have 100 head; now she's down to about 20. But then Alma has her spinning, and her quilting, and her knitting, and her sewing, and her loom, and her crewel and her rug hooking . . .

As we said, there just aren't enough hours in the day for Alma Campbell.

Bruce H., another retiree, is taking a class in advanced camera techniques; it's an adult education course held in a neighborhood public school. Bruce says he and his wife travel a lot, with particular emphasis on off-the-beaten-track places like the jungle areas of Mexico and the beaches of Tahiti. Bruce wants to take more professional-looking slides to submit in competitions, which is the reason he's in the class.

So it goes. Whether they get their learning in museums, Y's, public school adult education programs, libraries, churches, senior citizens' centers or elsewhere, and whether they study the French impressionists, camera techniques or myriad other subjects, older citizens are flocking to educational centers in record numbers.

The hunger on the part of older people to learn new things is, fortunately, matched by the expanding opportunities to learn them. A growing number of colleges and universities is tailoring programs specifically to senior citizens. The majority are two-year institutions (either community or junior colleges),

but more state-supported and private colleges are joining in. In fact, roughly 30 states have policies recommending free or reduced tuition for the elderly at state-supported institutions. (The minimum qualifying age varies from place to place, ranging from 60 to 65.) Continuing education programs offer educational opportunities, as do senior citizens' centers, financed by the cities in which they operate. The point is that opportunities for learning are everywhere and cost need not be a deterrent.

A LEARNING VACATION

A particularly interesting educational adventure can be had by joining the Elderhostel movement. And quite a movement it is. A nonprofit corporation run from a national office in Boston, Elderhostel is the ingenious brainchild of Marty Knowlton, a self-styled "guerrilla educator and social activist" who himself is in his early sixties.

Combining the European ideas of youth hostels and "folk schools," where adults can return for short tastes of academia throughout their working lives, Elderhostel offers a summer's grand adventure. The opportunity to spend a week at a college, taking a variety of noncredit courses, mingling with other students in the dining hall, sharing room space (or whatever accommodations are arranged) with other participants in the program—are all offered through Elderhostel at a moderate cost. Each older group is limited to 30 or 40 people; they're usually housed in the same location on campus. How good is the food? How good are the accommodations? These vary from college to college. Don't expect luxury, however, because this is a hosteling-learning kind of experience—an adventure for the senses and the mind.

The first Elderhostel movement started in the summer of 1975 with 200 students enrolled at five colleges. It was so enthusiastically received—meaning it immediately filled such a need—that the enrollment has been mushrooming ever since. By 1982 more than 400 educational institu-

Moderately priced Elderhostels provide both vacation and education. You spend a week at a college, taking noncredit courses and rubbing elbows with those of like interests.

tions in the United States and abroad were participants in the program—a genuine international phenomenon attesting to older people's energy, initiative and will to learn.

The courses offered—each taught by a regular faculty member of the participating college—cover an amazingly wide area of interests. Collectively, there really is something in Elderhostel to please everyone, no matter how conventional or esoteric your tastes. If you're a crime novel buff, you might be interested in The Mystery of Crime Solving (a class in modern forensic techniques). If you're a birder, The Idiosyncracies of Birds would be your thing. On the other hand, you might be keener on Philosophy and the Arts, Parapsychology, Meditating, Poetry, Clowns and Humorists. (The complete catalog of courses and costs can be obtained by writing to Elderhostel, 100 Boylston Street, Suite 200, Boston, MA 02116.)

"It's a perfect match," says Elderhostel national president Bill Berkeley, explaining the program's success. "It's such a positive experience for the elderly, and it's also something colleges enjoy putting on and doing well."

Apart from the Elderhostel movement, there's tremendous excitement, too, among older people who make a full-time commitment to start, continue or finish up undergraduate or graduate degree work. It's no longer unusual, as it once was, to see men and women in their fifties and sixties sitting in the college classrooms and just as intent on getting a B.A. or M.A. as the "youngsters" who are expected to be there.

Whatever educational opportunities you might be thinking about, if you haven't been in a classroom for 30 or 40 years, it may be a little hard at first to adjust to learning again. You might have mixed feelings—wanting to study, but resisting the idea as well. When you ease into it, you'll find the resistance melting and the challenge and stimulation of the experience taking over.

As for specific study hints to ease the way and facilitate learning, educational gerontologists offer the following pointers: Accept the reality that there is a difference between older and younger students—give yourself plenty of time to learn new material and to recall it for tests and other purposes. Don't pressure yourself; take breaks as you need them and don't waste your energy. If some material or assignment seems too complicated at first glance, break it down into small parts or segments. Trying to understand or absorb new material all at once usually leads to feeling confused and overwhelmed. Avoid distractions when you study; choose study places where you won't be interrupted. Be sure to read and study in good light, all the more so if the type is small; dim light causes eyestrain and headaches. And avoid acquaintances who are so wrongheaded as to insist that older people can't learn!

WORLD-WIDE WANDERING

You see them everywhere, all over the globe. They have the time and the money to travel. You see their gray heads bent back to view the ceiling of the Sistine Chapel. You see their tanned and shining faces in Pamplona, Paris, Pompeii and even Pittsburgh. Here are the Selfridges— he's in his late seventies, she's a few years younger—clambering over the hardened volcanic ash that forms the soil of this particular island. Which one? South Plaza—one in the chain of islands known as the Galapagos, 600 miles off the coast of Ecuador, in the Pacific. These are uninhabited bits of volcanic leftover, home to giant turtles and iguanas, sea birds and walruses and a fantastic array of birds, some of which are found nowhere else on earth. The Selfridges were exploring these remote bits of land along with some 60 other people, almost all of them retired, under the auspices of the National Audubon Society.

And here are the Lewises, who are in their second year of retirement and don't have any far-flung stardust in their eyes. They like their travel close to home, meaning they want to see something of their own

TIPS FOR NEW STUDENTS

1. Don't worry that your memory might fail you; to relax helps to recall.

2. Before an exam, say out loud or write down what you want to remember.

3. When you read a course book, ask of each main point "who, what, where, when, why and how."

4. Vary reading speed according to the subject matter at hand.

5. When you write a college paper, take notes on index cards; you can easily shuffle them into the proper order.

6. Ask about tests like CLEP (College Level Examination Program) and ACT (American College Test); you might earn credits by taking these tests.

country and they want to do so as comfortably as they possibly can. The Lewises have signed up for a motorcoach trip to the Grand Canyon and Grand Teton national parks; they'll be staying in very good, comfortable hotels and everything, including baggage handling, will have been arranged for them.

As if to dispel the rocking chair image with a vengeance, older Americans have been traveling to places near and far in what almost amount to mass migrations. According to U.S. government statistics, in 1980 alone almost 520,000 Americans 60 and older were issued passports for foreign travel. They travel in buses, planes, ships, cars and trailers, and the kinds of trips they arrange for themselves cover the gamut from strolling the boardwalk in Atlantic City to birdwatching in Patagonia to rock climbing in Switzerland. Why do they go? Basically because they know, instinctively or otherwise, that few activities are as rejuvenating as travel.

Let's talk it up for travel in retirement years. Why do we need to talk it up at all? Because some retired people tend to see travel—or, more broadly, vacations—as something that belonged only to the work-related time of their lives. It's part of the work ethic: You work hard all year so you need (and "deserve") a rest, a change, a getting-away-from-it-all. People who are confirmed in this view tend to see postretirement vacations as a contradiction in terms: Who needs a vacation when we're on vacation, so to speak, the whole time?

The answer is: We all do. Routine is routine, sameness is sameness, whether you work or not. A change stimulates and energizes us; shakes us up in a positive way, makes us look at and think about things a little differently. Travel is enriching—we meet people who aren't exactly like us, see things we're not accustomed to seeing. We can enjoy great art, memorable surroundings, interesting new foods. Travel gets us out of the rut; even if it's exciting, it's still relaxing, and everyday cares slide away as we react to new scenes and experiences.

Seasoned travelers are aware of this; they don't need convincing and they know what to do—in terms of health, comfort, suitability, etc.—to make their trips successful. Others may not be so experienced, but even

Travel trailers—those mini-homes on wheels—are a preferred mode of travel for many retirees. Here, for example, the Wally Byam Caravan Club Intl. assembles for a holiday by the sea.

older people who have never been more than a couple of hundred miles from home can embark on enjoyable, satisfying travel.

First of all, you have to think about what it is you want—or very definitely don't want. If you don't want to do anything in the way of roughing it, neither rock climbing in Switzerland nor an ordinary camping trip is for you. Trips in which everything is taken care of might, under the circumstances, be very much for you. Cruises, tour bus trips, rail and even some air package trips fill that bill. Another obvious eliminating factor can be cost. If money is very much the object, it eliminates luxury travel, cruises and jaunts to most far-off places.

To stretch a thin travel budget, think both "off-season" and "group." Assuming you have a lot of flexibility as to when you can travel, it makes sense to consider going at a time when most people are home working—it's not only a lot cheaper, but also less crowded. Of course, it all depends on where you're going and what the weather at your destination will be like. Paris in midwinter can be quite cold; Aruba, in the Caribbean, can be quite

Benefits of Group Travel

Travel is for the birds and other winged things, you say. Another's dream vacation is your woolly nightmare. You fear being stranded in a place where no one accepts American Express and the natives look wilder than Shriners at a convention.

But where this bad trip ends, the glories of group travel begin: Here are all the thrills of travel without its risks and rigors. Here luggage, language, itinerary, reservations, tickets, passport, papers and all the usual cares and chores of travel are handled for you. Meals can be prepaid and prearranged.

A tour guide can explain the mysteries of Mont-Saint-Michel or currency exchange.

Some group tours are geared exclusively toward people who're over 55 and retired. About a dozen tour operators in the country offer travel packages designed not only for the elderly but also for those confined to a wheelchair, handicapped or infirm. For a full listing of these tours, write to the nonprofit Society for the Advancement of Travel for the Handicapped (SATH), at 26 Court Street, Brooklyn, NY 11242; enclose a stamped, self-addressed envelope.

pleasant in midsummer because of cooling trade winds—and half the peak winter season cost.

Think "group" because group rates are often considerably cheaper than individual rates. Some group operators sell comprehensive tours that take care of all the details, large and small, that travelers would otherwise be responsible for handling, including restaurant meals and baggage transfers to and from hotels. Such tours are usually known as "fully escorted" and are especially appealing to people with little travel experience. There are, however, many variations on the theme. You can also find groups that are simply "hosted" —meaning that only transportation and accommodations are provided for on a group basis, while in other respects (transfers, meals and per-

Tips for Healthy Traveling

1. Visit your doctor well in advance.

2. Stock up on any medications.

3. Get copies of prescriptions for drugs (the generic names) and glasses.

4. Leave medicines in their original containers and carry them with you.

5. If you have a serious medical problem, carry an I.D. or a detailed description of your condition.

6. Pack a small first aid kit.

7. If you need special meals, be sure to arrange them when you make your reservations.

haps sightseeing) travelers are on their own. When considering a group tour, be sure to find out what is—and is not—included in the price.

When considering a tour, be sure to take the pace into account. If you want slow, relaxed travel, many tours are definitely not for you; often it's up at sunrise and five cities to "do" in three days. The pace can be frantic as the tour operator or travel agent tries to cram as many activities as possible into the shortest time possible. If you want a more relaxed pace, be sure the tour offers it.

At least a couple of commercial operators specialize in tour packages for older people and at fairly reasonable rates. Such tours and related activities are specifically geared to persons in their fifties and up on the supposition (as in retirement communities) that such people will find it more enjoyable to be with peers than to travel in groups that include young adults and families with children. If you want more information on such tours, write to: Grand Circle Travel, Inc., 555 Madison Avenue, New York, NY 10022. Or call their toll-free number: (800) 221-2610. Also, Saga International Holidays, Ltd., Park Square Building, Suite 1162, 31 St. James Avenue, Boston, MA 02116.

Wherever in the world you decide to go—or even begin to think of going—start the adventure by doing as much research on it as you can. Read guidebooks and other kinds of travel books on the area. Send away for tourist literature. Many foreign countries have government tourist offices located in the major cities, while most states maintain at least one tourist information office. If possible, talk to people who have been to the area; while your experiences may turn out to be different, pointers from these people can be invaluable. Doing research on the place is both informative and fun; the more you find out about a locale, the more excited you're apt to become about actually going there.

Consider engaging the services of a good travel agent, especially if there's a complicated itinerary involved or if it's a long-distance trip. If the travel agent has been on that particular tour or been to the area, so much

the better. Travel agents receive their commissions from transportation companies, hotels and tour operators; they should be able to give you thorough—and free—information on schedules and cut through the maze of special restrictions on discount fares. They also make hotel recommendations (be sure you don't get booked into a room that costs more than you can afford) and they can offer advice on passports, vaccinations, sightseeing and the like.

Whether or not you use a travel agent, thoroughly explore the possibility of getting senior citizen discounts on ground and air transportation, hotels, admissions to museums and parks and so on. Greyhound and Trailways both offer senior citizens 10 percent discounts on regular fares. Greyhound, Trailways and Amtrak also sell special passes that allow you unlimited travel within a limited period of time. These aren't always the bargain they seem, though; compare the cost of the pass with the cost of the trip using regular fares. As for hotels and motels, many chains give discounts of 10 percent or more on rooms rented by members of the American Association of Retired Persons, but you must ask for the discount ahead of time.

On to matters of health. You may hesitate to go on a trip, especially a lengthy one, if you're not sure that your health is up to it. Often such a fear is needless, but take the precaution of having a talk with your doctor about your proposed trip. Explain in detail where you want to go, for how long and something about the pace of the trip. Find out if it's permissible for you to fly, should that be your mode of transportation, and what precautions —if any—you need to take. Certain countries require inoculations. (If you're going to Africa, India or other countries where there may be a health risk, you may want inoculations beyond those officially required. For example, gamma globulin to protect against hepatitis is often advisable. The infectious diseases department of a major teaching hospital in your area may provide such information—or tell you where to get it.)

If you're on medication, that's

Obtaining Medical Assistance around the World

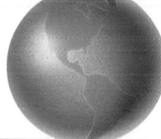

Below are a few key phrases to help you find a doctor and secure medical care when you are traveling abroad.

English	Spanish	German	French	Italian
I am ill.	Estoy enfermo (a).	Ich bin krank.	Je suis malade.	Mi sento male.
Call a doctor right away.	Llame a un médico immediatamente.	Rufen Sie sofort einen Arzt.	Appelez un médecin immédiatement.	Chiami subito un dottore.
Take me to a doctor right away.	Lléveme con un médico, immediatamente.	Bringen Sie mich sofort zu einem Arzt.	Emmenez-moi chez un médecin immédiatement.	Mi porti subito da un dottore.
Is there a doctor in the building?	¿Hay un doctor en este edificio?	Gibt es einen Arzt im Haus?	Y a-t-il un médecin dans cette maison?	C'è un dottore in questo edificio?
I cannot speak [Spanish, German, etc.]. Please call this number for me.	No sé hablar español. Por favor hable a este número de mi parte.	Ich kann kein Deutsch. Bitte wählen Sie diese Nummer für mich.	Je ne peux pas parler français. S'il vous plaît, appelez-moi ce n° de téléphone.	Non so parlare italiano. Per favore, chiami per me questo numero.
Take me to a hospital right away.	Lléveme al hospital immediatamente.	Bringen Sie mich sofort ins Krankenhaus.	Emmenez-moi à un hôpital immédiatement.	Mi porti subito a un ospedale.

another matter to discuss with your physician. Be sure you have enough medication with you and an extra prescription just in case.

If you hesitate to fly long distances because you're on a special diet and know you can't eat a regular airline meal, don't worry. Airlines can provide vegetarian, salt-free and other kinds of special diets (including kosher); however, you must make your need known at the time you make your reservation.

As for a final major health concern — getting sick far from home, especially out of the country — there are ways of preparing for that unlikely eventuality, too. You may contact the United States consulate or embassy to obtain the name of an English-speaking doctor wherever you are. Alternatively, you can take a list of such physicians with you. The International Association for Medical Assistance to Travelers (IAMAT) provides lists of English-speaking doctors in foreign countries who will treat you at stipulated fees. IAMAT also provides rules for safe eating and drinking (as well as climate information, for an extra $15)

for whatever areas you plan to visit. There's no charge for this service, though a donation would be appreciated. Because of a heavy backlog of requests, you should ask for the information six to eight weeks before you need it. IAMAT is at 736 Center Street, Lewiston, NY 14092. The telephone number is (716) 754-4883.

A PET STROKE OF LUCK

"I don't believe in miracles but I'd say this was something like one. And it wasn't love at first sight, either. Kerry and Bill just kind of eyed each other for about three days. You could see they were studying each other, not really sure — and then, on the fourth day, she jumped into his lap and started purring. That was it."

The speaker was a woman named Susan, a participant in a round-table discussion on pets in relation to physical and emotional health. Eight months earlier, Susan explained, her husband, a dynamic businessman, had suffered a massive

159

stroke. It left him, at 59, confined to a wheelchair. He had to resign from active participation in a successful fur business; and though money wasn't a problem, his loss of purpose in life was. He became withdrawn and depressed. Although still mentally alert and capable of being somewhat more active, he refused to do more than watch television.

Everything changed, however, when Susan acted on a hunch and brought home a beautiful young Abyssinian cat—Kerry. Kerry turned out to be cute, fun and loving—and she triggered something in Bill. The spark came back. Bill became more responsive. He started to think about ways of keeping himself busy and involved in life again. Though he had trouble speaking, he taught himself to use a typewriter and became actively involved, working with conservation groups to protect endangered and near-endangered animals.

A growing number of pet-related studies have made it clear that pets of all kinds are good for us, all the more so as we grow older. They enhance our physical and emotional health. There may even be a positive relationship between pet ownership and longevity. Consider some of the evidence.

A pet offers more than simple companionship. Surprisingly, it also can provide certain health benefits.

- At the University of Maryland Hospital, 93 patients who had suffered heart attacks or were subject to the pain of angina were studied in relation to their social attachments. Pet ownership was one of the facets the investigators looked at. This is what they discovered. After one year, only 3 of 53 patients who were pet owners had died. But of the 39 other patients who didn't have any pets, 11 had died. That was quite a striking difference in the death rate of the two groups, but then the researchers were struck by the thought that there might be a very logical reason to account for that difference. Could it be that most of the pet owners who survived were dog owners who walked their dogs and therefore got more healthful exercise? In order to find out, they eliminated dog owners from the study, which still left 10 other pet owners who survived after a year—the pets being cats, horses, chickens, goldfish and even one iguana. None of these pet owners exercised their pets, so the key to their survival had to be the owning of the pets rather than any exercise connected with them.

- In a study undertaken at the University of Pennsylvania, Aaron Katcher, M.D., a psychiatrist, found that when people "talk" to animals, it has a distinct and beneficial effect on blood pressure. He and his colleagues first measured the blood pressure of people reading an unexciting text, then measured it while they were enthusiastically talking to, stroking and patting their dogs. Despite the vigor they expended while greeting the animals, these volunteers nevertheless had significantly lower readings while greeting their pets than while reading.

- The *Canadian Medical Association Journal* has reported on still another unusual animal-related experiment. Toronto's Sunnybrook Hospital has a special "animal room" where a few special cats are housed. Each day the animals are taken to visit elderly hospital residents. Every cat has a special person it visits, so that—in effect—each patient has his or her own pet. This project has been developed to determine what effect this loving interaction has on these hospital residents. If other studies are any indication, the results should be positive.

What is there about the emotional connection between animals and humans that creates this kind of response? According to Gerald Jay Westbrook, a research project developer at the University of Southern California's Leonard Davis School of Gerontology, "Pets increase feelings of responsibility, usefulness, self-worth and being needed," which are exactly the things that some people lose, he points out, when they retire.

Studies in England and elsewhere have shown that one of the things dog owners prize most about their pets is attentiveness. The dogs make contact. The dogs acknowledge their masters' presence. One could say that the dogs make their masters feel more human—which is hardly stretching the point, since another study has shown that many dog owners actually see their pets as "human" members of the family rather than merely as companion animals.

Gerontologist Westbrook points to other significant benefits we gain from keeping and caring for a pet. One is a more regular eating pattern. For instance, older men and women who live alone tend to skip meals, Westbrook says, but "if you are feeding a pet, you're more likely to fix something for yourself, too. And having a pet around makes meal times not so lonely."

Exercise is another benefit. People who live alone sometimes tend to have a hard time getting up in the morning. They become lifeless, lying or sitting around. Owning a pet—particularly a dog that needs to be walked—gives some structure to the day; it forces you to get some

Fish Tanks Lower Blood Pressure

Fish tank gazing may not be a miracle cure, but it does demonstrably reduce high blood pressure. Psychiatrist Aaron H. Katcher, M.D., says, "Anything that turns your attention outward to the natural environment around you is a powerful way of controlling tension."

Fish, open fires, lapping waves—whatever is always changing yet always the same soothes us.

fresh air and exercise.

Owning a pet—again, especially a dog—can also help bring more human companionship into our lives. Two senior citizens walking their dogs in the park, for instance, are much more apt to stop, chat and maybe strike up a friendship than if they were simply taking their strolls alone.

Of course, Westbrook and other experts add, not everybody is psychologically or financially suited to pet ownership. You have to like animals—or at least a particular kind of animal—to own one. You have to be able to afford the expense of feeding and otherwise taking care of the pet. Also, you have to be sure to get a pet that's appropriate to the way you live. If you're away from home regularly, it makes more sense to have a cat than a dog because cats—unlike dogs—can stay by themselves for a day or two at a time. Such cautions aside, pet ownership can add immeasurably to our well-being.

EARNING, WORKING, GIVING

Irene E. Best of Chicago loves being a hospital volunteer. Her awesome schedule proves it: four days a week she works as a volunteer in Northwestern Memorial Hospital's cardiac surgery intensive care waiting room. What she does there is to help calm the anxious family members of patients who have undergone surgery. She's ideally suited for the task; in addition to her natural strength and optimism she brings a special sensitivity to the task—she herself has had two heart attacks. But counseling those family members is only one of the volunteer jobs she has set for herself; she also does a stint at the hospital coffee shop and she prepares mothers-to-be for their hospital stays by giving them tours of their section of the hospital. "I've had a wonderful life, and I'd like to give something back," she says. "And I don't let things slow me down."

Volunteers like Irene Best are rare. Few people, no matter how responsive they may be to the idea of community service, can be expected to have that gargantuan an appetite for it. Nevertheless, millions of people of all ages do find the idea of contributing their time, skills and energy to help others has tremendous appeal. As for retired people specifically, literally hundreds of thousands are involved, at any given time, in some kind of volunteer effort in the communities in which they live. In fact, the federal government has set up volunteer programs especially geared to the needs and abilities of older people.

There's far more to the appeal, of course, than merely keeping busy. Volunteers who are absorbed in what they're doing certainly find, to their delight, that the hours fly. But, more than that, these are happy, rewarding hours. People who enjoy their volunteer work invariably feel it has a rejuvenating effect on them—even if they don't exactly put it like that. What they often say is that it brings some more meaning to their lives. What they say is that in helping others they find themselves enriched. What they say is that it somehow makes them feel more connected to the world—yes, more alive.

You find retired volunteers literally all over, both in geographical terms and in terms of diverse activities. According to the National Center for Voluntary Action, there are 96 different kinds of services waiting for volunteers to carry them out. Many volunteers like the idea of utilizing in volunteer work the skills they utilized in their jobs or professions. For instance, retired lawyers can be found in Legal Aid offices, donating their time and expertise to indigent persons who need legal advice. Retired businessmen, accountants and management experts work through the federally sponsored SCORE, giving advice to new or faltering small businesses. A retired bookkeeper has set up an accounting system for a community action program in her city. A retired baker bakes for a nursing home. Whatever your expertise, you can make some good use of it in your community.

Lots of other volunteers enroll in programs that tap skills different from the ones directly relating to their life's work. Fed up with TV watching and talking to her daughter on the phone, 66-year-old Edna P. joined a volunteer program run by New York City's Community Service Society. Now she works with a retarded, institutionalized boy— talking to him, playing with him, helping him to find himself. There's a good result: The boy is more alert now and, for the first time, interacts with the other children. In Los Angeles, a 72-year-old man, Henry F., who had spent most of his days aimless and alone, now has a good reason for getting up in the morning: He teaches English and math on a tutorial basis to a fourth-grader, a delightful little girl who's a recent arrival from Nicaragua. Henry got started when he read about this church-sponsored after-school tutorial program in a flier posted on a bulletin board of his local supermarket —and he now says it's the best thing that's happened to him in years.

So it goes. Churches, schools,

"Grandma love" is a precious commodity, and just as good to give as to receive. Here, a participant in the Foster Grandparent program shares the wealth with a delighted youngster.

hospitals, libraries, the Red Cross, day care centers, senior citizens' centers, shelters for the homeless and for runaway youths all need volunteers. Specific skills aren't always required. Enthusiasm for the work and a willingness to serve are often the top qualifications needed. A retired mechanic spends his lunchtime helping to feed homeless people at a soup kitchen set up by his community. A widow, who has had no practical work experience, reads stories to children twice a week at her neighborhood library. In Gainesville, Florida, 50 residents of nursing homes, though they themselves have serious medical problems or physical impairment, are volunteers in the Alachua County Retired Senior Volunteer Program. Their objective: to work in a variety of ways to enhance the quality of life in nursing homes. They also engage in other good works, such as fund-raising; volunteers at the Convalescent Center of Gainesville, for example, raised over $9,000 for the Heart Fund.

The landmark Foster Grandparent Program affords low-income persons 60 and older the opportunity to give love and care to physically, emotionally or mentally handicapped children. Volunteers work in pediatric wards of hospitals, institutions for the mentally retarded, group homes and other such places. In addition to the rewards of serving, volunteers receive a transportation allowance and other benefits. Another volunteer program—the Senior Companion Program—is also geared to low-income volunteers and offers benefits.

For information on this and other federally administered programs, write to ACTION, 806 Connecticut Avenue, NW, Washington, DC 20525—or call the toll-free number, (800) 424-8580.

Admittedly, volunteer work isn't for everyone. Some people want to keep busy and revitalize themselves at something structured, but they're not really rewarded by donating their services. They like the idea of getting paid for what they do. Some others find they simply can't afford to do something for free because they need to supplement an income drastically reduced at retirement. For such

persons part-time or full-time jobs may fit their needs more exactly.

Where do persons past the age of 60 or 65 find work?

Julian Brodie of Retirement Program Services says that sometimes retired people find part-time jobs doing the same things they did on a full-time basis—whether that be clerical or computer work, typing or sales. There's a trend among many firms to hire more part-time and fewer full-time workers, the reason being that part-timers don't have to be worked into a pension plan and don't receive other benefits. Some employees also make arrangements following retirement to work for their former companies a few hours a day or a few days a week.

If you're looking for either a part-time or a full-time job, try visiting your state employment service (it's free). You can also explore federally sponsored job programs that hire older persons to work in nutrition programs, community beautification programs and the like. Your regional office of the Department of Labor has the information. Also, you could visit employment agencies; they sometimes place older workers. (They also sometimes charge placement fees.) Mature Temps, with branches in more than a dozen cities, places older employees in temporary jobs in business and industry.

Have you considered a second career? Many imaginative senior citizens—people in their sixties and older—have begun new careers and new businesses, often with great success. The most striking example is Colonel Harland Sanders. At 66 he was out of work, with only a small amount of savings and a $105-a-month Social Security check between him and abject poverty. Then he got the idea to start his Kentucky Fried Chicken business, which became so spectacularly successful he later sold it for $2 million. On a much smaller scale, some retired accountants and bookkeepers and other specialists have started at-home businesses to service small accounts in their communities. Think of all the possibilities.

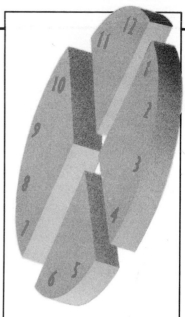

Part-Time Jobs

Part-time jobs are out there, the only question is where to look for them. First, check to see if a group like Chicago's Operation Able is in your city. Such lately sprung, nonprofit organizations find part-time work for older or retired persons. Also contact the state job service and your local Area Agency on Aging for a possible part-time job in a nonprofit agency under the federal Title V program.

Source Notes

Chapter 1

Page 2

"The Great Divide" compiled from information from the Bureau of the Census, U.S. Department of Commerce.

Page 6

"Pleasure Travel" adapted from *Travel Market Yearbook 1982*, Penny Sarbin, ed. (New York: Ziff-Davis, 1982).

Chapter 2

Pages 20-21

"How Long You Live, by Country" adapted from *Demographic Yearbook 1980* (New York: United Nations, 1982).

Chapter 3

Page 39

"Foods Naturally High in Calcium" adapted from *Nutritive Value of American Foods in Common Units*, Agriculture Handbook No. 456, by Catherine F. Adams (Washington D.C.: Agricultural Research Service, U.S. Department of Agriculture, 1975) and *Composition of Foods: Dairy and Egg Products*, Agriculture Handbook No. 8-1, by Consumer and Food Economics Institute (Washington D.C.: Agricultural Research Service, U.S. Department of Agriculture, 1976).

Page 62

"Are You Hearing Less?" adapted from *Our Endangered Hearing* (Emmaus, Pa.: Rodale Press, 1977) and "Quieting: A Practical Guide to Noise Control," National Bureau of Standards Handbook 119 (Washington, D.C.: U.S. Government Printing Office, 1976).

Page 65

"Sound Levels and Human Response" compiled from information from the U.S. Environmental Protection Agency.

Chapter 4

Page 77

"Yoga Stretches" adapted from "Anti-Aging Exercises," by Helen M. Lennon, *The Herbalist New Health*, June 1981.

Chapter 6

Page 107

"Memory Quiz" adapted from *Use Both Sides of Your Brain*, by Tony Buzan. Copyright 1974 by Tony Buzan. Reprinted by permission of the publisher, E. P. Dutton, Inc.

Page 113

"Older Is Better" adapted from *Statistical Abstract of the United States 1981*, 102d ed., by the Bureau of the Census (Washington, D.C.: U.S. Department of Commerce, 1981).

Chapter 7

Page 121

"Average Frequency of Sex" adapted from "Sexual Activity in the Ageing Male," by Clyde E. Martin, in *Handbook of Sexology*, J. Money and H. Musaph, eds. (New York: Elsevier/North Holland Biomedical Press, 1977).

Page 125

"Divorce Rates" adapted from *Statistical Abstract of the United States 1981*, 102d ed., by the Bureau of the Census (Washington, D.C.: U.S. Department of Commerce, 1981).

Chapter 9

Page 159

"Obtaining Medical Assistance around the World" adapted from *The Special Diet Foreign Phrase Book*, by Helen Saltz Jacobson (Emmaus, Pa.: Rodale Press, 1982).

Photography Credits

Cover: Margaret Skrovanek. *Staff Photographers* — Christopher Barone: pp. 64; 81; 144; 145. Carl Doney: 66; 67; 82; 83. T. L. Gettings: 142, top and bottom. John P. Hamel: 45. Michael W. Koenig: 3, upper right; 11, lower right. Mitchell T. Mandel: 1; 10, upper left; 33; 50; 54; 60; 72; 103; 109; 126; 133; 136; 142, center; 160; 161. Margaret Skrovanek: 10, lower right; 17; 85; 93; 94; 120; 130; 154. Christie C. Tito: 52; 75; 76; 77; 84; 86; 87; 111; 127. Sally Shenk Ullman: 38; 69; 97; 100; 119; 147.

Other Photographers — Charles H. Anderson: pp. 157-158. Susan Biddle: 162. Candy Clemson: 116; 117. Conrad Collette: 8, upper right. Frank Driggs: 10, upper right. C. H. Scott Heist (copyright 1978): 11, upper right. Tom Hollyman: 3, lower right. J. Michael Kanouff: 26. Craig Lampa: 122. Jayne Mangino: 115. Robert Mapplethorp: 9, lower left. Martin Reichenthal: 114. Fred Smith: 23. John Zimmerman: 12.

Additional Photographs Courtesy of — The Bettman Archive, N.Y.: pp. 11, lower right. Biomedical Communication, Div. of the University of Nebraska Medical Center: 18. CBS News: 9, upper left. Mount Sinai Hospital: 3, lower right. National Gallery of Art: 11, upper right.

Illustration Credits

Susan Blubaugh: pp. 5; 27; 31; 35; 43; 44; 45; 48, lower left; 56, lower left; 62, lower right; 71; 74; 78-79; 81; 84; 88; 95; 96; 98; 101; 105; 106; 121; 123; 128; 129; 139; 144-145; 150-151; 152-153; 155; 157; Joe Lertola: pp. 2; 4; 6; 19; 20-21; 23; 24; 34; 37; 39; 40; 42; 48, upper left; 50; 52; 54; 56, upper left; 58; 60; 62, upper left; 65; 66; 89; 90-91; 99; 104; 107; 113; 124; 134; 137; 138; 140; 141; 149; 158; 159; 163. John Pepper: pp. 54; 73.

Index

Rodale Press, Inc., publishes PREVENTION®, the better health magazine.
For information on how to order your subscription,
write to PREVENTION®, Emmaus, PA 18049.